The Myth of Evil

The Myth of Evil
Demonizing the Enemy

Phillip Cole

Westport, Connecticut
London

Published in the United States and Canada by
Praeger Publishers, 88 Post Road West, Westport, CT 06881
An imprint of Greenwood Publishing Group, Inc.
www.praeger.com

English language edition, except the United States and Canada,
published by Edinburgh University Press Ltd., Great Britain

First published in 2006

Library of Congress Cataloging-in-Publication Data

Cole, Phillip.
  The myth of evil / Phillip Cole.
    p. cm.
  Includes bibliographical references and index.
  ISBN 0-275-99216-0 (alk. paper)
  1. Good and evil.   2. Psychology.   I. Title.
  BJ1401.C58 2006
  170–dc22
                       2006006634

ISBN: 0-275-99216-0

Printed in Great Britain by The Cromwell Press, Trowbridge, Wilts

Contents

Acknowledgements

I have received a great deal of support and encouragement during the writing of this book. Middlesex University ensured that I had two semesters free from teaching and administrative duties, which was, of course, invaluable. I am grateful to the institution and to my colleagues in the Philosophy group for making this possible. Many individuals have helped and encouraged me, in particular Paul Gilbert who was extremely supportive of the initial proposal and also helped to clarify some important issues during various conversations, especially concerning the motivation of Satan. Many other people have listened patiently and made helpful comments or recommended readings – I may not remember all these occasions but I would like to thank Gideon Calder, Bill McBride, Bob Brecher and Suzanne Uniacke. Sandy Pragnell read Chapter 6, and given her authoritative expertise on the questions I was exploring there, I'm grateful for her patience, feedback and encouragement. John Pitts also directed me towards extremely helpful readings for that chapter.

Some parts of the book were delivered as papers in research seminars, and the comments and criticisms I received on those occasions have been invaluable, leading me to develop particular arguments and abandon others. I would therefore like to thank all the students and staff who attended those sessions at Middlesex University (twice), University of Wales College, Newport, the University of Hertfordshire, and the University of Brighton. I also delivered a paper called 'The Vampires of Moravia: Towards a Philosophical History of the Undead', at the Meanings of Community conference, Palacky University, Olomoucs, in the Czech Republic, in July 2003, and while I may not have persuaded all that vampires are a crucially important subject for political philosophy, I would like to thank those who attended that session not only for their supportive and encouraging comments, but also for their good humour.

Edinburgh University Press has once more provided a secure and supportive context for writing an academic text. Jackie Jones was a particularly important figure. She strengthened what was initially a confused and vague idea, and proposed many of the topics for the chapters as well as providing insightful comments on the pieces she read. She also proposed the book's title. Not least, she was patient in the extreme as deadlines were consistently missed, and when I jokingly proposed that Dante should have reserved one of his circles of Hell for authors who miss deadlines, she did not disagree. Carol Macdonald took over the final stages of the book's production and her contribution to its final form was invaluable. Others who helped during this process were James Dale and Ann Vinnicombe.

The British Library was another source of assistance. It was not only an invaluable source for books, but it also provided a space to sit and work and think. The staff in Humanities 2 were always efficient, helpful and patient, especially during the final stages of checking when I was ordering ten books at a time and returning them within the hour with a demand for more.

The most important support came from Roshi Naidoo. The idea for the book arose during conversations with her as we walked along the coast of Pembrokeshire, and despite the pressure of her own work and writing she always found the time to listen to problems and read and comment on the text. Our intellectual partnership has been the foundation of my work, and our emotional partnership has been my foundation.

Chapter One

Terrorism, Torture and the Problems of Evil

Speaking of the Devil

This is a book about evil. More precisely, it is a book about human evil, and its central question is whether there can be a secular conception of evil, whether that idea can tell us anything about the human condition, explain anything about what human beings do, in the absence of its more familiar territory of the supernatural and the demonic. In seeking to understand human evil it asks the question whether evil exists at all, and one possible answer I take very seriously is that it does not. That this is a book about something that may not exist is, of course, a puzzle, and it may be more accurate to say that this is a book about the idea of evil, for that undeniably exists and has for thousands of years. But still, in the end this is not simply an exploration of the history or coherence of an idea, although that is clearly an important aspect of what follows. It is primarily concerned with the metaphysical problem of the existence of evil in the world. Although the first aspect is perhaps the most complex, this second metaphysical aspect is the deepest and most urgent, especially during what are troubled days for the 'civilised' world. After the horrific destruction of the World Trade Center in New York on 11 September 2001, carried out by the al-Qa'ida group, the leadership of the United States of America has identified an 'axis of evil' and has launched military attacks on, at the time of writing, two independent nation states, Afghanistan and Iraq, and overthrown their governments in the name of destroying that axis. Iran, Cuba and Syria remain on the list. They have been supported in this to varying degrees by other nations, such as the United Kingdom, partners who have been more reluctant to employ the discourse of evil to justify their participation, but who are now deeply engaged in what is a global 'war on terror', which is escalating horrifically each day. But the United States' leadership has created a new understanding of the global order, in which the world is divided into good and evil, something international relations theorists would not have thought possible only a few years ago.

However, at the same time as the United States is engaged in this global struggle against the forces of evil, something deeply disturbing has happened. In May 2004, the press and television began to show pictures taken by American forces of their own people engaged in ritual and humiliating violence against Iraqi prisoners held in Abu Ghraib prison near Baghdad, some of them smiling broadly, showing their clean white teeth in their bright young faces as they performed unspeakable acts against helpless, powerless human beings. Most horrifying of all, it was as though these pictures were taken as holiday snaps, with the same smiles and poses as you would see of a young person at the beach in California, except instead of them leaning against a surfboard they were leaning against a pile of naked, bound prisoners. Looking at them induced a deep nausea, as do the details of the allegations against American and British personnel, and raised the question, how is this possible? This led to a traumatic re-evaluation in the United States of what it believed it was doing, with sombre sessions of senate committees trying to understand how these events happened, and expressing deep shame that they did. The realisation is that evil may be within as well as in the world outside. Evil is something to be feared, and historically, we shall see, it is the enemy within who has been seen as representing the most intense evil of all – the enemy who looks just like us, talks like us, and is just like us. This is one of the traditional guises of the Devil, who is at his most dangerous when he appears not as a serpent or a demon, but as an ordinary person, passing among us undetected.

Speaking of the Devil, one curiosity is the extent to which he features in this book. I am, after all, a devout atheist and an analytical philosopher by training. As I researched the book, I found myself spending more and more time examining the figure of Satan, but I always thought this was a distraction, and that the vast pile of notes about him would be set aside when it came to writing the final work. But once I began writing, I found that I could not get away from him. What was meant to be one section about his place in the scheme of things grew into half a chapter, and then into a whole chapter. There are, of course, large parts of the book where I escape him, but he returns in the end, like a long delayed punch-line. Not that this book is intended as a joke. The point, of course, as everyone knows, is that the Devil is in the detail, and the more I examined the detail of evil, the more I sensed his presence – not a supernatural presence, but a political one. In a sense, this is a political philosophy of Satan. Others do, doubtless, sense a deeper presence. Images of the Devil's face can allegedly be seen in the patterns of smoke issuing from the burning World Trade Center after the September 11th attack, images that have not been manipulated. One came from CNN's film coverage, the other from a reputable freelance photographer, Mark D. Phillips. This is an instance of pareidolia, the predisposition to see faces within vague and unformed patterns. What this Devil in the smoke symbolises is, as always, ambiguous. Some have seen it as representing the diabolical nature of the attack, others as evidence that the Twin Towers were Satan's headquarters on earth.

Primarily, though, this is a book about human evil, and its central question is whether there can be a secular conception of evil, a conception we can use without the framework of supernatural powers. As we proceed, we will see that there are a number of different conceptions that are candidates, one of which is of pure or absolute evil. This is the most troubling understanding of what it is to be evil. We can understand, to an extent, why people do terrible things to other people in order to achieve some recognisable human end, such as the pursuit of power, or wealth, or popularity, or, very often, the greater good of the community or even humanity; but this is a kind of 'impure' evil, evil outcomes mixed with immoral intentions, or at least mundane intentions, or perhaps even good intentions. But pure evil includes not only the evil of outcomes, but the evil of intentions – it is the pursuit of the suffering and destruction of others for its own sake, and this verges on the incomprehensible, to such an extent that many thinkers have argued that mere human beings are incapable of it. Human agents can only be evil in the impure sense, while pure evil, if it exists at all, belongs to the supernatural. And so if we reject the supernatural, then it seems we must reject the reality of pure evil. However, the central question is whether it is true that human agents are incapable of pure evil, in the face of all the damning historical evidence to the contrary. Many of these seemingly evil acts can be understood as provoked by anger or ignorance or even misguided hope, but some stand out as unspeakable and incomprehensible. If such evil exists, the challenge is to make it comprehensible, and one way of doing this is to explore the figure of Satan, because one other common description of this pure or absolute evil is that it is diabolical. Diabolical evil has an obvious historical and conceptual connection with Satan in western thought, and one way in which diabolical evil can act as an explanation for the terrible things people do is that the Devil is acting through them to bring about his purposes. From a secular perspective, this explanation can play no role here. But it is still worth examining Satan's character, because if diabolical evil is a human possibility, although this does not necessarily imply the existence of Satan or other demonic powers, it does seem to imply that human beings can be like him. He is, in a perverted sense, a role model. And so even though this investigation remains secular throughout, Satan is a central figure.

The Borderlands of Humanity

Whenever I suggest that evil may not exist, that it may be a concept that belongs in fiction and mythology rather than in any description of reality, those listening become fervent in their belief that it does really exist, and that it is an accurate description of what happens. Even a degree of philosophical doubt provokes this response. One example given to me in such a conversation was of a woman who had been deserted by her husband, who then entered a relationship with another woman, a mother of two children. The deserted woman, one night, set fire to the house where the woman and children slept, killing them all. This, I was told, was a demonstration of the existence of evil; there was no other way to describe what happened. This may be right, but if we do describe this event as evil we need to be careful about what we are doing, and one problem with the idea of evil is the carelessness with which it is used. Evil is always something asserted with confidence, with determination, never with an uncertain shrug of the shoulders, never with philosophical doubt. Descriptions can take different forms and, although about the same event, can describe different things about it. If we describe this event as evil, is this a description of the suffering of the mother and children and the pain and terror they may have suffered? Or is it a description of the senseless loss of valuable human life? If either of these descriptions is meant, then it shouldn't matter what caused the fire that killed them; a natural event like a lightning strike could have caused something that was evil. But although the idea of natural evil is one with a long tradition, I don't think this is what people mean in this kind of case. There is a clear distinction made between natural and human evil, destruction caused by nature and destruction caused by human agency, and here there is a human agent – the woman who started the fire is an essential part of the description. Perhaps it's that children are involved that makes it especially shocking, and gives the certainty that this is an evil event. But again I don't believe that this is decisive here. In the conversation I was having it was clear that what was being described was the woman who caused the fire, and that what made this event evil was her sheer malignity; that it was a deliberate act with the intention to destroy three innocent lives is central to our understanding of it. But then the question becomes, what is it about this woman that we are describing?

The problem I'm getting at here is whether the description is meant as an explanation for what happened. Obviously not all descriptions are explanations, but some are, and so a description such as 'grass is green' can become '*because* grass is green' when it is the answer to some kind of 'why?' question, rather than simply asking what colour grass is. And so 'she was evil' can become '*because* she was evil' when it is the answer to the question, 'why did she do it?' The description is now an explanation – she performed this terrible act because she was evil. It is difficult to see how any description of this woman as evil can avoid being this kind of explanation for what happened, but then we are faced with the problem of how this is an explanation. To avoid this problem we could only employ the word 'evil' in a description of another level, of the whole state of affairs, in which case it is just an extreme way of describing terrible events. But I don't believe this is what people take the word 'evil' to mean when they use it in this kind of description, and there are plenty of other words that work well enough when describing terrible states of affairs – 'evil' brings with it another dimension, that of agency. The concept is supposed to be some kind of explanation for certain kinds of agency, and the question I am raising here is what sort of explanation is it? What exactly is being described and how does this description work as an explanation of anything? My suspicion, which I intend to develop into an argument as the book progresses, is that it only works as an explanation at a mythological level, and it only works here if we suppose there is some other force at work other than the woman in question, either some kind of force that chooses to work through her, or some kind of narrative force, a story unfolding in which she is simply a character playing a specific and prescribed role. In either case, she does not act on her own initiative. If we do not believe in the existence of these forces, then there is no explanation here at all, and the concept of evil has no role to play in a secular understanding of human behaviour.

There is an alternative answer, but it goes against the philosophical tradition concerning what human beings are like. According to that tradition, humans are capable of doing terrible things to others, but not in a diabolical sense, not for the *sake* of doing terrible things to others. Earlier I made the distinction between the pure conception of evil, an absolute malevolence which is diabolical and pursues the destruction of others for its own sake, and an impure conception, the pursuit of the harm of others for some other goal such as power, wealth, comradeship, or the collective good. What matters is the motivation. According to the tradition, human beings are only capable of this lesser, merely human evil, not the pure, diabolical kind; human freedom is constrained and it reaches its ultimate limit here. The human figure who pursues the destruction of others for its own sake is a fictional or mythological figure, but does not exist in reality. And so the woman in the example above was not driven by pure malevolence, but by some other factor such as despair or anger in the extreme. This means that, to an extent, we can understand what she did, because we know what it is to be in despair or angry in the extreme – she is not beyond human comprehension. The consequences she intends to bring about are so terrible that we can describe them as evil, and so we can say that she has evil intentions, but this is still primarily a description of the state of affairs she intends to bring about, not a description of her. What we do not understand is what it is like to be absolutely evil, to set out to destroy others purely for its own sake. Here it is not only that she intends to bring about evil consequences, and so not merely that she has evil intentions in this sense, but that her motivation is itself evil – *she* is evil. Such an agent would be beyond human understanding.

Now, it may be that the impure conception of evil is all we need in order to account for the terrible things people do to other people, but then there is something missing from our description of the woman who destroyed the mother and her children, and 'because she was evil' cannot be an answer, or at least not a complete one. We can use the idea of evil to describe her intentions, but this is, in the end, a description of the consequences rather than her, and there is now the further question of why she was evil, of how she came to have these intentions? The answer here might be, 'because she was in extreme despair', but then doesn't the concept of evil become redundant here? The question, 'why did she do it?' can be directly answered with 'because she was in extreme despair'. The idea of evil doesn't seem to add anything to our understanding of her, or if it does, it seems to be some kind of mythological added factor that we can do without in our account. And so the philosophical conception of impure, merely human evil has a built-in tendency towards the redundancy of the concept. All it seems to describe in the end are the consequences of her actions, the states of affairs she brings about, and that is not, I think, the intention behind its use. It is meant as part of an explanation of why she did what she did, not merely a description of the consequence of what she did. But if it is merely a description of states of affairs in the world, then this, too, has a tendency towards redundancy, because there seem to be other, more coherent descriptions of states of affairs in the world. The only way in which the description of states of affairs in the world as evil makes any sense at all is because of the connection between those events and agency, but once we move towards the explanation of that agency, the concept of evil becomes obscure, difficult, and, in the end, deeply unhelpful. Perhaps we can retain the concept as the expression of an attitude towards the act, describing it as evil in order to condemn it, but this is not a metaphysical theory of evil anymore, and there is nothing left in the world which the concept describes. According to the metaphysical possibilities we are exploring, the word 'evil' must be part of a description of the actual world, and not something about our attitude to the world. And, crucially, the part of the world it describes is human agency. The puzzle we are left with is how it describes/explains anything to do with human agency.

The alternative answer I hinted at above, however, moves beyond the traditional understanding of human nature and allows that human beings can be purely evil. If we make this move then the idea of evil can play a full role in an explanation of human action. 'She did it because she was evil' is a complete description with nothing missing, and I think it is this kind of explanation people believe they are offering when they use the word. But whether or not humans have the capacity for pure evil, whether the concept of evil can ever act as a complete explanation for what some people do, is a deeply divisive and urgent question. We seem to believe that there is a level of immorality, of depravity, which removes people from the 'merely' immoral into the realm of evil; and here again there is another level, between the 'merely' human evil, and pure evil of the radical kind. C. S. Lewis expresses this in his comedic but deeply serious character of Screwtape in *The Screwtape Letters*, the high-ranking demon who gives advice to his naive nephew Wormwood, and who, in his toast at the annual dinner of the Tempters' Training College for Young Devils, complains bitterly of the thin quality of the human souls they have to dine on. 'Oh to get one's teeth again into a Farinata, a Henry VIII, or even a Hitler! There was real crackling there; something to crunch; a rage, an egotism, a cruelty only just less robust than our own. It put up a delicious resistance to being devoured. It warmed your innards when you'd got it down' (Lewis 2002: 188). He then complains of the little people on offer at the feast: a municipal authority figure who took bribes, 'a grubby little nonentity who had drifted into corruption....'; the lukewarm adulterers, 'who blundered or trickled into the wrong beds in automatic response to sexy advertisements...'; the trade unionist who 'quite unknowingly, worked for bloodshed, famine, and the extinction of liberty' (Lewis 2002: 189). All these insipid characters, Lewis seems to think, belong in hell, punished for eternity in dreadful ways for their lukewarm deeds alongside a Hitler, but still there was something 'special' about a Hitler. Is there a genuine distinction here between the pure, radical evil of such a figure, and the blundering or even unknowing deeds of Lewis' other inhabitants of hell?

The danger, however, with the notion that evil can be a complete explanation is that it closes off all possibility of understanding. If we seek to understand the social, psychological, historical conditions that act as the background for horrific acts, the notion of pure evil may disappear – indeed the idea of evil may disappear in its entirety. In 1993 two boys, Robert Thompson and Jon Venables, both aged ten, were tried in the United Kingdom for the murder of James Bulger, aged two. They beat him with bricks and iron bars on a railway siding, leaving his body lying across the tracks to make it look like an accident. Writing in *The Guardian* newspaper on 2 February 2003, after Thompson and Venables were released from serving their sentences, Blake Morrison comments on the media frenzy that surrounded the killing, of the demonisation of the two boys as 'child-monsters'. But it was not just the media who deployed the language of evil. The trial judge in his sentencing also used the word to describe them, and the Prime Minister of the day, John Major, pronounced that, 'We must condemn a little more, and understand a little less.' Morrison observes that in this atmosphere 'Thompson and Venables lost the right to be seen as children, or even as human,' and, 'The word used about them stopped all arguments. They were evil.' The alternative view, which struggled for expression at the time, was that they were damaged – that they each had an appalling history, that, if understood, could act as a more coherent explanation for what happened. The challenge, however, for this alternative view, is that there may be many other children who emerge from a similar appalling history who do not kill. Richard J. Bernstein points out that however much we use the social disciplines and psychology to account for a person's actions through their background, training, education, character and circumstances, this 'never adds up to a *complete* explanation of why individuals make the choices they do. There is always a gap, a "black hole", in our accounts' (Bernstein 2002: 235). One attraction of the idea of evil is that it can fill that hole. The problem remains, however, that the concept of evil itself may be a black hole, a gap, and so all we have is the illusion of closure.

This is an exploration of the borderlands of humanity, a study of what it is to be a human being, but also of what it is not to be. The people who will form much of the subject matter for the arguments in this book have done things which 'normal' human beings find unthinkable, unspeakable; they have crossed the border from the human into the inhuman. And yet in making that judgement about them we must be supremely confident about where that border lies, and the very fact that they can cross it at all surely shows that this confidence has a fragile basis. For these are inhuman/ humans – they are people who are much like you and me, and that they are capable of such dreadful acts raises the possibility that you and I are capable of them too. The young Americans in the images of torture in Iraq, we learned from their families and neighbours and friends, were just ordinary people, not monsters. Some people who do dreadful things are clearly mentally disturbed or under extreme circumstances. These people were not mentally ill, but were they operating under extreme pressure? They were not under the extreme situation of the combat zone, but they were in an alien country doing a difficult job, and there is evidence that they were under pressure from superior officers to help gain intelligence results and that they were encouraged to pursue degrading treatment of prisoners as a method of getting those results. As the prosecution of seven guards at Abu Ghraib began in June 2004, the United States government was anxious to dispel such notions, and released secret papers to show that the kind of treatment that took place there was not condoned. However, Rupert Cornwell reported, in *The Independent* newspaper on 23 June 2004, what those documents also revealed was that harsh treatment, which included stripping prisoners, placing them in hoods and using dogs to terrify them, had been approved for some months, although these measures were officially revoked in April 2003. And the documents failed to dispel the suspicion that the government 'tacitly condoned' the use of tougher techniques that did amount to torture. The pressure on those involved at Abu Ghraib was to make interrogation more 'productive', and there was a background assumption that if information could be obtained that averted an attack, torture was justifiable. This, it was argued, led to the 'anything goes' approach at the Abu Ghraib prison. Cornwell reports that senior members of al-Qa'ida in custody were threatened with shooting or drowning under secret rules approved by the Central Intelligence Agency and the Justice Department. Guy Womack, attorney for one of the accused, told the media as the trial progressed that although there were no specific orders to handle prisoners in the manner they did, the personnel were following orders they believed to be lawful. 'Under the environment as it existed at Abu Ghraib, it appeared to be lawful'. And when the unit of which his client was a member arrived at the prison the activities were already ongoing (CNN, 21 June 2004). Given this background, we can begin to understand why those people prosecuted for their actions in Abu Ghraib may have believed they were doing their duty. This suspicion gained ground in May 2005, when one of the key figures being prosecuted, Lynndie England, had her guilty plea to seven charges rejected by the military judge hearing her case. The guilty plea had been entered after negotiations with the prosecution in the hope of re-ceiving a lighter sentence, but the judge argued that the testimony entered on her behalf as mitigation in order to reduce her sen-tence implied her innocence, and he entered a not-guilty plea on her behalf (news.bbc.co.uk/1/hi/world/americas/4514839.stm). Private England had argued during earlier hearings that she had been following orders. Four British soldiers were courtmartialled on similar charges. The incidents took place at an aid depot near Basra shortly after the end of the Iraq war, after 'trophy' photographs were discovered (*The Independent*, 24 February 2005). During the courtmartial it was claimed 'that the men were scapegoats to hide a culture of brutality which had "infected" the camp with the connivance of senior officers.'

However, we return here to Bernstein's problematic black hole, that in any such situation people at some point make a choice whether to perform such actions or to refuse them. Under extreme circumstances it may be that refusal could have drastic consequences, but there is no evidence here that the American or British personnel under investigation would have suffered dreadful consequences if they had refused to participate in the humiliation and torture of prisoners. And so we need to understand why, given the unspeakable nature of the actions, those involved made the choice to carry them out. All the factors I've outlined that made up the background of pressure or condonment can only go so far as an explanation. This is where the concept of evil begins to take on its explanatory power: there is nothing that can explain why these people did what they did, no mental disease, no extreme circumstances, except that they were evil. Perhaps they managed to conceal their evil nature from their family, friends and neighbours, but then perhaps the capacity for this kind of evil lies in all of us, waiting for the right circumstances to emerge. Here the circumstances seem to be the power to do anything they wanted to the Iraqis under their supervision, together with a view of their prisoners that reduced them to objects for sport, not human beings at all. It may be that this capacity – to suspend or set aside our knowledge that others are human beings and so entitled to our protection and respect, and to see them instead as objects for pleasure, subjects of power – is human evil in the absolute sense. But this is only the appearance of a solution to the problems of evil, because the question now is why anybody would seek to set aside this knowledge, to take part in such a knowing self-deception. In some cases we may want to say that these people have made a genuine mistake, that they have been so conditioned, brainwashed, to the extent that they cannot be held responsible for what they do. But in other cases it may be very difficult to make out that they have made a mistake and Abu Ghraib may be one of those cases – the evidence may point to a deliberate choosing to suspend knowledge of the humanity of others, and it is this deliberate, free act which lies at the centre of the idea of absolute evil. Such agents do terrible things to others, not through madness or necessity or mistake, but because they have freely, rationally, deliberately chosen to do them. Such a choice, according to the philosophical tradition, is impossible, but the evidence of its possibility confronts us every day. In *The Independent* newspaper on 7 June 2004, there is the story of gangs in Afghanistan who are kidnapping children, and killing them in order to extract their organs to sell them. Even though I wish to deny its reality, the spectre of diabolical evil as a basic human capacity keeps confronting me.

Possibilities of Evil

It confronted others too. Richard von Krafft-Ebing, in his *Psycopathia Sexualis*, first published in 1886, examined terrible cases of sexual perversion and violence. One of the most shocking case studies is that of Gilles de Rais, the fifteenth-century Marshall of France who fought alongside Joan of Arc, and who was responsible for the torture and murder of perhaps 800 children (Benedette 1971). Krafft-Ebing tells of Rais' history of 'mutilation and murder', and, as a professor of psychiatry at the University of Vienna, is confident that 'Satisfactory proof of Rais' insanity has been given' (Frayling 1991: 391). But it is not clear what that evidence is beyond the nature of the acts Rais committed, and elsewhere Krafft-Ebing's scientific confidence slips, as he describes him as 'the inhuman wretch', and 'the monster' (Frayling 1991: 390). These throwaway descriptions hint at the view that Rais is not a human agent at all, but something other than human, capable of actions no human could ever contemplate. Here are two very different understandings of evil at work within the same text, an enlightened, scientific view of human psychology, and a radically disturbing view of human beings as monsters. In another aside Krafft-Ebing describes the Marquis de Sade as a 'sexual monster' (Frayling 1991: 394), and takes great satisfaction from the fact that he died in an asylum for the insane, in, no doubt, sordid and extremely miserable conditions. As we have seen, while the scientific approach seeks to understand, the opposing view seeks to condemn. This contest needs to be resolved, and the purpose of this book is to resolve it one way or the other. Although it may seem to be a contest between two opposing viewpoints of human evil, one denying its possibility, the other asserting it, in fact we can distinguish between four different positions.

The monstrous conception

The first secular possibility is that human agents are capable of pure evil, such that evil is a complete explanation for what they do. But here, to complicate the possibilities, there are still two options. The first I will call the monstrous conception, that some humans can freely and rationally choose to make others suffer purely because this is what they want to do and for no other end, but these people have crossed the border beyond humanity. According to the monstrous conception, these are monsters in human shape, human/inhumans, or inhuman/humans, who are willing to inflict suffering on others purely for its own sake, capable of pure evil precisely because of their monstrosity. The important point about this conception is that these monsters constitute a distinct class, different from the rest of humanity, with a different *nature* – they are not like you and me. This conception of evil is a powerful vision and we can see that power in the world of fiction. Both heroes and villains take on superhuman powers and even the most traditional monster like the vampire and the werewolf continue to live on in our imaginations, filled with malevolence towards us.

Although it may be tempting to describe the monstrous conception of evil as primitive, in fact it has its sources in modernity. Of course it does have obvious connections with pre-modern thought and David Pocock, in an anthropological study of evil, points out that this conception of the inhuman/human is precisely how evil persons were understood in 'primitive' societies, a 'belief in creatures who are and are not human beings, at once within and beyond the limits of humanity' (Pocock 1985: 48); someone who is 'paradoxically, not human' (Pocock 1985: 49). The motives of the truly evil person are therefore beyond understanding, incomprehensible to normal human beings, and it is precisely the inability to explain that leads to the use of the concept of evil (Pocock 1985: 49), as though the idea of evil itself provides a full explanation. However, if the motives and actions cannot be understood, they cannot be judged. Pocock says: 'the evil act itself is beyond the comprehension of human justice' (Pocock 1985: 52). However, another element of the oldest philosophies of evil is that of ambiguity. In ancient Greek thought, for example, we find the 'daimon', a force or energy between God and humanity (Flint 1999: 280). These are in-between creatures, a mixture of the human and the divine, and they are ambivalent between being helpful and being harmful. They are a mixture of divine powers and human emotions and this combination makes them extremely dangerous, but none of them are purely evil or purely good. The monster which emerges in modern fiction is something else, for here we have pure evil, not some powerful, unpredictable force which we can, if we are careful, exploit for beneficial purposes, but a figure of pure malevolence who wants nothing other than our extreme suffering and destruction and who very often can only be resisted at the very last moment with extreme effort and massive cost, or, in Gothic tales with horrific twists, not resisted at all. Another aspect of the ancient view is that the 'daimons' are agents of more divine forces, capable of carrying messages between heaven and earth, for example. The modern monster has no message for us, is an independent agent, pursuing nothing other than our destruction. Or, if she or he does carry a message, it takes the form of metaphor.

The problem which undermines the credibility of the monstrous conception of evil is how to explain why certain human beings have a radically different nature to other human beings – how they can be inhuman/humans. This is not so much of a problem for fictional representations, as the nature of characters is often simply given without any attempt at explanation, and in mythologies it is given by the character's fundamental role in the narrative: certain characters are evil because this is their narrative function. However, quite often in fiction and mythology the presence of the evil character is explained in terms of a two- (or more) world model – the evil monster came from another world, and in order to explain their presence in *our* world all we have to do is describe their journey; as we have no understanding of their world, there is no requirement to explain their nature. This model is most obvious in science-fiction narratives of alien invasion, always highly potent and popular. But the two-world model can appear in horror narratives as well. In the enormously popular American television series *Buffy the Vampire Slayer*, Buffy and her comrades protect the Californian town of Sunnydale – and the rest of the world – from vampires and other evil monsters. Sunnydale is a site for evil activity because it is built on a 'hellmouth', a gateway between our world and a demon dimension. Although some of the monsters Buffy encounters spend their time in our world, the worst enter from that demon dimension, and often her struggle is an apocalyptic one, to prevent her evil enemies from opening the gateway, collapsing the boundary between the human and demon worlds, and so destroying humanity.

But although the monstrous conception of evil, with or without the two-world dimension, has its obvious home in fiction and mythology, a recurring theme of this book will be how often this fictional portrayal of evil agency, this particular myth of evil, is employed as a real-world description of specific groups and individuals. The popular media are quick to identify murderers, rapists and others as monsters. The problem is, of course, that these people, because of their monstrosity, are more or less than human and, like all monsters, are extremely dangerous and deserve little more than to be eliminated. They are not, after all, genuine human beings. Worse, if the authorities do not eliminate them, then ordinary people will mobilise to do it. In August 2000 the *News of the World* newspaper in the United Kingdom began a campaign to identify convicted paedophiles following the murder of an eight-year-old girl. As a result of the identification of these people as monsters, campaigns of intimidation and violence were carried out by 'concerned' members of the public to drive them out of their communities, if not to kill them. One commentator described these campaigns as a witch craze.

The pure conception

The pure conception of evil shares the basic characteristics of the monstrous conception in its understanding of evil, that human agents have the capacity to freely choose to pursue as a project the destruction of others for its own sake. Once more, evil is a complete explanation for human action. But there is one radical difference, that according to this understanding, there is no sharp boundary between humans and monsters – the capacity for pure evil lies in all human agents without distinction. Those who commit such acts are not monsters, not inhuman/humans, but are all too human. It is not that they exist beyond the boundaries of humanity, but that we have put the border in the wrong place. We use the monstrous conception of evil in its traditional form to hide not from monsters, but from ourselves. At the heart of the pure theory of evil is a conception of human freedom, a radical freedom, the freedom to choose any possibility, however awful. Joan Copjec describes evil as 'uniquely the product of a free humanity' (Copjec 1996a: xi). If we assert the possibility of free will against the determinism of social and psychological forces, then one possibility has to be to choose to pursue the destruction of others for its own sake. How can philosophers of freedom deny this possibility?

The impure conception

But deny it they do, and this leads us to the third secular possibility, the conception of evil developed within modern moral philosophy, which I described above as impure. This philosophical conception rejects absolute evil as a human possibility. Normal human agents cannot be evil in the pure sense of willing the suffering of others for its own sake. However, they are capable of the impure form of evil, a merely human evil, which is the causing of suffering to others for some other human end, such as power, wealth, security, or the greater collective good. Colin McGinn is one contemporary writer who makes this distinction, between what he calls pure evil and instrumental evil. Pure evil is 'malice for its own sake, not as a means to achieving some other goal', while instrumental evil occurs in cases 'in which a person does something to harm another in order to reap some benefit, as with violent theft or fraud or some such: here the pain of the other is not the *goal* of the act, only a necessary (and perhaps regretted) means towards achieving something else' (McGinn 1997: 63). According to the philosophical conception, the evil person is now someone who is willing to make others suffer in order to achieve his or her goal, but the goal is distinct from the suffering. This is the conception of evil we find in a tradition of moral theory which includes the deeply pessimistic Thomas Hobbes, who, although he never expects much from his fellow human beings, nevertheless says, 'that any man should take pleasure in other mens great harmes, without other end of his own, I do not conceive it possible' (Hobbes 1985: 126). It also includes the sceptical David Hume, who makes the point that mere indifference to virtue is not sufficient for evil. 'A creature, absolutely malicious and spiteful, were there any such in nature, must be worse than indifferent to the images of vice and virtue. All his sentiments must be inverted, and directly opposite to those, which prevail in the human species' (Hume 1975: 226). This, observes Hume, is to make the truly evil person someone inhuman, and this is an impossibility. 'Absolute, unprovoked, disinterested malice has never perhaps place in any human breast' (Hume 1975: 227). And most importantly, it includes Immanuel Kant, the most influential and important thinker who denies the possibility of pure evil in *Religion within the Limits of Reason Alone.* But it is precisely Kant who provides the most radical theory of human freedom as unconstrained by the phenomenal world of our experiences, and the puzzle here is how we can hold that human agents are radically free to choose any possibility except this one. Is the limit Kant and others impose upon human freedom merely the expression of wishful thinking?

The psychological conception

The final secular possibility is to reject the existence of evil as a human capacity altogether and shift attention from human freedom to the human condition. According to the psychological conception, where humans commit what we are describing as evil acts there must be an explanation which does not involve them freely and rationally choosing to do them. Instead, a proper explanation will rely on empirical causes, to do with their social or psychological history, or the physiological state of their brain, or the extreme circumstances under which they are forced to act. To put it crudely, this is explanation through madness or necessity. If madness, then those humans' means/ends reasoning has broken down due to a loss of contact with reality, so that they pursue what may be perfectly reasonable ends through means which make sense to them but which are out of all proportion to those ends. For example they may want peace and quiet so they can read a book undisturbed in their garden, and so they shoot dead everyone who lives on their street. I include here compulsive behaviours, by people who have been so socially conditioned through their social or psychological history that we no longer hold them morally responsible for their actions in any real sense, although this is to enter into the borderlands of the debate about mental health and moral responsibility. But there are always borderlands rather than clearcut boundaries. If the explanation is through necessity, then they have been forced to pursue normal human ends through extreme means because their immediate circumstances have closed off all other options for them. More than this, the human ends that are being pursued through these extreme means are ends which no normal human being should be expected to give up, or at least it is arguable whether they cannot be given up. To pursue a normal but mundane human end through extreme means on the basis that no other less extreme means were available – there is no other way to achieve peace in the garden other than slaughtering the neighbourhood – would again be to enter the realms of insanity. A proper example of the necessity explanation would be a crew lost at sea in a lifeboat with no supplies and no immediate prospect of rescue who kill and eat one of their members to survive. What they did is arguably morally understandable. Again, there are borderlands here. Is the occupation of one's nation state by a foreign army an example of such extreme circumstances that one has no choice but to pursue horrific and brutal acts of resistance? Here we enter the 'war on terror' from both perspectives. What is crucial for the madness/necessity explanation is that freedom or rationality of choice have been removed. Either mental illness has made rational choice impossible or circumstances have made free choice impossible. What is ruled out is that human agents can freely and rationally choose to do such things simply because they want to.

I will look at all these possibilities in later chapters. The aim is to discover whether the idea of evil has any place in a secular understanding of humanity, or whether it is an irredeemably religious or supernatural or mythological concept. The fundamental problem is one of explanation, and whether the concept of evil can play any constructive or useful role in explaining human action. Is 'because she was evil' ever an explanation, even a partial one? On the other hand, if we abandon the concept of evil altogether, as the psychological conception insists we must, is there not a huge gap in our understanding of humanity? In the end, is a world view without the concept of evil one that can make any sense to us? Are none of the examples of grotesquely violent and cruel behaviour committed by humans against other humans evidence that there is such a thing as evil? And we must remember Bernstein's critical challenge to the psychological conception, of the gap it leaves in our accounts, and that the attraction of the idea of evil is that it can fill that gap. When we are asking why the American guards in the Iraqi jail inflicted gross suffering upon their victims while others in the identical situation chose not to, then 'because they were evil' completes our accounts of them, and tells us everything we need to know.

However, in defence of the psychological conception, we can ask whether the 'black hole' has genuinely been filled, whether we have, instead, fallen back into mythology. 'Because they were evil' presents the illusion of understanding, and we may have failed to understand anything if we resort to it. Indeed, the 'black-hole' problem afflicts even the most traditional understandings of evil. If we submit the Devil to any detailed examination to try to understand why he afflicts humanity, 'because he is evil', paradoxically, fails spectacularly to explain anything about him and his motivations. Having said this, though, the psychological conception, although it may give us the correct understanding of the metaphysics of evil – its radical non-existence – does fail to supply any sort of account of why the idea of evil has such a powerful grasp on our imaginations, such that, even though we see it belongs within a dream, we constantly confuse that dream for reality. This account has to be a central component of the rejection of evil as myth. One possibility is to explore our own psyches, to try to discover what we are so scared of. Here we move beyond the psychological to the psychoanalytic, a journey into the unconscious to find the true form of the supernatural monsters that haunt us. One place where the unconscious can be explored, of course, is the world of fiction, where these monsters, demonic and human, are the stuff of everyday experience. Another possibility is to understand the concept of evil as a disciplinary discourse that regulates an oppressive sense of the human, drawing on the work of Michel Foucault. The third possibility is to understand evil against the background of mythology, such that each time we describe someone as evil we are placing them within a mythological narrative, giving them a specific role to play in a world history. Evil, in this sense, is the grandest of grand narratives.

Behind the question of the meanings of evil lies a more fundamental one, of the meaning of humanity, for each conception of evil has as its partner a conception of what it means to be human. If we discover the need for a new conception of evil, we will also discover the need for a new model of the human as the accepted borders between humanity and inhumanity collapse. This has enormous implications for moral and political philosophy, because at their foundation is a conception of the limits of the human, and the idea of evil both reinforces those limits and disrupts them. It also has profound implications for those cases where people do transgress those limits and our capacity to judge and punish them. On the one hand, judgement is impossible and punishment may itself be inhumane. On the other hand, perhaps such judgements have to be made and punishment owed as retribution for what has been done, precisely in order to maintain the boundaries of the human. We may have to accept that some of the most dreadful acts in our history have been freely chosen by rational agents.

This possibility haunts us at the level of our community and our individuality. It haunts us at the level of the community because of the deep dilemmas we face when it comes to the treatment of the disturbingly many people who transgress their humanity. It haunts us at the level of our individuality because at stake here is our own humanity and our own insecurity about who we are and what we are capable and incapable of doing. Bearing witness to the dreadful things so many people have done to so many others confronts us with the possibility that we have the capacity to do the same or worse. It may be that one possible meaning for the concept of evil is that we use it to hide from ourselves.

On Philosophical History

I will make two final points before I close this first chapter. First, my previous work has been on political theory and immigration (Cole 2000). It is worth noting the connections between that work and this current project. In that book I argued that the borders and boundaries peoples draw in order to identify themselves as distinct from others are imaginary and have no real basis. The point there was to argue that those borders and boundaries could play no legitimate role in any genuinely ethical view of what it is to be a member of a community. Here the boundary is that of humanity but the problem is the same, that if this boundary is imaginary then we have no genuinely ethical view of what it is to be human. The idea of evil is supposed to play a role in marking out that boundary, but what I have argued here and will continue to argue throughout the book is that in fact it undermines it drastically, because what we will discover is that the enemy is always within – the one fact we cannot escape is that if pure evil does genuinely exist in the world, it is human beings who put it there. We may be able to shore up the border by declaring all such human beings to be deviant monsters, or insane or helpless against overwhelming circumstances, and so not *really* evil at all, or not really human. But then all such defences may fail, and, in Judith Halberstam's terms, the attempt to 'make the human a refuge from monstrosity' may be futile (Halberstam 1995: 188).

The second and final point is that I use the idea of philosophical history to propose a method of tracing the possible meanings of evil and drawing on a range of sources from different fields. I take the idea of philosophical history from Jonathan Rée (Rée 2000).

This is to approach evil as a phenomenon, and, says Rée, 'to treat something as a phenomenon means approaching it not as an object, but as a topic or theme: a great onion, as you might picture it, made of nothing but layer upon layer of more or less intelligent experiences – a topic of human perceptions, weighed down by history, saturated with memories, fears and desires; a theme of love, hatred, obsession and fascination; in short a hubbub of conflicting interpretations, accessible only through the multiple obliquities of a philosophical history' (Rée 2000: 7). A philosophical history will 'devote itself to metaphysical notions that have infiltrated ordinary common sense and become real forces in the world, guiding our individual choices and even determining the destiny of whole groups or classes...' (Rée 2000: 382). The concept of evil seems an ideal subject for such a method, to be treated as a 'metaphysical notion that has infiltrated common sense', and a concept that has become a real force in the world. At the end of such a history we may be in a position to judge whether the concept of evil has a legitimate role to play in a philosophy of humanity.

Conclusion

Although I have identified four possible secular conceptions of evil, in the end I believe the contest is between the pure conception of evil and the psychological rejection of it, and of the two my preference is for the psychological rejection. I do not supply any decisive philosophical refutations of the pure conception, but rather supply moral, political and psychological reasons why we should reject it. It is, I believe, a highly dangerous and inhumane discourse and we are better off without it. In Chapter 3 I look at the philosophical, impure conception of evil, and show why it is incoherent, and one might assume that once this is done the book would take the form of a debate between the pure and psychological views. However, although I have already dismissed the monstrous conception of evil, we will find that we encounter it over and over again because, as in Krafft-Ebing's text, it keeps erupting into view at certain crucial points.

And so the book is not simply a debate between the pure and psychological conceptions, but is also a record of the ways in which the monstrous conception keeps rising up and dominating the field. We will confront it in Chapter 4 when we study the historical phenomena of the witch trials of Europe and North

America of the sixteenth and seventeenth centuries, and the vampire epidemics that swept through eastern Europe in the eighteenth century. It was this myth of monstrous evil that was mobilised to attack 'witches', and to persuade people to obey religious authorities in order to be protected from the living dead that were rising from their graves. In Chapter 5 I pose the question, what are we scared of? What is it that enables authorities – religious or political – to exploit our fears and insecurities so effectively? I look at psychoanalytic accounts, such as those of Sigmund Freud and Julia Kristeva, approaching them through the presence of evil in fictional form in film, television and literature. Here, again, it is fear of evil monsters, often invaders from another world, that keeps recurring as a theme.

One of the enduring images in fiction is the evil child, for children in their innocence are especially terrifying, and in Chapter 6 I examine the demonisation of children in reality, looking at the case of the killers of James Bulger and how they were treated both culturally and legally. Here the psychological conception directly battles against the myth of evil monsters, as I argue against the view that children who kill cannot be 'real' children, but are monsters in disguise. Chapter 7 returns to philosophical argument to examine the idea of 'character', and whether it makes sense to talk of 'evil' characters. John Kekes argues that we must use the concept of evil to condemn such characters, and I examine his views in detail. But once more, we find the monstrous conception lurking beneath the narrative, in that if we *can* identify people with evil character, we must condemn them, shun them, and deny the possibility of redemption. Chapter 8 confronts the Holocaust, the most difficult challenge for anybody who wishes to deny that the concept of evil has any useful role to play in describing human agency. Nevertheless I argue that the idea of evil fails to help us to understand how such events happen, and so I question its importance even here. It is the monstrous conception of evil that is at work once more, in the anti-Semitism that drove the Nazi leadership and its supporters in their conviction that the Jewish people were a demonic enemy bent on the destruction of Germany and human civilisation in general. But we also find it in the portrayal of the Nazi leadership and those who participated in the Holocaust – they could not be 'ordinary' Germans, but had to be some kind of demonic presence.

Finally, in Chapter 9 I look at 21st-century mythologies, such as that of global terrorism, where once more we find ourselves confronted by a demonic enemy with supernatural powers devoted to our destruction. The myth of monstrous evil will not go away, and what we have to understand is the extent to which political communities are constituted by fear of imaginary monsters. And so, while I intended to write a philosophical treatment of the concept of evil, a detached, dispassionate study, I found myself facing a profoundly un-philosophical creature, and instead have written what is, for the most part, an enraged polemic against that monster. I conclude that the idea of evil is not a philosophical concept, certainly not a psychological one, and not even a religious one. It is a mythological concept that has a role to play in grand narratives of world history. To describe someone as evil is not to say anything about *them*, but is to place them as victims of a narrative force, as characters in a story in which they play a specific and prescribed role. In Chapter 2 I look at the history of the idea of Satan, and argue that this history shows that the figure of the Devil has always played a political role in mobilising a community through fear of the evil enemy, and that this enemy is usually to be found *within* the community, in the figure who appears to be one of us, but who is a monster in disguise. In the concluding chapter I return to this theme, and argue that Satan is only a coherent figure in the context of a mythology – outside of that mythology both Satan and the idea of evil make no sense. In the absence of any mythological grand narrative of world history, we should abandon the idea of evil.

Chapter Two

Diabolical Evil – Searching for Satan

Introducing Satan

Each day on the television or in the newspaper I am confronted by the evidence that human beings are capable of the most dreadful acts against other human beings. If, like me, you regard animals as carrying ethical significance then the catalogue of atrocity becomes even longer. One way of understanding at least some of these actions is to see them as diabolical or demonic, a commitment to the suffering and destruction of others for no other reason than that destruction itself. Many of them can be understood as provoked by anger or ignorance or even misguided hope, but some stand out as unspeakable and incomprehensible. It is here that 'because she was evil' becomes a complete answer to the question 'why did she do it?', a total explanation, but one that seems to take us to a baffling dead end. Both the monstrous and the pure conceptions of evil which I described in Chapter 1 seem to rest on this possibility of diabolical evil and so do seem to take us to this dead end – if they are going to be truly illuminating we need to understand how they can act as explanations of human behaviour at all.

Diabolical evil has an obvious historical and conceptual connection with the figure of Satan or the Devil in western thought, and one way in which it can serve as an explanation is that Satan is acting through people to bring about his purposes. I will examine this explanation more closely later in this chapter because a great many people, some of them 'enlightened' and highly educated, believe it. In the first parts of the chapter, however, I will examine the history of the idea of Satan closely, and although this may seem to be an unnecessary detour into the interpretation of ancient religious texts when there are more urgent contemporary problems of evil to discuss, there is a good secular point for doing it. The monstrous and pure conceptions of evil do have a strong connection with diabolical evil, and although I do not take the monstrous conception – that there is a distinct set of monsters in human form – seriously, I do take seriously the pure conception – that all humans have the capacity for pure evil. This does not mean that Satan must exist for the pure conception of evil to make sense, but it does mean that we must have the capacity to be like him, and so in understanding Satan's character we begin to understand our selves.

Jeffrey Burton Russell, in his extremely valuable and detailed studies of the history of the Devil, identifies four kinds of evil: moral, '...when an intelligent being knowingly and deliberately inflicts suffering upon another sentient being' (Russell 1989: 1); natural, '...the suffering resulting from processes of nature such as cancers and tornadoes' (Russell 1989: 2); metaphysical, '...the necessary lack of perfection that exists in any created cosmos, since no cosmos can be as perfect as God is perfect' (Russell 1989: 1); and cosmic. Cosmic evil aims at the destruction of the cosmos itself, and is the Devil's business. 'Inflicting suffering for the sake of suffering, doing evil for evil's sake, the Devil is by definition the personification of cosmic evil' (Russell 1989: 2). He raises the question, though, 'whether the concept of the Devil makes any sense' (Russell 1989: 2). If we find that it does not, then it may be that the most disturbing conception of human evil fails to make sense too. The question we will find ourselves facing is, paradoxically, whether Satan is capable of diabolical evil? The notion of diabolical evil may be so incoherent that not even the Devil can engage in it, unless he, too, becomes a radically incoherent figure.

Satan in the Old Testament

The investigation of the Satanic figure in western thought must start by asking where it comes from, and an obvious beginning is the Hebrew Bible, the Christian Old Testament. However, this obvious beginning is, unfortunately, highly misleading, and in fact we will have to do a great deal of detective work and search other sources, historical, mythological and fictional, for the Devil's origins. Before we do that work, the fact that looking at the Old Testament is a mistake needs explanation, and the first part of this explanation is that although the Bible is, for Christians, the most authoritative text that has ever existed, it is, especially the Old Testament, the product of a series of translations over thousands of years, and translations are notoriously ideological. For example, the order of the Old Testament is very different from the Hebrew Bible for ideological reasons. In Judaism the Hebrew scriptures are known as the *Tanakh* (Sarna 1987: 152). This is an anacronym, TaNaKh, representing the three parts of the book, the Torah, the *Nevi'im* (the Prophets), and the *Ketuvim* (the Writings). The Torah consists of the first five books, Genesis, Exodus, Leviticus, Numbers and Deuteronomy, known to Christians as the Pentateuch, covering the creation of the world to the death of Moses and the arrival in the promised land. The *Nevi'im* consists of the former prophets which continues the historical narrative ending in the Babylonian exile up to 560 BCE (I use BCE and CE here, as Before the Common Era and the Common Era, to avoid using the Christian dating system), and the latter prophets, works of literary prophets in Israel and Judah from the eighth to fifth centuries BCE. The *Ketuvim* is made up of a collection of different kinds of writings gathered together in a way which suggests it was added to the other two sections later, although some elements of it are older than the *Nevi'im*. The Hebrew Bible was translated into Greek, the *Septuagint*, a project started in the 3rd century BCE and completed around 132 BCE, to meet the needs of the hellenised Jewish community in Alexandria. There was some rearrangement and divergence here but it is not clear why (Sarna 1987: 155). It was this Greek version which became the official Bible for the Christian Church, with the books of the New Testament being produced between 50 CE and 150 CE. The Latin version was produced in 405 CE, the *Vulgate* of St Jerome. The first English translation appeared in 1395 under the direction of John Wycliffe, although some elements of it had been translated prior to this. Most significantly William Tyndale translated and printed an English version in 1525.

At an early stage in the history of the Christian Church the Old Testament was rearranged into four parts, the Pentateuch, the Histories, the Poetical Works and the Prophets, and Robert Carroll and Stephen Prickett, editors and commentators on a recent edition of the King James Authorised Version written in 1611, argue that this rearrangement alters the character of the text taken as a whole. The Hebrew arrangement is 'at once timeless and open', pointing to 'the pattern of perpetual exile and questioning of God' (Carroll and Prickett 1998: xiv). The Christian arrangement is 'a polemical and even a doctrinal pointer to what is to follow it in the New' (Carroll and Prickett 1998: xiv), making it 'a dynamic and purposeful sequence, rather than an open quest' (Carroll and Prickett 1998: xv). Most significant is the placing of the Prophets last to point to the New Testament, and closing the canon with Malachi, who declares: 'I will send my messenger, and he shall prepare the way before me' (Carroll and Prickett 1998: Old Testament 1038), and that the day of the Lord is approaching. Sarna comments: 'the variant sequence was best suited to express the claim of the church that the New Testament was the fulfilment of the Hebrew scriptures of the Jews' (Sarna 1987: 156). And of course the process of translation itself was ideological, or at least doctrinal. In that process, 'the actual terms of the translation were also being themselves transformed – sometimes with radically new meanings' (Carroll and Prickett 1998: xvi). With this in mind we must approach the appearance of Satan in the Old Testament with a great deal of caution, because his presence there is precisely an example of mistranslation from the Hebrew, and if we take Carroll and Prickett's point then this mistranslation may be intentional, with an ideological or doctrinal purpose. If this is right, then the figure of Satan himself may have an ideological or doctrinal role to play, and this reflects significantly on our understanding of diabolical evil – it, too, may have an ideological role, and this, possibly, may be all there is to it. We may have evidence here to deny the reality of diabolical evil at least, and so be in a position to reject the pure conception of human evil and question the ideological motivations of those who choose to employ the idea of evil in attempting to achieve political purposes.

The Book of Job in the Old Testament begins: 'There was a man in the land of Uz, whose name was Job; and that man was perfect and upright, and one that feared God and eschewed evil' (Carroll and Prickett 1998: Old Testament 607). The story is a familiar one and contains all the main characters:- God, Satan, and a tormented human being. Job is made to suffer by Satan in order to test his faith, and everything that Job has reason to thank God for is destroyed. Throughout his sufferings Job remains steadfast and the story proves the power of faith and the futility of Satan's task in the face of such faith. The moral of the story is, of course, that if we have faith in God then Satan cannot really hurt us. But this fails miserably as a reading of the Book of Job because Satan *does* hurt Job terribly, and many innocent people connected to him suffer too, mere bystanders in this cosmic experiment – Job's seven sons perish and his servants are all killed, and although they are mostly replaced by the end of the story, there is no acknowledgement that they have been the innocent victims of a cosmic prank. Most disturbing of all, Satan has God's permission to do all of this and God remains fully aware of everything that happens. This, say Carroll and Prickett, is both 'baffling and haunting' (Carroll and Prickett 1998: 353), and makes Job one of the most 'disturbing books in the Bible' (Carroll and Prickett 1998: 353–4). But the fact is that none of the characters here are quite who we think they are. Certainly the God we encounter is not the God of Christianity, who would never deliver a good and faithful servant into the Devil's power for any reason, let alone what seems like a celestial wager. And neither is Satan here the character who stands as the opponent of God and Christ in the New Testament and later writings.

Russell points out that the God of much of the Old Testament is both light and darkness, good and evil (Russell 1989: 28). Here we have a monotheistic religion with a dualistic God. 'The Old Testament God is powerful and benevolent, but he had a shadow side, and that shadow is part of the background of the Hebrew Satan' (Russell 1989: 29). Neil Forsyth agrees that here is an ambivalent God who has 'a destructive as well as creative side' (Forsyth 1987: 109). Gradually this ambivalent God is transformed into a wholly beneficent God, and evil is seen as having another source. There were two strategies to account for this, first an emphasis on the alienation of humanity, that the people have strayed too far from God and so are justly punished by him (Russell 1989: 30–1), and second the existence of a supernatural being opposed to God who attacks the faithful and makes them suffer (Russell 1989: 31). This, of course, raises problems for a monotheistic faith like Judaism, and the result is 'a tension between monotheism and a kind of practical, implicit dualism, a tension that became typical of late Hebrew religion and Christianity' (Russell 1989: 31). Either, it seems, we have a dualistic God, both good and evil, or we have a religion with elements of dualism. Later Judaism and Christianity, as Russell points out, take the latter path, making space for the figure of Satan.

In the Book of Job, says Russell, 'Satan is already a personality with the function of accusing, opposing, and harming human beings. He is not yet the principle of evil, for he is still one of the heavenly court and does nothing without God's consent and command' (Russell 1989: 37), but there is still a hint of opposition here. 'Satan works as the shadow, the dark side of God, the destructive power wielded by God only reluctantly' (Russell

1989: 37). Elsewhere we encounter the *mal'ak Yahweh*, an evil messenger of God, an evil spirit God sends out to do mischief in his name. The *mal'ak* is a dark spirit who lies and deceives at God's command. In books such as Judges, Kings and Chronicles the *mal'ak* slowly gains independence from God: '... gradually its destructive aspect was emphasised; finally it became the person-ification of the dark side of the divine nature. The *mal'ak* was now the evil angel, Satan, the obstructor, the liar, the destroying spirit' (Russell 1989: 38). It is this character that is taken up and developed in other writings during the intertestamental period and who emerges more or less fully formed in the New Testament as the Devil, the opponent of God and Christ, with a clear role to play in the Christian version of world history.

The Old Testament without Satan

According to this reading, then, a character emerges in the Old Testament and develops into the figure we can identify as Satan. However, this interpretation is disputed, and in another reading of the Old Testament no such figure can be identified, and so the idea of Satan has to have some other source. This idea of Satan found its way into the Old Testament through mistranslation of Hebrew terms at a much later time, a time when the idea we now have of Satan was more fully developed – at the time that the Old Testament texts were written, this notion of Satan did not exist at all. But before we identify Satan's true source, what evidence is there that he has no place in the Old Testament texts? Breytenbach and Day make out this case, observing that the name Satan is an anglicisation of the Hebrew word *satan*, which is commonly linked to verbs in Hebrew which mean to stray, to revolt, to se-duce, all roles Satan will play. But this linking is questionable and, they say, probably results from 'interaction between popular etymological speculation and developing traditions about Satan' (Breytenbach and Day 1995: 1369). In other words, it is the idea of Satan which shapes the meaning of these words rather than the other way round. In fact, they point out, the noun *satan* has no cognates in texts prior to or contemporary with the biblical texts, and so 'the meaning of the noun *satan* must be determined solely on the basis of its occurrences in the Hebrew Bible' (Breytenbach and Day 1995: 1370). It appears there nine times, and in five refers to human mortals and in four to celestial beings. When referring to human beings it is not a proper name but a common noun meaning 'adversary' or 'accuser', depending on the context. In the four celestial occurrences there is only one where it might function as a proper name and in the other three it works as a common noun again (Breytenbach and Day 1995: 1370). The first of these celestial contexts is Numbers 22: 22–35, where God sends his celestial messenger, the *mal'ak Yahweh*, to block the road travelled by Balaam, who has set out on a journey which God opposes. Here in the Hebrew the *mal'ak* is described as a *satan*, although in the English translation of the Authorised Version we have only 'the angel of the lord' (Carroll and Prickett 1998: OT195). Breytenbach and Day comment: 'the heavenly being who acts as a *satan* in Numbers 22 has very little in common with later conceptualizations of Satan. He is Yahweh's messenger, not his archenemy, and he acts in accordance with Yahweh's will rather than opposing it. Indeed, Yahweh's messenger here, as elsewhere in the Hebrew Bible, is basically an hypostatisation of the deity' (Breytenbach and Day 1995: 1372). In other words, the *mal'ak* is to be understood as an element of God himself, as he appears before Balaam.

The Authorised Version of King James first mentions Satan in the Book of Job. Here we see a gathering of the 'sons of God', and among them is a being named in the Hebrew as *hassatan*. This is the common noun preceded by the definite article, so here we are in the presence of 'the satan', but not Satan. Breytenbach and Day point out that although this is usually translated as the accuser, a specific legal title, there is no evidence of such a post in the legal systems of Israel or in celestial divine councils. Where the definite article is used elsewhere, its force is 'to de-emphasise precise identity and focus on the status of the character as it is relevant to the narrative plot' (Breytenbach and Day 1995: 1373). Therefore, they argue, we can assume that *hassatan* at Job 1: 16 has a similar sense: 'that a certain divine being whose precise identity is unimportant and who has the current and temporary status of accuser is being introduced into the narrative' (Breytenbach and Day 1995: 1373). This reads against the development of a continuing character we can connect with the traditional idea of Satan, and rather sees *satan* as a description of different characters filling a rather loosely defined role in different narratives.

This argument is reinforced by the other two references to a celestial *satan* in the Old Testament. In Zechariah 3, the Authorised Version has 'Joshua the high priest standing before the angel of the Lord, and Satan standing at his right hand to resist him'

(Carroll and Prickett 1998: Old Testament 1027), and God rebukes Satan for his opposition to Joshua as high priest. Once more in the Hebrew we have *hassatan*, the satan, accusing Joshua, but we also have the *mal'ak Yahweh*, the angel of the Lord, defending Joshua, and so one obvious conclusion is that the *mal'ak Yahweh* and *hassatan* are distinct characters here at least. Again *satan* is not a proper name, say Breytenbach and Day. Rather, the figure in this text represents a political dispute within the Jewish community, embodying elements of that community who opposed the status of Joshua as high priest, and possibly the office of high priest itself. What is clear is that this is not the same celestial being we encountered at Numbers 22, and there is no reason to suppose that it is the same figure that tormented Job (Breytenbach and Day 1995: 1375).

In the first book of Chronicles 21: 1 we have a more complex problem. The Authorised Version says: 'And Satan stood up against Israel and provoked David to number Israel' (Carroll and Prickett 1998: Old Testament 510). This provokes God's anger. Here in the Hebrew the noun *satan* appears without the definite article, and say Breytenbach and Day, the majority of scholars believe we have the proper name Satan here (Breytenbach and Day 1995: 1376). In the second book of Samuel the same story is told, but here God provokes David into taking the forbidden census. Breytenbach and Day argue that since the writer of Chronicles is using Samuel as the source text, 'it is clear that the Chronicler has altered his source in such a way as to take the burden of responsibility for the sinful census away from Yahweh. Some scholars interpret this to mean the Chronicler was striving to distance Yahweh from any causal relationship to sin, or to rid Yahweh of malevolent behaviour in general' (Breytenbach and Day 1995: 1376). However, this doesn't make complete sense, as there are other passages in Chronicles where Yahweh is clearly causing people to sin, and an alternative account is that the Chronicler is altering the text to present David, not Yahweh, in the best possible light, distancing him from events that reflect badly on him in Samuel. The census could not be omitted because it is too central to the story, but now the sin lies with another character, Joab, for not taking the census properly (Breytenbach and Day 1995: 1377). This matters, argue Breytenbach and Day, because the Chronicler's motivation tells us how we should take the word *satan* in this text. If he really is trying to separate Yahweh from wicked behaviour by inserting a new character in the text, then we have the beginnings of a moral and spiritual dualism that fits the distinction between the Christian God and Satan, and translating *satan* as Satan here is 'quite appropriate' (Breytenbach and Day 1995: 1377). However, if *satan* here is in the text to serve the ideological function of idealising David, and not to do with the problem of Yahweh's malevolence at all, 'then even if *satan* in this passage is a proper name, the term is still a long way from connoting Satan, God's evil archenemy' (Breytenbach and Day 1995: 1377). They favour the latter reading, citing the additional evidence that Chronicles was written around 520 BCE, in which case it is contemporary with Zechariah, which does not use *satan* as a proper name, and the earliest texts that do only appear more than 300 years later. It would therefore be extremely unusual if the *satan* who appears at 1 Chronicles 21: 1 is *the* Satan.

Breytenbach and Day conclude: 'the four Hebrew Bible texts that mention a celestial *satan* are most probably dateable to the 6th century BCE or later, and it is clear that the *satan* envisaged in Zechariah 3 is not the same divine being who acts as a *satan* in Numbers 22. Moreover, in none of the four texts is *satan* indisputably used as a proper name. Given these data, it is difficult to maintain, as many scholars have, that we can see in the Hebrew Bible a developing notion of Satan' (Breytenbach and Day 1995: 1377–8). And so, with Breytenbach and Day, I am inclined to conclude that there is no such character as Satan in the Old Testament, not even a developmental one.

Satan's Story

However, Satan is indisputably present in the New Testament as the major opponent of Christ and the ruler over the kingdom of darkness. There Satan appears 33 times, and another 32 times as the Devil, and occasionally under other descriptions such as Beelzebub, Belial, the evil one, the prince of demons, and the enemy. Here Satan is a 'distinctive personality' (Gaster 1962: 227), and there is a clear struggle taking place. Russell says: 'In the New Testament world view, either you follow God or you are subject to Satan. Because of sin, the world lies under the Devil's power; Christ comes to break that power and to heal the alienation between humanity and God' (Russell 1989: 44). The Devil is therefore associated with this world, with flesh and death: 'Since the moment of original sin, the Devil has been increasing his power over this world, until now, at this latter day, his sway has become nearly complete. But now God sends Christ to break the power of the old age and to replace it with the new age, the Kingdom of God' (Russell 1989: 44). Satan now comes complete with a role in a world history – he was there at the beginning in heaven with God, and will be there at the end of that history, at the final battle when he will be defeated. He also, crucially, comes with a host of demons, an army of evil spirits, and one major sign of Christ's battle with Satan is the casting out of demons and the curing of disease. 'The exorcism of demons represents no quirk here, no ir-relevant accretion of superstition, but rather is central to the war against Satan and therefore to the meaning of the gospels' (Russell 1989: 47). But the question remains, where did he come from, if not the Old Testament?

His first appearance in Jewish and Christian writings is in the bodies of work known as the *Apocrypha* and the *Pseudepigrapha*. The *Apocrypha* is a collection of Jewish writing between 300 BCE and 70 CE which has a disputed canonical status. Judaism does not accept them as canonical and neither do many Christian churches. The *Pseudepigrapha* is a collection of writing, some Jewish some Christian, from around 200 BCE to 200 CE. It is in these writings, says Gaster, that Satan 'begins to emerge as a distinctive person-ality' (Gaster 1962: 225), and Russell identifies the emergence of 'a being who personified the single origin and essence of evil', which is the figure of Satan, 'the development of the concept of a single principle – or, better, principal – of evil' (Russell 1989: 33). The *Pseudepigrapha* was especially influential, made up of books of apocalyptic revelation produced when the Jewish people were suffering under first Syrian and then Roman occupation, and re-flecting a sense of despair and disbelief that this scale of suffering could have been brought upon them by anything they did. The Book of Enoch, for example, develops the theory that this suffer-ing had a spiritual cause, and so develops a mythological history which explained why the world was dominated by evil (Russell 1989: 31). Gaster comments on the growing dualistic view, that the world was under the control of an evil principle 'who was re-sponsible at once for the massive sinfulness that had occasioned God's displeasure and for the vicious malevolence of Israel's op-pressors' (Gaster 1962: 225). What emerges is the figure of an arch-devil, 'who was the ultimate cause of evil' (Gaster 1962: 225). This arch-fiend is named as Satan, but also as Belial, Mastema and Sammael. But, says Gaster, there was 'a certain fluidity about the concept, for the Evil One sometimes retained his earlier character of a servant, rather than an opponent, of God' (Gaster 1962: 226). The mythology of this figure is constructed by the re-telling of Old Testament stories, including Genesis. Genesis 6: 2–6 tells the story of the sons of God who lusted after human women and entered into sexual relations with them, producing a race of giants. This is followed by the great flood and the story of Noah. In the Book of Enoch in the *Pseudepigrapha* these are the Watcher Angels, because of their interest in human women, and they have a leader, and they are ejected from heaven because of their lust and pride (see Charlesworth 1983, volume 1: 15–16). In the Book of Jubilees, also in the *Pseudepigrapha,* the figure named Mastema is the principle of evil who now takes on the malevolent aspects of God. And so when in Genesis 22 God commands Abraham to sacrifice his son Isaac, in Jubilees it is Mastema who deceives Abraham (see Charlesworth 1983, volume 2: 90–1). It is here, also, that the serpent in Eden is identified as a manifestation of Satan (see Charlesworth 1983, volume 2: 260). What emerges here and continues in the New Testament is a mythology of Satan which has basic elements that vary. Satan falls from heaven due to moral lapse or loss of dignity or voluntarily; he falls from heaven to earth, or from heaven to an underworld, or from earth to an underworld; and he falls at the beginning of the world, or from envy of Adam, or with the Watcher Angels at the time of Noah, or with the advent of Christ, the passion of Christ, the second coming of Christ or one thousand years after the second coming (Russell 1989: 48). But there is an overall pattern, that Satan is lord of this world, leader of an army of demons and evil humans, who stands in opposition to Christ. This is a war which Christ will win and the kingdom of God will be established for eternity with Satan's final defeat.

Thus Spake Zarathustra

And so it is in a collection of intertestamental writings that the fig-ure of Satan is developed, which explains why when he appears in the New Testament he is a definite character with a definite role to play in the Christian world history. But this is only part of the story, because we still face the question of why Satan appears at this time in this form, and whether there is another, older source. In fact there is such a source, Zoroastrianism, founded in pre-Islamic Iran by Zarathustra, perhaps as early as 1500 BCE (Boyce 1984: 280), and adopted by the Persian rulers in the early sixth century BCE. Zoroastrianism is a monotheistic faith with elements of a radical dualism, but Gherardo Gnoli argues that this is not necessarily a conflict. Dualism is 'a necessary and logical consequence' of monotheism – 'its purpose is to explain the origins of evil. The basis of dualism is essentially ethical' (Gnoli 1987: 581). In the Zoroastrian sacred texts, the *Avestas*, the monotheism is expressed in the supreme being of Ahura Mazda, and the dualism in two opposing spirits, Spenta Mainyu, the spirit of light, representing good, and Angra Mainyu, the spirit of darkness, representing evil, who are both products of Ahura Mazda. These two spirits have good or evil natures based on their choices. 'The good or evil nature of the two spirits derives from his own moral choice and is not, as suggested by some scholars, innate, ontologically given, or predetermined' (Gnoli 1987: 581). Therefore 'they act as a prototype of the choices that face each man as he decides whether to follow the path of truth or that of untruth' (Gnoli 1987: 581). And so: 'In Zarathustra's conception, a dualistic vision is almost a natural consequence of monotheism, for dualism explains the evil that resides in the world and afflicts it' (Gnoli 1987: 582). And so the presence of evil in the world is not metaphysical but ethical, the result of choice, not nature. It is worth noting here how important this point is for our secular understanding of evil, because it marks a clearer boundary between the two conceptions that draw on the notion of diabolical evil, the monstrous and the pure – the monstrous conception can now be understood as claiming that there are human beings who are monstrous by nature, and it is only these humans who have the capacity for diabolical evil, and the pure conception can be understood as claiming that all human beings have the capacity for diabolical evil, and the difference between those who pursue that capacity and those who do not has nothing to do with nature, but is down to the choices people make.

As Zoroastrianism developed it acquired a highly elaborate hierarchy of spirits, a demonology and angelology. Gnoli comments that these 'theological elaborations led to a precise structuring of a pantheon and a pandemonium; each is characterized by analogous hierarchical structures and precise interrelations between the worlds of good... and that of evil... so that each positive or beneficent entity has a corresponding negative or maleficent entity' (Gnoli 1987: 583). There also developed a more radical dualism, a version of Zoroastrianism known as Zurvanism, in which Ahura Mazda became one of the two opposing spirits, rather than the supreme being. However, the most important element for our interest is the battle between a prince of light and a prince of darkness for control over this world, aided by complex hierarchies of angels and demons. Jews would have encountered Zoroastrianism during the Babylonian exile after 586 BCE, and the hypothesis is that the influence of Zoroastrianism starts to appear in the Jewish writings during the intertestamental period, and is subsequently incorporated into the Christian mythology which takes in this Jewish mythology virtually intact. And so G. J. Riley writes that the inspiration for the appearance of Satan and his demons in the Jewish writings of this period 'was the encounter during the Exile and later with Zoroastrian dualism' (Riley 1995a: 450). For T. H. Gaster, 'Satan was, to a large extent, simply a Judaized version of the Avestan figures of Angra Mainyu...the inveterate foe of the supreme god Ahura-mazda...or of Druj, the spirit of deceit' (Gaster 1962: 226). This thesis is, of course, disputed, but in a detailed study of the similarities between Zoroastrianism and Judaism, Shaul Shaked concludes: 'It does not seem at all likely that so many similarities could have been formed in parallel independently, and, despite the chronological difficulties of the documentation, in most of the parallel points one may feel quite confident that the ideas were indigenous to Iran' (Shaked 1984: 324).

The most striking parallels are found in the writings of the Jewish sect of the Essenes, who settled the Qumran community from between 150 and 140 BCE to 68 CE, and were responsible for the libraries discovered in 1947. These writings, commonly known as the Dead Sea Scrolls, are believed by some scholars to be highly influential on the early Christian community. One Essenes text, the 'Treatise of the Two Spirits', states that the Spirit of Light and the Spirit of Darkness were created by God to determine the fate of each human being (Koch 2000: 1012). The Sons of Light were to be led by the Prince of Light against the demonic host led by Satan (Vermes 1987: 53). And so we can trace the development of the figure of the Prince of Darkness from Zoroastrianism into the Jewish apocalyptic writings, especially those of the Essenes, and into Christianity.

The Ideological Satan

Finally, I think, we know where Satan comes from, but the other part of our question was why he emerged at this time, and it is here that we start to see Satan as playing an ideological role for the Jewish and Christian communities of this period. Valerie Flint explains the appearance of Satan and his demons in terms of the insecurity of these communities: 'A people battling to defend its religion and self-identity, and without hope of victory in military terms, has a special need of a different kind of victory, and to categorise internally all that is most hostile to it. The evil "daimones" offered themselves readily to Judaism for the task. They were seized upon therefore with enthusiasm' (Flint 1999: 293). Elaine Pagels in her study of the origin of Satan takes a similar view, but makes the point that the primary enemy feared by these communities was not external, but internal. The Jews taken into Babylonian exile were freed by Cyrus the Great when he conquered Babylonia in 539 BCE and introduced religious toleration. He offered funds for the reconstruction of Jerusalem and the rebuilding of the Temple that had been destroyed by the Babylonians (Pagels 1996: 43). These returning exiles were regarded with some suspicion by those who had remained in Israel, as 'agents of the Persian king', and out to 'retrieve the power and land they had been forced to relinquish' (Pagels 1996: 44). Another empire was established by Alexander the Great in 323 BCE, a Hellenistic dynasty which created more conflict within the Jewish community between those who wanted to conserve traditional Jewish practices and those who wanted more secular influence or to adopt practices of other cultures such as the Greeks. The Jews gained their independence in 168 BCE, but the disputes continued as radical separatists formed who wanted to keep the purity of the Jewish traditions. 'More radical than their predecessors, these dissidents began increasingly to invoke the *satan* to characterize their Jewish opponents; in the process they turned this rather unpleasant angel into a far greater – and far more malevolent – figure. No longer one of God's faithful servants, he begins to become what he is for Mark and later Christianity – God's antagonist, his enemy, even his rival' (Pagels 1996: 47). Satan became increasingly important as a figure, the ultimate enemy in that he had been a trusted friend in heaven before his fall, one of the highest angels. He represents, therefore, one of the most dangerous of enemies, the enemy within.

Pagels argues that the texts of the *Pseudepigrapha* where these stories are developed can be read for their sociopolitical content. In the first Book of Enoch the story of the Watcher Angels is told, of how they fell because of their lust for human women, giving rise to a race of giants and demons (see Charlesworth 1983, volume 2: 16). Pagels says, 'these stories involve sociopolitical satire laced with religious polemic' (Pagels 1996: 50), perhaps aimed at the Greeks who believed people were descended from gods, or factions in the Jewish priesthood who married Gentile women (Pagels 1996: 50–1). Jubilees, written around the same time, expresses the same concerns about the abandonment of tradition, and emphasises a change in the traditional lines separating Jew from Gentile (Pagels 1996: 53). Jewishness is now a moral identity, not an ethnic one – being a Jew is not enough to be one of God's chosen. Satan and his demons are not metaphors standing for the oppressors of the Jewish nation, but for fallen Jews, those who abandon tradition, the enemy within the community. Radical sectarian groups, like the Essenes at Qumran, 'placed this cosmic battle between angels and demons, God and Satan, at the very center of their cosmology and their politics' (Pagels 1996: 56). The Essenes are especially important here. 'Had Satan not already existed in the Jewish tradition, the Essenes would have invented him' (Pagels 1996: 58). They place 'at the center of their religious understanding the cosmic war between God and his allies, both angelic and human, against Satan, or Beliar, along with his demonic and human allies' (Pagels 1996: 58). Russell says this theme continues within Christianity. The early Church was insecure, and so St Paul warns in Ephesians 6: 11–13: 'Put on the whole armour of God, that ye may be able to stand against the wiles of the devil. For we wrestle not against flesh and blood, but against principalities, against powers, against the rulers of darkness of this world, against spiritual wickedness in high places. Wherefore take unto you the whole armour of God, that ye may be able to withstand in the evil day . . . ' (Carroll and Prickett 1998: New Testament 244). But the most important enemy was not, once more, pagans, but schismatics and heretics who threatened its unity. Heretics were the agents of Satan (Russell 1989: 53). The enemy is not physical flesh and blood but supernatural. This belief in a supernatural enemy of great power and cunning comes to dominate the Christian Church, and we see its ultimate expression in the witch trials of the sixteenth and seventeenth centuries, as witches were the ultimate heretic, those who had pledged themselves to the service of Satan.

This chapter is called searching for Satan, and has been a search for his origins as a mythological character. What we have shown is that Satan has a specific ideological role to play in Judaeo-Christian mythology, and it may be that the idea of diabolical evil itself has a similar role. This should lead us to question the motivation of those who choose to employ the idea of evil for political purposes, and also lead us to suspect that the concept itself may be so thoroughly imbued with ideological purposes that we should abandon it. In Chapter 4, though, I want to look at another way to search for Satan, a way that emerges from the political nature of his presence. There is evidence that the figure of Satan emerges at its most intense within communities which consider themselves to be under threat, not from an external enemy, but from an internal one, the kind of enemy who threatens to transform the identity of that community and change it into something else, and the kind of enemy who appears to be a close and loyal ally but turns out to be plotting this kind of destruction. But Satan is a supernatural enemy, and his moral agents are human beings, some of whom are unknowing, but many of whom know clearly what they are doing and why they are doing it. The search for Satan therefore becomes the search for his human allies. Here we may find more evidence that the idea of diabolical evil has played an important ideological role, to such an extent that we should treat it with extreme caution. I will return to this political philosophy of the Devil in Chapter 4, but next I turn to the question of the relationship between the Devil and diabolical evil. It may be that if we study that relationship in enough detail, we shall see that not even he is capable of diabolical evil, which would suggest that the idea of it is incoherent, and this has important consequences for how we should understand human evil. I suggested that Satan was a perverted role model, but in fact he may not serve as a model at all, except to the extent that he demonstrates the disturbing complexity of the relationship between humanity and evil.

The Devil and the Intellectuals

We may reject the idea of the Devil as a primitive, pre-Enlightenment left-over, and assume that when we engage in intellectual argument with religious believers we are facing a theodicy that has no place for such a 'prince of darkness' figure. Two facts should caution us here. First, considerable numbers of people do believe in the existence of the Devil. Second, while we may want to dismiss such people as non-intellectuals who have not thought about the subject clearly or have not read enough books, there are intellectuals who believe in the existence of the Devil just as strongly and who have both read a great many books and written a great many too. The intellectual need for Satan arises primarily to solve the problem of the relationship between God and evil rather than between humanity and evil. In solving the former, religious thinkers may argue, we also solve the latter – but this does not necessarily follow at all, as I will argue later in this chapter. The traditional problem of evil takes the shape of five propositions, outlined by Peter Vardy in his book, *The Puzzle of Evil*: (1) a God exists that created the universe from nothing; (2) this God has a continued interest in its creation; (3) God is good; (4) God is omnipotent; and (5) God does not wish for suffering to take place (Vardy 1992: 81). Suffering *does* take place, and so it looks as though one of these propositions must be false, and yet all of them seem essential for Christian theology. The most coherent general reply to the problem, argues Vardy, is the free-will defence: that it is better that God created humanity with free will rather than eliminate all suffering, because it is good that people discover a loving relationship with God, than be turned into 'programmed robots' (Vardy 1992: 38–9). However, although the free-will defence makes the five propositions logically compatible, this position on evil is still vulnerable to another form of attack, not on its logic but on its compassion, or rather lack of it. There is, according to the argument, a higher good which justifies human suffering, but can it ever be worth it (Vardy 1992: 72)?

This is the question posed by Ivan Karamazov in Fyodor Dostoyevsky's *The Brothers Karamazov*. In a debate with his brother Alyosha, a novice monk, Ivan claims he is an atheist who believes in God, one who has rejected God's authority utterly. His focus is on the 'sufferings of children', who are 'as yet guilty of nothing' (Dostoyevsky 2003: 310–11), illustrated with a series of real examples Dostoyevsky took from the Russian newspapers while he was writing the novel (Vardy 1992: 72). The first is a report of Turkish atrocities in Bulgaria in 1875–6: 'Imagine: a mother stands trembling with an infant in her arms, around her the Turks who have entered. They contrive a merry little act: they fondle the infant, laugh in order to amuse it, they succeed, the infant laughs. At that moment a Turk points a pistol at it, four inches from its face. The baby boy laughs joyfully, stretches out his little hands to grab the pistol, and suddenly the artist pulls the trigger right in his face and smashes his little head to smithereens' (Dostoyevsky 2003: 312). In the second, the parents of a five-year-old girl subject her 'to every torture one could think of. They beat her, flogged her, kicked her, themselves not knowing why, turned her whole body into a mass of bruises; at last they attained the highest degree of refinement: in the cold and freezing weather they locked her up for a whole night in the outside latrine because she did not ask to be relieved (as though a five-year-old child, sleeping its sound, angelic sleep, could learn to ask to be relieved at such an age) – what is more, they smeared her eyes, cheeks and mouth all over with faeces and compelled her to eat those faeces' (Dostoyevsky 2003: 316). The third tells of the owner of a large estate who hunted with dogs. One day a serf boy, eight years old, threw a stone which bruised the leg of the owner's favourite hound. When he learned of this, the man kept him locked up overnight, and the next day had him stripped naked and made to run as the hounds were sent after him. 'He hunted him down in front of his mother, and the dogs tore the child to little shreds!' (Dostoyevsky 2003: 317).

The point of all this, says Ivan, is to challenge the view that human suffering serves a higher goal. 'Tell me yourself directly, I challenge you – reply: imagine you yourself are erecting the edifice of human fortune with the goal of, at the finale, making people happy, or at last giving them peace and quiet, but that in order to do it it would be necessary and unavoidable to torture to death only one tiny little creature, that same little child that beat its breast with its little fist, and on its unavenged tears to found that edifice, would you agree to be the architect on those conditions...?' (Dostoyevsky 2003: 321). And from the point of view of the people for whom the edifice is being built, could they 'agree to accept their happiness being bought by the unwarranted blood of a small tortured child and, having accepted it, remain happy for ever?' (Dostoyevsky 2003: 321). This, says Peter Vardy, constitutes 'the most effective attack against God ever produced' (Vardy 1992: 72). He concludes that, 'rationally and on balance Ivan's attack succeeds. I can see no way of defending the claim that the suffering of innocent children is worth any ultimate end, no matter how glorious' (Vardy 1992: 82). There are two responses to Ivan's challenge, the first to become an atheist, the second to claim that we can never understand God's scheme and so make it an unfathomable mystery which we should never question (Vardy 1992: 87). This latter option, of mystery, is a highly respected and traditional one in Christian theology. The *Catholic Dictionary of Theology*, in its discussion of evil, concludes: 'Thus the place of evil in the world remains mysterious' (Davis et al. 1962: 249).

This is precisely because evil is a 'privation permitted to intrude into the work of God only for the sake of some greater good', and this greater good will 'be seen only by the light of Glory' (Davis et al. 1962: 248). However, Vardy himself takes a third and very different approach, which is to modify one of the five propositions that make up religious belief, by limiting God's power (Vardy 1992: 113). And one way in which he limits God's power is to draw in the figure of Satan as an oppositional force of evil, perhaps an appropriate response to Dostoyevsky's novel, for, according to David McDuff: 'The Devil is the central character in *The Brothers Karamazov*' (McDuff 2003: xxiii).

According to Vardy, God has limited power over his creations: 'a much more restricted view of God's omnipotence is required and . . . one of the major reasons that Christians have intellectual difficulties in believing in God in the face of evil in the world is that they have a too exalted view of God's power. God's power is much more restricted than is generally supposed' (Vardy 1992: 113). In the traditional Judaeo-Christian narrative God's power is clearly limited. In the Old Testament, although he controls human history, he rarely acts directly and usually works through human agencies. In the New Testament it is clear that the world is under the power of the Devil. 'The only real power God has is the guarantee that he provides that anyone who anchors himself or herself wholly on him will not be overcome by the forces of darkness' (Vardy 1992: 116). But rather than talk of the Devil, with all its superstitious baggage, Vardy talks instead of 'forces of evil', and poses the the central question: 'whether there are such forces, and, if so, whether they are entirely locatable within the human psyche' (Vardy 1992: 169).

He argues that the existence of an independent force of evil is made plausible by two other ideas. The first is the notion of the last judgement: 'The idea of judgement after death or at least the decisive effect of the kind of life individuals live in this world on what happens in the next, is not an optional extra in Christianity which can be discarded because it gives rise to unpleasant thoughts. It is, rather, a central part of traditional Christian belief and of God's purposes. Without any idea of judgement, the idea of God creating human beings and giving them freedom becomes pointless' (Vardy 1992: 174–5). But if we accept the idea of final judgement, then the idea of heaven and hell becomes crucial; and 'Similarly if God exists as traditionally defined, then the possibility of a force of evil similarly existing is also opened up' (Vardy 1992: 175).

The second notion is that of free will, for if God created creatures with free will, then the traditional Christian idea of rebellion in heaven becomes plausible. 'If there is such a realm with free will, then the existence of a force of evil, representing those heavenly forces that have turned away from God, follows logically from the initial assumptions' (Vardy 1992: 178). The world of humanity is therefore 'not wholly in God's control' (Vardy 1992: 178); and 'The existence of a force of evil independent of the human psyche will have profound consequences for any understanding of God's power in the world and its limitations' (Vardy 1992: 179–80).

The Explanatory Gap

We should keep in mind here that Vardy's project is to make religious belief coherent, rather than persuasive, and the fact that we need to bring the figure of Satan, or in Vardy's terms, forces of evil independent of the human psyche, into that world view in order to achieve coherence may fail to convince non-believers that this is the way to approach the wider problem of evil. Gordon Graham is more ambitious – he believes that by bringing Satan into the picture we *do* make the religious framework more persuasive. In *Evil and Christian Ethics* he asks how we can engage in moral endeavour in a world so full of human suffering that none of us can hope to make any significant difference? Such endeavour only makes sense in the context of moral faith, and the only coherent source of moral faith is a traditional Christian theology – a theology in which the Prince of Darkness exists. We cannot make sense of human evil without appeal to the existence of supernatural powers.

For Graham, 'evil is something that cries out to be explained' (Graham 2000: 161); and it must be explained in two respects: 'First, there is the necessity of providing a philosophical explanation of its intrinsic character, its reality as evil. Second, there is a need to explain its occurrence' (Graham 2000: 163). But the modern, scientific world view fails in both respects. This world view has two aspects. The first is humanism, the view that moral values derive from humanity and not from some external source, and is therefore a form of moral subjectivism. 'It believes, in an ancient phrase, that "man is the measure of all things", that the valuable is the *humanly* valuable' (Graham 2000: 109). But, in this form, humanism cannot take evil seriously: 'humanism cannot adequately account for the moral significance of evil; it cannot, that is to say, properly capture what we might call its evaluative darkness' (Graham 2000: 120). Something can only be 'evil' if somebody thinks it so, and if no one thinks it so, then it cannot be evil. This leads to the absurd situation where we could make all evil disappear by ensuring that no one cared about it, an implication most would reject because we believe that 'evil is disturbing whether or not anyone is disturbed by it' (Graham 2000: 163). The second aspect is naturalism, the scientific approach to explaining human behaviour – what I have called the 'psychological' conception – and it is here that we have the most dramatic and serious failure to explain. Graham looks at the phenomenon of the 'multiple' murderer (Graham 2000: 121). There are two reactions to these cases, says Graham. 'The first is to condemn the perpetrators as evil; the second is to declare them mad or mentally ill'. The two are connected if we take it that evil is ' "unnatural" in the sense of being the radical dysfunction of normal psychological-cum-physiological processes.' Indeed, 'there is some plausibility in the suggestion that multiple murder arises from a psychology gone drastically wrong' (Graham 2000: 122). But whether such explanation is adequate is not itself a psychological question but a philosophical one (Graham 2000: 122), and so we can ask: 'Can multiple murder *always* be explained in terms of a pathological condition? Are multiple murderers *necessarily* mad?' (Graham 2000: 124). He contests whether 'madness *must* be the explanation' and whether it is even 'an adequate account of what it is about their behaviour that is properly described as "evil"' (Graham 2000: 124).

Graham concludes that many multiple murderers cannot be counted as 'mad' in the sense that they have lost their grasp of reality, because they are completely aware of the facts about the world and what they are doing (Graham 2000: 132). If they are going to count as mad then the *ends* they choose to pursue have to be considered, but the naturalistic humanist approach, with its subjectivism, cannot diagnose madness in this sense. Such killers may well have 'abnormal desires and aspirations as a result of atypical personal and psychological histories', but 'none of this shows that their mental condition is tantamount to madness in the sense of radical dysfunction, and none of it explains why we should think of them as evil' (Graham 2000: 135). There is another approach which can explain both of these things, and that is the traditional Christian world view, that 'the fundamental explanation lies not with malfunction, but with evil' (Graham 2000: 137). The interesting psychological feature of many multiple killers is 'the sense of psychological compulsion', where they knew what they were doing was horrific and yet they still felt drawn towards it. 'Both features are accommodated by the idea that they come under the influence of spiritual powers' (Graham 2000: 138). Such people have been *seduced* by evil – the seducer does not override their will, but works through it, such that they come to want to do these things, even though they know they should not. But if they are being seduced, there must be a seducer.

The most detailed case Graham examines is that of Eric Harris and Dyland Klebold, two teenagers who shot and killed twelve children and one teacher and then killed themselves at Columbine High School in Denver, Colorado, in April 1999. One response to the question why they did it was to look at their background, and there we find that they were exposed to violent pornography, and this is taken to explain, to some extent, their actions. 'To very many people such a contention seems hardly more than common sense. Yet those who would defend the claim that, at some level or other, the depiction of violence causes violence, have to explain why it is that vast numbers of other young people, similarly exposed, never come near to committing acts of this magnitude' (Graham 2000: 147). And so we have an explanatory gap, a black hole, into which Graham inserts supernatural forces of evil. In the end 'neither the exploration of personal psychological histories, nor attention to unusual external causes gets us very far in answering the question "Why did they do it?"' (Graham 2000: 150). This represents the double failure of our modern world view. 'Humanism cannot explain (so to speak) the evil of evil, and naturalistic science, even of a well-informed psychological kind, cannot explain its occurrence. So, if there are alternative explanations that do accomplish these tasks, there is reason to prefer them' (Graham 2000: 154). The alternative explanation is 'that Harris and Klebold were seduced by evil' (Graham 2000: 156), and so by the rule of inference to the best explanation – that where one explanation explains more than the other then it should be chosen – we should develop this view further.

But one thing Graham has to explain if he is going to develop his position is why Harris and Klebold in particular performed these evil actions. He claims: 'these boys were *chosen*, just as a seducer chooses his victim, and they were worked upon, not by straightforward deception, bribery or psychological manipulation, but through their own agency. In their taste for violent pornography they displayed a susceptibility that made them suitable candidates for Satanic purposes, individuals who could be successfully seduced by evil. There was a spirit, in short, that saw them as *willing victims'* (Graham 2000: 157–8). And so we have a relatively simple explanation: 'the battle between elemental forces of good and evil – a battle in which the Prince of Darkness was on this occasion assisted by the wealth of technology readily available to those who were, as a result of their engagement with it, more readily seduced into becoming his agents' (Graham 2000: 159). And the reason we have to believe this account is 'that it provides us with the best available explanation of evil, and since evil is something which cries out to be explained, we ought to believe the best explanation' (Graham 2000: 161).

The Devil's Psychology

One objection that Graham faces is that his argument is circular: 'Does the appeal to an evil spirit really explain anything?' (Graham 2000: 194). This is an objection articulated by Colin McGinn: 'the answer does not really explain what needs to be explained anyway. It does not tell us what the evil person finds appealing about the pain of others: it simply offers to tell us what causes him to have the evil impulses to begin with. Moreover, the invocation of the devil simply raises the same question about his psychology: why does he find the pain of others worth pursuing? The devil's psychology raises our puzzle in its most intense form without resolving it. What *does* make Satan tick?' (McGinn 1997: 72; taken from Graham 2000: 194). Graham interprets this as a double objection: first, that 'to appeal to such a force at best identifies the external cause of evil character, and does nothing, therefore to illuminate its nature' and second, that 'it explains the evil psychology of the wrongdoer in terms of the evil psychology of the cause (Satan) and is thus no explanation at all' (Graham 2000: 194). In other words, if we simply say that Satan causes human evil and go no further, we have no explanation of the *nature* of human evil – what makes it *evil*; and we have no explanation of *why* humans would want to *be* evil. If Graham's explanation of human evil is this simplistic, then he does face failure.

However, while there are problems with Graham's explanation here, I don't think this captures them. We are explaining how human evil is possible by positing the existence of a supernatural evil agency, but there are three reasons why it cannot be simply that the supernatural evil agency *causes* human evil agency, why it cannot be a *causal* argument in any straightforward way. First, there is another cause in the chain, God, and God contains no evil, and so the evil in the supernatural agency has no causal explanation – it does not come from anywhere. Second, we don't have a causal chain here at all, in fact – God causes both the supernatural and the human agencies, but, crucially, he cannot cause them to be evil. Third, in this model the presence of evil within human agency is causally determined by Satan, but this would undermine the free-will argument which lies at the centre of the defence of God against the charge of causing evil. We have to remember that human beings must *freely* choose evil.

The proper explanation, and the one offered by Graham, is that *both* the supernatural agency and humanity come to be evil through their own free choices. We may need the idea of a seducer, according to Graham, but this seducer 'works upon and through the will of the seduced' (Graham 2000: 194). Such an explanation is not causal in a simplistic, mechanical sense:- it is necessary that human agents turn away from God at least to some extent in order to open themselves up for seduction. If we look at Screwtape's advice to his demon nephew Wormwood in C. S. Lewis' *The Screwtape Letters*, all Wormwood can do is plant seductive suggestions in the mind of the 'patient' he must recruit for hell, such that the human comes to want to turn away from God: he cannot simply *make* him commit sins. Importantly, Graham points out that there are human beings who need no seduction because they 'share his [Satan's] hatred' (Graham 2000: 198). And so at the heart of the choice of evil lies human freedom and we do not have here the sort of crude causal model that risks circularity. If we ask how Satan and the other fallen angels became evil we have the same kind of explanation: they freely *chose* to oppose God and it is this that caused their fall from heaven. Here Graham accepts St Augustine's account of this fall: 'Others . . . delighting in their own power, and supposing that it could be their own good, fell from that higher and blessed good which was common to them all and embraced a private good of their own' (quoted in Graham 2000: 200). Graham concludes: 'Precisely this (or something very like it) is to be seen at work in the episode at Columbine, I am inclined to say. We can understand it, without imputing necessary and sufficient conditions, which is why the talk of conditioning by violent pornography on the internet is both inept and inadequate' (Graham 2000: 203).

However, this is to overlook notorious problems with St Augustine's account. According to this approach, evil is the result of a free-will choice, whether that choice is made in heaven by rebelling angels or on earth by human beings. But Jeffery Burton Russell points out that St Augustine faces a dilemma here: 'On the one hand, both sets of angels (that is, all the angels) must have been created absolutely equal, or else God would be responsible for their inequality and thus the ultimate cause of the sin of those who fell. But on the other hand, if there was no initial difference between them, no cause of their fall could be discerned, and the only explanation would be absolute freedom' (Russell 1989: 102). In other words, either God is responsible for creating the difference between the angels and is therefore responsible for evil, or the angels freely chose evil and this demonstrates that God's power is limited – he could not prevent this choice. St Augustine's solution is that the angels were capable of sinning if left to their own devices, and so God, not wishing them to fall, strengthens some of them through grace, giving them a deep understanding of the cosmos so that they are now incapable of sinning; however, he withholds this grace from another group of angels who freely choose sin and so become demons. God therefore does not cause the defect in the will of the rebelling angels, he merely permits it. But, says Russell, 'for God to decide to save some of the angels and not others is an inexplicable act of apparent injustice' (Russell 1989: 102); it is to simply randomly choose between the angels which will be retained and which allowed to fall. And anyway, says Russell, even if God did not initially create two varieties of angels, in effect he does by the later strengthening of the will of a group of them, and so this is a 'blundered argument'. Instead, the 'simplest and most elegant explanation' is that 'some angels chose God and others chose sin, both with an absolutely free motion of the will that had no cause' (Russell 1989: 102). We now have no need of a cause, 'since nothing can cause a free-will choice' (Russell 1989: 98). Not only that, but we should not look for the origins of this choice in the internal nature of the rebellious angels, as this would once more make God responsible for their choice. Michael Galligan comments: 'these decisions could not be attributed to anything in their nature, that is, any other components of their being, and so could not be blamed in any way on God' (Galligan 1976: 22). Once more we see the crucial distinction between the monstrous and pure conceptions of evil – whether evil arises from *nature* or by *choice*. The rebellious angels, including Satan, are *not* monsters – if they were, God would be responsible.

However, if we take this option and explain the presence of evil in heaven through the free-will choice of Satan and other angels, then it is no longer clear what Satan is doing in the picture at all. If the evil of the supernatural agency needs no further explanation other than that it was the free choice of that agency to turn away from God, then surely the evil in human agency can have the same explanation, for if the evil of Satan needs no external cause, then the evil in humanity needs no external cause. Rather than the argument being circular, the problem is that it takes us to a dead end. If we can explain Satan's choice of evil, then we no longer need him, because that explanation can be directly applied to human evil itself. If we cannot explain Satan's evil – if it has to remain mysterious – then we have no explanation here at all, and again we do not need Satan because we may as well accept that human evil is internally mysterious rather than posit a mysterious external cause. And so McGinn is right that the crucial question is what makes Satan tick. What Graham's argument establishes, if anything, is that human agents can be diabolically evil – remember that he allows that some human agents do not need to be recruited by Satan at all because they have already made the choice to be evil. But if human agents are fully capable of diabolical evil, we already have diabolical agency and there is no need for an added level of *supernatural* diabolical agency. If we are going to look to medieval philosophy for assistance here, we should perhaps look in the direction of William of Ockham, who in the fourteenth century proposed what is now known as Ockham's Razor: do not multiply entities without necessity. In other words, keep things simple.

Graham insists that evil is something that cries out to be explained, but in the end we can ask what exactly he has explained. According to him, the psychological approach fails because it cannot tell us why Harris and Klebold chose evil while others with similar backgrounds did not. I will argue in Chapter 6 that in fact the psychological conception *can* explain this difference, but for now we can ask whether Graham's account can do any better. His explanation is that the forces of evil chose Klebold and Harris because they had displayed themselves as suitable candidates for seduction through actions such as viewing violent pornography.

But either the supernatural agency chooses its recruits at random, which is simply to make the whole process mysterious and therefore not an explanation at all (as well as being manifestly unfair if we suppose, as we must, that Klebold and Harris are destined to eternal damnation); or we suppose that Klebold and Harris were *especially* weak willed and *especially* addicted to pornographic violence in ways in which no other boys were, such that they *stood out* for recruitment. But there is no evidence for this latter thesis other than the fact that they committed the evil actions while the others did not, and this is exactly the sort of argument Graham would not accept. And anyway, if we suppose that they *were* especially addicted in this way, then Graham's central objection to the psychological account – that it cannot explain the difference between Harris and Klebold and the other boys who did not kill – disappears. Graham is right that the difficult question is not so much why Harris and Klebold committed such horrific crimes, but rather why they did so when so many others did not, but he is wrong to suppose that the supernatural gets us any closer to answering it. If Graham has any explanation at all, it is a general explanation of the presence of human evil in the world, rather than an explanation of why some choose evil and some do not. But even as a general explanation it has to fail through its appeal to supernatural evil. For God to be free of responsibility for human evil, humanity must be capable of freely choosing to be diabolically evil. But if human beings can freely choose to be diabolically, purely, evil, Satan and his demons are redundant. Graham might object that his crucial example is of 'the sense of psychological compulsion', where people know what they are doing is horrific and yet they still feel irresistibly drawn towards it. There are two final points we can make, though. First, his choice of Klebold and Harris doesn't fit this model, as there is no evidence that they were at all repelled by what they planned to do, and therefore no need to suppose that they needed to be seduced. Second, even if we find we have no explanation for this kind of compulsion, we can believe, rightly in my view, that we are more likely to find a coherent explanation for it – and for the many other kinds of compulsive behaviours – within the rich and complex structures of human psychology than within the realm of the supernatural.

How, then, do we explain the presence of Satan? We explain it, I think, not so much as a metaphysical presence as a literary one. Neil Forsyth says: 'Satan is first, and in some sense always remains, a character in a narrative' (Forsyth 1987: 4). Satan fulfils a narrative/mythological purpose. Forsyth says: 'one may best understand him not by examining his character or the beliefs about his nature according to some elaborate and rootless metaphysical system, but rather by putting him back into history, into the narrative contexts in which he begins and which he never really leaves. That is, we must try to see him as an actor, or what Aristotle called an "agent" with a role to play in a plot, or *mythos*' (Forsyth 1987: 4). Neither Graham nor Vardy may object to this, as Graham himself notes that what his account requires is 'cosmic narrative' (Graham 2000: 178), a traditional Christian cosmic history that includes the struggle between God and Satan for control of the world (Graham 2000: 178–9). But now, in order to make sense of human evil, we have to take on a whole cosmological historical narrative. We may wonder if there are other, more economic ways to understand the idea of evil. I will come back to Satan in the closing chapter of this book to look more closely at the notion of his narrative role. In the next chapter, however, we move towards a picture of evil that leaves the supernatural behind.

Chapter Three

Philosophies of Evil

Faust and the Philosophers

In a world without Satan, how are we to make sense of evil? An enlightened Christian world view would, of course, attempt to account for evil without a supernatural prince of darkness, but as we saw in the previous chapter, such a theodicy is notoriously unstable and the dark prince keeps coming back into the picture. The central question of this book is whether a secular world view can do any better in accounting for evil, or whether the concept becomes empty in a world without God or the Devil, or any other supernatural powers. Can there, in the absence of such powers, still be evil agencies which are the cause of much of the evil humanity suffers? In Chapter 1 I briefly described three secular possibilities, which I called the pure, the impure and the psychological conceptions of evil. According to the pure conception, human beings can be malevolent, diabolical agents, pursuing suffering and destruction for its own sake. According to the psychological conception, evil is not a category that can be meaningfully applied to human behaviour at all. We should find some other, more human, way of describing what happens. The impure conception seems to be a compromise between these two oppositions – that human agents cannot be evil in the pure sense, but are capable of an impure form of evil, a merely human evil. This consists in willing the suffering of others, but not for its own sake, rather for the sake of some other understandable human end, such as power, wealth, security or the greater good of humankind. It is this impure conception that has developed with the tradition of modern moral philosophy.

What is at stake here is whether there are *evil people*, rather than merely evil consequences of human action. Does it make sense, within a secular viewpoint, to suppose that the evil that exists in the world is caused, to some degree, by evil human agencies? The pure conception says yes; the psychological conception says no; and the impure conception gives a rather muddled and confused answer. But it is this conception that has dominated moral theory. The 'great' philosopher of evil in the impure sense is Immanuel Kant, who rejects the possibility of a human being choosing evil as a principle of action. In this broad philosophical view, evil is held to be a privation, a lack, some kind of going wrong or mistake, or an outbreak of irrationality, rather than a positive, rational choice. Paul Barry Clarke contrasts this philosophical position with what he describes as the Faustian view, that such an active, positive choice of evil is a human possibility. We encounter this Faustian account of human evil through literature and other kinds of fiction, and some of the greatest works of literature, such as those based around the Faust narrative, develop it with great subtlety and power. Clarke comments: 'in the literary tradition evil is frequently regarded as the choice to follow an evil principle, to adopt the course and precepts of the Devil' (Clarke 1996: 352). Here we have that traditional clash between philosophy and literature, between the philosophers and the poets, with two distinct representations of human possibility, and many, certainly the majority of ordinary people, generally believe that the poets have got it right.

However, while Clarke takes Faust as the paradigm of such a literary figure, if we look at him closely we face the same problem that arose when we examined Satan as a mythological figure – just as the Devil cannot be understood to make diabolical choices, it is highly questionable whether we can understand Faust as making the kind of choice Clarke and others would describe as Faustian. The Faust that emerges from the text is in fact a profoundly human figure. Alfred Hoelzel, in his study of the various Faust texts, comments: 'today's popular mind identifies Faust in two deeply divergent, almost antithetical ways: on the one hand, the reckless villain who goes so far as to traffic with the devil in order to enjoy forbidden fruit, and, on the other hand, the brave hero who even dares to traffic with the devil in his progressive quest for knowledge and experience' (Hoelzel 1988: II). Faust is at least, then, a deeply ambivalent figure. His major sin, according to Hoelzel, is not some base desire for pleasure, nor even his desire to expand his knowledge and experience (hardly a sin!) – rather, his transgression lies in his decision to compete with God in the pursuit of knowledge, a 'Luciferian striving for power' (Hoelzel 1988: 4).

There are strong parallels, says Hoelzel, with the Fall of Adam and Eve as well as that of Lucifer himself, for both Faust and Adam and Eve commit the great sin of defying God, but their motivation for doing so arises out of a fundamentally central human virtue, the desire for knowledge of the world (Hoelzel 1988: 15). Although the Fall was, of course, catastrophic, it was also beneficial for humankind. In Paradise Adam and Eve were happy and content but lacked any creative or progressive motivation, and humanity's creative and progressive powers follow precisely from their decision to defy God. Although their lives are filled with hardship, there is no suggestion in any scriptural text that they have lost God's long-term support, nor that they will be punished further in the afterlife. Indeed it was deemed heretical to suggest that Adam was damned, and verses 1–2 in chapter 10 of the Wisdom of Solomon in the *Apocrypha* was taken to imply his salvation (I'm not aware of any debate about the long-term fate of Eve). There was also a widespread belief that Adam was buried at the foot of the cross at Calvary, and that the blood of Christ flowed into the grave to redeem him. Faust, too, 'elicits much sympathy and admiration for his motivation of intellectual curiosity' (Hoelzel 1988: 21).

Certainly the figure of Faust remains ambiguous in the texts. In the most popular early version, by Johann Spies printed in 1587, Faust does appear as 'a rather sinister character' in some parts of the story (Hoelzel 1988: 26), as 'a malicious troublemaker, who delights in molesting innocent people, deceiving honest traders, and entertaining himself with trivial acts of magic' – here he fulfils a traditionally evil role (Hoelzel 1988: 27). But in other parts of the text we find a very different Faust who 'displays considerable generosity, courage, honesty, and great dignity in the face of death' (Hoelzel 1988: 27). Christopher Marlowe's *Dr Faustus* (1604) is represented as more clearly in pursuit of knowledge (Hoelzel 1988: 50) and more clearly as a victim of the struggle between God and Satan (Hoelzel 1988: 48). 'Instead of merely replicating a brilliant but naive and gullible adventure-seeker who becomes easy prey for the shrewder and much more powerful Mephistophilis, Marlowe has created a hero with a far more clearly defined moral and intellectual profile' (Hoelzel 1988: 55). Hoelzel also notes that the figure of Mephistophilis himself is drawn more sympathetically by Marlowe. 'We see in him, at least momentarily, less the embodiment of pure evil, much more the pitiful *victim* of evil who, as he himself admits, seeks in Faustus another soul to share his own misery' (Hoelzel 1988: 56). As such: 'He seems a strangely subdued hellion, one who speaks regretfully about his own status and even warns Faustus to desist from his intentions. The realms of good and evil seem suddenly less clearly demarcated than ever, and their roles in the interaction between Faustus and Mephistophilis much more difficult to sort out and define' (Hoelzel 1988: 57–8). And in Goethe's version of the tale, published in two parts in 1808 and 1832, the story ends with a battle between the forces of Mephistopheles and God for Faust's soul, which God's angels win, and Faust is taken to heaven – hardly the conclusion one would expect if Faust was the embodiment of pure evil. (Interestingly, Goethe's *Faust* begins with God entering into a wager with Mephistopheles, giving him permission to tempt him; - Faust's temptation and alliance with Mephistopheles therefore has God's 'blessing'.)

Of course there are figures in fiction which fit more closely Clarke's Faustian villain than Faust, but the suspicion has to be that such villains are drawn in a psychologically crude and unsophisticated way, and that the more deeply the fictional villain is explored, in genuinely revealing and moving works of literature, the less easy it becomes to regard them as agents of pure evil – they become, like Faust himself, ambivalent, impure figures. Mary Midgley presents this case for another great literary villain, Milton's Lucifer in *Paradise Lost*. She argues that Milton presents in Lucifer not 'a figure of complete and unqualified evil' (Midgley 1984: 133); rather, Lucifer is, like all great tragic figures, fatally flawed. For all his grandeur, he lacks the one quality whose absence will bring about his fall, and that is an inability to tolerate anybody standing above him (Midgley 1984: 133). This exhibits itself as excessive pride, which leads him to rebel against God. But Satan as a rebel is not a heroic figure, although he is sometimes presented in this way, because his motivation, says Midgley, is mean and vicious rather than magnificent: he lacks any reforming purpose in his rebellion, and all we are left with is a spiteful destructiveness (Midgley 1984: 135). But all this makes Satan intelligible as a figure. 'The story of Satan is there so that we can understand his motives, not so that we can honourably refrain from thinking about them on the grounds that we are in no position to judge him' (Midgley 1984: 138). His motives remain intelligible because their 'centre is the violent hatred and rejection of all that seems to be superior to oneself, and their familiar names are pride and envy' (Midgley 1984: 138).

Adam Morton warns against the cruder representations of evil in fiction. Certainly, we expect a close connection between the 'psychology of fiction' and the 'psychology of psychologizing' (Morton 2004: 93), in that the plots and the villains who act within them have to be plausible in order to be at all satisfying. 'But that doesn't mean that a good story really does give us insight into why people do things. Far from it. An appealing story line can seduce us into thinking that people frequently act in ways they rarely do, and for reasons that seldom apply' (Morton 2004: 93). One particular form of fiction that Morton warns against is that about serial killers. Serial killers have entered the popular imagination very recently, and their motives are complex and hard to understand, such that in fiction 'the difficulty of understanding the criminal turns him into a diabolical monster, something like a vampire or a werewolf. The fictional image of a serial killer combines this half-human category with that of a more traditional killer, with motives and means that the detective has to uncover. The result is plots which combine an intellectual puzzle with a primeval horrified fascination' (Morton 2004: 95). But while this form of fiction has wide appeal, it also presents problems for an understanding of evil. 'Characters have to make some kind of sense, and the danger is that the criminal will turn out to be a force of nature rather than a motivated character' (Morton 2004: 95). Morton discusses the figure of Hannibal Lecter, the serial killer central to Thomas Harris' hugely popular novels, *Red Dragon*, *The Silence of the Lambs* and *Hannibal*, all made into films (two versions have been made of *Red Dragon*). Certainly here Lecter seems to be a force of nature, verging on the supernatural. Morton comments: 'Lecter has a supernatural understanding of human motive and emotion, based largely on his almost superhuman intelligence, and no sympathy for human feeling' (Morton 2004: 97). At times Lecter, despite his comparative age, seems also to be supernaturally physically powerful, simply overwhelming and destroying any who stand in his way. In the film version of *The Silence of the Lambs* he is represented as an irresistible force – any who oppose him are doomed, unless he takes a liking to them.

Morton looks at the novel *Red Dragon*, the first in the series, an encounter between Lecter and the detective Will Graham, who is pursuing another serial killer, and seeks out Lecter, held in a

secure institution, for his advice. Graham is highly intuitive, able
to get into the killer's mind and so have an intuitive certainty
of who he is and what he will do (Morton 2004: 97). Lecter is
the opposite, with no intuitive grasp of others, but an extensive
scientific, psychological understanding of human motivation. Together they combine to enable Graham to track the killer down. But
in order for the novel and its companions to work, says Morton,
they 'need to postulate killers with individual themes and traits'
(Morton 2004: 98) – they each follow specific patterns in select-
ing their victims and in executing them in particular ways. 'Very
few real killers are like this. Overwhelmingly, serial killers target
a fairly wide class of victims, defined by gender, sexuality, and
age, and then kill in whatever way comes easily to them' (Morton
2004: 98). Our popular image of the serial killer is shaped by fiction. 'The appeal of the idea that serial killers have very individual
psychology as killers, a kind of artistic style that a sufficiently intuitive person could understand and anticipate, comes from thinking of them as both diabolically alien and also as rich characters.
In the fictional genre of serial killers both assumptions are needed,
but in fact serial killers are much harder to understand than this
supposes' (Morton 2004: 98). The danger of fiction here is that
it appeals to 'a kind of imaginative laziness'. Morton says: 'We
prefer to understand evil in terms of archetypal horrors, fictional
villains, and deep viciousness, rather than to strain our capacities
for intuitive understanding towards a grasp of the difficult truth
that people much like us perform acts that we find unimaginably
awful' (Morton 2004: 102). The antithesis to the Lecter novels
and films is *Henry: Portrait of a Serial Killer* (1986), which deeply
shocked and disturbed people precisely because the central character displays no pattern in carrying out a series of killings, and
displays no supernatural powers or complex character. What is
truly horrifying and disturbing, and which makes the film almost
impossible to watch, is that Henry is so ordinary (but of course
even this film cannot be taken as an accurate representation of serial killers, nor of the figure that 'inspired' it, Henry Lee Lucas). By
representing serial killers as diabolical monsters we make them
easier to detect, and to realise, as Morton says, that they are people much like us makes them far *more* terrifying than Lecter could
ever be. This is by no means a rejection of fiction as a way of approaching the concept of evil, and in Chapter 5 I will examine
what horror fiction in particular reveals about how we *imagine*

it, but it is less obvious that fiction can help us to understand it. Because we seek to *understand* evil we must, for now, turn away from literature towards philosophy.

Kant and Radical Evil

Philosophical discussions of evil commonly take place against the background of two famous descriptions of it, Hannah Arendt's notion of the banality of evil from a comment she makes in her report of the trial of Adolf Eichmann (Arendt 1976), and Kant's idea of radical evil, which he describes in his *Religion within the Limits of Reason Alone* (Kant 1960). One difficulty, however, is that neither writer is that clear about what they mean by these ideas, and much of the philosophical debate about evil is taken up with trying to untangle their obscure comments. I will examine what Arendt might have meant by the banality of evil in Chapter 8, but for now we turn to Kant and radical evil, as he gives the most sophisticated and detailed account of what I have described as the philosophical or impure conception. In *Religion* Kant tackles the problem of moral evil, and his most important contribution to the philosophical understanding of evil is his rejection of human devilishness. For Kant, moral evil is any deviation from what morality demands, as expressed through our power of reason and stated by the moral law or the categorical imperative. Reason tells us that we must follow the demands of reason and do our duty to others, whatever feelings or emotions or other non-moral incentives we may have to do otherwise. However, because we are free beings, we are not *forced* to follow the moral law, but can choose instead to follow those non-moral incentives. Notoriously, for Kant even acting to benefit others through feelings of sympathy for them, rather than because we recognise that it is our duty to help them, is an example of moral evil. Richard J. Bernstein, in his invaluable discussion of Kant's theory, explains that for Kant, 'we call a man evil not because he performs actions that are evil', just as we would not call a man good because he performs actions that are good (Bernstein 2002: 18). The only thing that matters for Kant is the will, and as long as the will pursues non-moral incentives that lead away from compliance to the moral law, then we are engaged in evil. What is crucial for Kant is the principle or maxim which forms the basis of our action: 'Whoever incorporates the moral law into his maxim and gives it priority is morally good; and whoever fails to do this, but gives priority to other nonmoral incentives (including sympathy) is morally evil' (Bernstein 2002: 18).

However, what Kant insists is that human beings cannot renounce the moral law altogether. They cannot will evil for its own sake, and make the kind of declaration made by Milton's Lucifer, 'Evil be thou my good' (*Paradise Lost*, Book 4, 11.110). John Silber comments: 'Not even a wicked man wills evil for the sake of evil. His evil consists in his willing to ignore the moral law and to oppose its demands when it interferes with his non-moral incentives' (Silber 1960: cxxiv). Here Kant opposes literature, as Clarke suggested in section one of this chapter. Silber explains: 'To assert, then, as is often done in literature and in the popular imagination, that there can be devilish beings who defiantly and powerfully reject the moral law itself, presupposes a conception of freedom which, according to Kant, is hopelessly transcendent and without foundation in human experience' (Silber 1960: cxxv). Devilish figures in literature are the result of either 'transcendent superstition' or are humanly evil. Silber identifies Milton's Lucifer as an example of transcendental evil, the rejection of the moral law itself. 'Such an image beckons to men with its romantic illusions about the grandeur and heroism of wickedness' (Silber 1960: cxxv). This contrasts with the Mephistopheles of Goethe's *Faust* Part 1, who, 'though less imaginatively drawn than Satan and far less attractive, has the weakness of personality required by Kant's analysis' (Silber 1960: cxxv). The romantic possibility represented by Milton's Lucifer is denied to humans, according to Kant, and Mary Midgley warns against even taking Lucifer too literally when he declares 'Evil, be thou my good' (Midgley 1984: 134). 'What Milton wrote about the devil is not – once we drop the purple spotlight of romantic partiality – at all flattering. Satan's personal motives are mostly mean and claustrophobic centring on competitive self-assertion. His grandeur stems from his original nature, which is not of his own making ... The phrase "Evil be thou my good" is no sublime manifesto of creative immoralism, but a competitive political move to establish a private empire' (Midgley 1984: 151). Whatever we think of Lucifer and his motivations, for Kant humanity cannot reject the moral law as such, cannot reject morality. 'Man (even the most wicked) does not, under any maxim whatsoever, repudiate the moral law in the manner of a rebel (renouncing obedience to it)' (Kant 1960: 31). No one is that depraved that they can violate the demands of morality without feeling some degree of guilt or misgiving. No human being, then, can be purely evil, to be 'devilish' in this romantic, rebellious sense, for, as Bernstein points out, 'this would mean that some human beings are not really human' (Bernstein 2002: 38). He concludes: 'To be a human being is to be a person who *recognizes* the authority of the moral law regardless of whether one chooses to do what it requires' (Bernstein 2002: 39).

What Kant is trying to explain is why human agents are willing to put up with a bad conscience, the awareness that they are resisting the demands of the moral law for the sake of non-moral ends. The capacity for immorality, as well as morality, has to be explained in the terms of being human, when being human includes not only our physical needs and desires but also our power of reason, and therefore our capacity to recognise what morality demands – we know, except in difficult circumstances, what the right thing to do is, and yet we often do not do it. How is that possible? We have already seen that one explanation that will not do for Kant is that we are free to be devilish and renounce morality altogether, for if that were so we would experience no guilt. For Kant we are free to disobey the moral law but not without penalty, and that penalty is the guilt we feel, and the existence of the moral law and our knowledge of it is demonstrated through that guilt. Kant also rejects the explanation that we do wrong because our rational self is overwhelmed by our passionate self, our desires overcoming our reason. Moral evil remains the free, conscious choice of a human agent – we commit immoral acts for the sake of some recognisable human end. Therefore if we commit a selfish act for the sake of acquiring more wealth, for example, we cannot claim that we were overwhelmed by our desire for wealth, for we freely chose the pursuit of wealth over the pursuit of morality. Joan Copjec says Kant conceives of evil as 'a positive fact, firmly rooted in reality', and this makes evil a moral and political problem for the first time by making it an aspect of human freedom itself: 'evil is uniquely the product of a free humanity' (Copjec 1996a: xi). Animals can do what strike us as horrific things through their desires, but they remain incapable of evil because – as far as we are aware – they do not freely choose to do them.

This is to fully grasp the concept of humanity embodied in the Enlightenment, of free individuals who have control over their actions through their power of reason, and it makes explicit the double nature of that Enlightenment concept: that free and rational human beings are capable of both bringing about great benefits to their fellows, and also of bringing about great destruction to them. Human evil is not the product of forces beyond our control, whether those forces be supernatural, psychological or circumstantial. It is a human responsibility brought about through human freedom. In Chapter 1 I raised the example of the torture and abuse that happened in the Abu Ghraib prison in Iraq and of the defence raised by some of those American personnel brought to trial – that they were under pressure from superiors and circumstances to abuse their prisoners. What Kant insists upon is that there is always a moment at the heart of the affair when one makes a choice, and at that moment one's freedom and rationality are intact and one bears responsibility for that choice. When we commit evil acts it is not because we have been overcome by our primitive or primeval selves, or anything else, but because we have chosen to act on self-interested principles rather than moral ones. We choose this freely, although the price is the guilt we experience because we know precisely what morality demands of us, and we know what we ought to have chosen.

But the question remains: how is this possible? It cannot be accounted for by a human capacity for pure evil or by the power of our desires over our capacity to reason. Bernstein explains that in *Religion* Kant makes a distinction between the faculty humans have for unconstrained free choice, which he calls *Willkür*, and the *rational* aspect of our volition which he terms *Wille*. The former 'is neither *intrinsically* good nor *intrinsically* evil; rather, it is the capacity by which we freely choose good or evil maxims' (Bernstein 2002: 13). The latter 'does not act at all; it does not make decisions' (Bernstein 2002: 13). The *Wille* is the legislature, the normative aspect of the human will, identifying the demands of morality, and the *Willkür* the executive, our capacity to choose whatever we will, and therefore our capacity to choose to prioritise non-moral incentives over moral ones. This is why our wrongdoing cannot be explained away as the defeat of reason by desire. Claudia Card explains: 'Although we do not choose our desires or inclinations, we choose what importance to accord them. In acting wrongly, we accord our desires or inclinations more importance than duty. We are not simply determined by them. We choose to let them determine what we do' (Card 2002: 77). Therefore our capacity to choose non-moral incentives over moral ones is explained through the concept of *Willkür*, and the alleged fact that we cannot reject the moral law as such – and so be free of guilt – is explained through the concept of *Wille*.

Fortunately, the extent to which this helps to make sense of human evildoing need not delay us here, for what we are pursuing, and so far have not encountered, is Kant's concept of *radical* evil. The kind of moral evil Kant has in mind so far amounts to *any* deviation from the moral law, such as, as we saw earlier, acting out of sympathy rather than duty. This is hardly the account of evil we were after. In fact Kant identifies three levels of moral evil. The first can be understood as weakness of the will or human frailty (Kant 1960: 24–5), where we acknowledge the demands of morality but sometimes we prioritise our non-moral incentives over them. The second is to do with the problem of mixed motives (Kant 1960: 25), where it may appear to others and even to ourselves that we act according to the demands of morality but in fact our actions are contaminated by non-moral incentives. The third is human wickedness (Kant 1960: 25), the deliberate and systematic subordination of moral incentives to non-moral ones, although knowledge of the moral law, and therefore guilt, remains. Card identifies this third level, where we have 'reversed the order of our practical principles', with radical evil (Card 2002: 77), but it is not obvious that this is what Kant means by the term. Bernstein comments: 'Despite the striking connotations of the term "radical", Kant is not speaking about a special *type* of evil or evil maxim' (Bernstein 2002: 20). And so radical evil is not one of the three levels of moral evil Kant describes, nor a fourth one (and is certainly not to be confused with the pure, devilish evil he rules out as a human possibility). The sense in which evil is radical for Kant is perhaps that it cannot be *eradicated* from the human condition, rather than the extremity of what is willed. One meaning of the word 'radical' in the *Concise Oxford English Dictionary* is 'relating to, or affecting the fundamental nature of something', and its Latin origin lies in the idea of 'root' or 'rooted', and this is perhaps the sense of radical we find in Kant. Bernstein explains: 'Human beings are tempted to disregard the moral law, to adopt evil maxims – maxims that give priority to nonmoral incentives. It is this tendency or propensity... that Kant seeks to isolate with the introduction of the concept of radical evil' (Bernstein 2002: 28). What Kant means is that 'there is a propensity... not to do what duty demands', and this tendency is '*rooted* in human nature...' (Bernstein 2002: 28). Kant describes this as a 'corrupt propensity' which is 'rooted in man' (Kant 1960: 28); a 'natural propensity, *inextirpable* by human powers' (Kant 1960: 32). He says: 'Hence we can call this a natural propensity to evil, and as we must, after all, hold man himself responsible for it, we can further call it a *radical innate evil* in human nature (yet none the less brought upon us by ourselves)' (Kant 1960: 28). We have a natural tendency towards moral evil – the prioritisation of the non-moral over the moral – and the presence of this tendency is itself an evil, and a radical one in the sense that it is rooted in our nature, and also because 'it corrupts the ground of all maxims' (Kant 1960: 32). This tendency or propensity, therefore, can be regarded as radical in these two senses: it is ineradicable from human nature, and every principle of action we arrive at is corruptible by it. Which sense of 'radical' Kant intended is not completely clear, although he only ever uses the word in relation to the second possible meaning. Bernstein himself seems to take the first meaning, as he elsewhere characterises radical evil as 'evil that goes to the root . . .' (Bernstein 2002: 95).

What can we take away from Kant's discussion of evil? We have two important insights. First, humanity cannot be evil in the pure, devilish sense – Kant has clearly set out the impure, philosophical conception of evil. Second, human agents freely choose to perform evil actions and so are responsible for them; they cannot be explained away in terms of our physical, animal nature. This, Joan Copjec has pointed out, is to establish that evil is a moral and political problem for the first time. However, although Copjec may be right about this, we can ask whether Kant has taken us any closer to a solution of that problem. In the first place, his characterisation of radical evil seems disappointing. It does not name a special kind of evil, but simply the human propensity for immorality (and for Kant's rather severe characterisation of immorality). Bernstein comments: 'There is no evidence that Kant means anything more than this' (Bernstein 2002: 28), and 'The more we focus on the details of Kant's analysis of radical evil, the more innocuous the concept seems to be' (Bernstein 2002: 33). Indeed, Bernstein questions whether Kant's conception of evil explains anything at all: 'Ultimately, we cannot *know* why one person chooses to follow the moral law and another person does not' (Bernstein 2002: 25). The monstrous and pure conceptions of evil gave us an explanatory framework and enabled us to answer the question, 'why did she do it?', with the answer 'because she was evil'. The impure conception, at least as Kant presents it to us, seems to have given up the project of explanation. All we are left with is description, and the grounds of good and evil become mysterious. Raimond Gaita accepts this implication of the Kantian approach: 'Good and evil are essentially mysterious, which is why no metaphysical or religious explanations will penetrate their mystery' (Gaita 2000: 39). He accepts that 'the concept of evil has no explanatory power' (Gaita 2000: 46), and so understands why many would be sceptical about it: 'there are few circumstances in which appeal to an evil intention or to an evil character will explain a person's actions' (Gaita 2000: 44). However, we must keep the concept, he argues, because the project of moral description requires it, and moral description can bring understanding. 'Our need to understand is not exhausted by our need to explain why things occur. We sometimes need the concept of evil to describe adequately what we are confronted with and also to characterise adequately our responses to certain actions, as their perpetrators, their victims or as spectators of them' (Gaita 2000: 47). The moral descriptions of certain situations 'are sometimes only adequately represented by a distinctive concept of evil' (Gaita 2000: 52). I will look more closely at how the concept of evil works in this kind of moral description in Chapter 7, but will for now simply note how hard it is to prevent 'evil' being the description of agency, and once it is a description of agency, it is even harder to prevent it from being an *explanation* of what that agency does.

Another criticism of the Kantian conception of evil is that it is incoherent. What his, and the philosophical conception in general, insists is that there can be a human agent who freely chooses evil means in order to achieve their human goals. They could have chosen to act morally, but they have chosen not to. But if an agent is understood to have freely chosen evil methods to get what they want, then non-evil means must have been available to them. Colin McGinn points out the basic structural weakness here. His example is of a person who inflicts pain on another in order to achieve a human end when there were other more reasonable ways of getting what they want. He comments: 'any theory that tries to treat causing pain as a means of satisfying some further desire will face the problem that pain is valued for itself by the evil person' (McGinn 1997: 76). There were other options available, but they chose this evil method above all others, and so there must have been something about the evil method which attracted them. But then it becomes an end in itself to the extent that makes the impure conception of evil incoherent. We can no longer say of them that they chose evil means to achieve a human end so that they remain within the realm of the human, because their choice of the evil means in preference to others makes that evil, even here, an end itself – it is chosen for its own sake, and its choice becomes an example of pure, rather than impure evil. Devilishness enters the realm of the human. We can explain why some people want power or companionship, but we cannot explain the very thing that cries out for explanation – why they choose to make others suffer in order to get it, when there are other options open to them.

We can therefore ask whether Kant is right to place the category of pure evil beyond human possibility. John Silber says that, 'in dismissing the devilish rejection of the law as an illusion, Kant called attention to the limitations of his conception of freedom rather than to the limits of human freedom itself' (Silber 1960: cxxix). The distinction between human and inhuman evil cannot be maintained simply by dismissing all evidence of the latter. 'Kant's insistence to the contrary, man's free power to reject the law in defiance is an ineradicable fact of human experience' (Silber 1960: cxxix). All evidence points to the fact that 'man's freedom can be diabolically, no less than heteronomously, expressed' (Silber 1960: cxxix). Bernstein agrees that Kant's analysis cannot rule out the possibility of the 'devilish' human agent at all. At the base of Kant's treatment is a conception of human freedom that is in principle unlimited. This is why a person's choice of good or evil is mysterious to us, and also why, in order to be consistent, Kant must allow for the possibility of pure evil. '*There is no free choice . . . unless there is the free choice to be morally evil, and even devilish*' (Bernstein 2002: 42; italics in the original).

The philosophical conception of evil may therefore be difficult to maintain. It is equally difficult to maintain the concept of evil as purely descriptive, either of the consequences of certain kinds of human agency or of that agency itself, without it taking on an explanatory role. It is my argument in this book that 'evil' has no explanatory role to play whatsoever, and that when it does take on that role it is positively harmful and dangerous for our understanding of why people perform certain kinds of actions, and so it is better to find other ways to describe the world and the people in it. It is better to ask why people use the concept of evil itself – it is the *idea* of evil that needs explanation. Claudia Card thinks this is a mistake, and one for which she blames Friedrich Nietzsche and his critique of morality. 'Nietzsche's critique has helped engineer a shift from questions of what to do to prevent, reduce, or redress evils to skeptical psychological questions about what inclines people to make judgments of evil in the first place, what functions such judgments serve' (Card 2002: 28). My own view is that this is not a mistake at all, because the making of such judgements is itself a major cause of the kind of harm and suffering Card wishes to use the concept of evil to describe. If we can expose and dismantle the idea of evil, we may have found at least one way of preventing, reducing or redressing some of the intolerable harms that have been inflicted in its name. But Card is correct to identify Nietzsche as the central figure in exposing and dismantling the idea of evil, and so we examine his critique in the rest of this chapter.

The Nietzschean Turn

The key Nietzschean text is *The Genealogy of Morals*, published in 1887, and written, some would argue, when Nietzsche was at the height of his creative powers. In it he engages in a devastating critique of Christian morality, which Nietzsche takes to stand for the general humanistic morality that dominated European thought. In particular, he wishes to account for the morality that takes 'good' and 'evil' as its opposite poles. How did this morality come about, and what *value* do its central values themselves fulfil (Nietzsche 1996: 5)? For Bernstein, Nietzsche 'is engaged in a critique of morality – a critique directed to exposing our distinction between good and evil, our moral prejudices' (Bernstein 2002: 110). Famously, Nietzsche constructs a genealogy which traces the development of contemporary morality from a historical conflict between two classes, the 'masters' or the nobility, and the 'slaves' or the masses, who each possess their own distinct moralities, a conflict which the slaves win, such that it is slave morality which comes to dominate the European tradition. However, the slave morality develops as a *reaction* to the master morality. Within the master morality there are the two concepts of 'good' and 'bad', and it is the idea of 'good' which is primary and the idea of 'bad' is derived from it. But within the slave morality the two basic concepts are 'good' and 'evil', and here it is 'evil' which is primary and the notion of 'good' is derived from it. Contemporary ethics is this reactive slave morality, and it is the product of what Nietzsche calls *ressentiment*, a notion which, for Bernstein, is Nietzsche's most important contribution to the critique of morality. *Ressentiment* drives the slaves forward in their revolt against the nobility, and continues to shape our morality in important and damaging ways. Brian Leiter explains that *ressentiment* here is a German word derived from the French but differing in sense from that origin and from the English equivalent – in the German it is stronger than simply resentment, a kind of 'grudge-laden resentment' (Clark 1998: 854). Leiter explains: '*ressentiment* draws on the resources of more familiar emotions such as hatred and vengefulness' (Leiter 2002: 203). And so: '*Ressentiment*, then, is Nietzsche's term of art for a special kind of festering hatred and vengefulness, one motivated by impotence in the face of unpleasant external stimuli, and that leads (at least among the impotent) to the creation of values that *devalue* (or at least make sense of) those unpleasant stimuli' (Leiter 2002: 204). But to grasp the idea of *ressentiment* and to see how it can help us to understand the concept of evil, we have to look in some detail at Nietzsche's version of the history of morals.

In the first essay of the *Genealogy*, Nietzsche explains the development of morality and the ideas of good and evil. 'The judgement "good" does *not* derive from those to whom "goodness" is shown! Rather, the "good" themselves – that is, the noble, the powerful, the superior, and the high-minded – were the ones who felt themselves and their actions to be good – that is, as of the first rank – and posted them as such, in contrast to everything low, low-minded, common, and plebeian' (Nietzsche 1996: 12). The aristocracy, therefore, name 'good' after themselves and their own qualities, and name anything below them as 'bad': – 'the pathos of nobility and distance, the enduring, dominating, and fundamental overall feeling of a higher ruling kind in relation to a lower kind, to a "below" – *that* is the origin of the opposition between "good" and "bad"' (Nietzsche 1996: 13). However, within the ruling aristocracy there emerges a priestly caste – 'the political concept of rank always transforms itself into a spiritual concept of rank' (Nietzsche 1996: 17) – and the conflict arises between the warrior caste and the priestly caste within the aristocracy; the slave revolt in morals is not led by the masses, but by this priestly elite. The priests hate the warriors not because they are repressed by them, but because the masses look up to them and show loyalty to them rather than the priests (Clark 1998: 854). In order to win over the masses, the priests have to create a new morality in reaction to the old one, and reverse the noble concepts of 'good' and 'bad'. The priests lack the power to confront the warriors directly, and it is this impotence that leads to hatred: 'Priests are, as is well-known, *the most evil enemies* – but why? Because they are the most powerless. From powerlessness their hatred grows to take on a monstrous and sinister shape, the most cerebral and most poisonous form' (Nietzsche 1996: 19). The way the priests attack is through a radical transvaluation of values, 'an art of *the most intelligent revenge*' (Nietzsche 1996: 19). The priests, because they lack physical power, have to become clever, far more clever than the warriors. 'Human history would be a much too stupid affair were it not for the intelligence introduced by the powerless' (Nietzsche 1996: 19). And so we get '*the slave revolt in morals...*' (Nietzsche 1996: 20).

The revolt is driven by *ressentiment*: 'The slave revolt in morals begins when *ressentiment* itself becomes creative and ordains values: the *ressentiment* of creatures to whom the real reaction, that of the deed, is denied and who find compensation in an imaginary revenge' (Nietzsche 1996: 22). The revenge is the reversal of morality, so that what was noble becomes 'evil', and the 'qualities' of the priests become 'good'. 'The reversal of the evaluating gaze – this *necessary* orientation outwards rather than inwards to the self – belongs characteristically to *ressentiment*. In order to exist at all, slave morality from the outset always needs an opposing, outer world; in physiological terms, it needs external stimuli in order to act – its action is fundamentally reaction' (Nietzsche 1996: 22). The primary focus of the new morality therefore becomes the idea of evil, projected on to an outer enemy, and the good person becomes whatever the evil person is not. The aristocratic morality did not have this outward 'gaze': 'There is, in fact, too much nonchalance, too much levity, too much distraction and impatience, even too much good temper mixed up with this aristocratic contempt for it to be capable of transforming its object into a real caricature and monster' (Nietzsche 1996: 23). And: 'The "well-bred" *felt* themselves to be "the fortunate"; they did not have to construe their good fortune artificially through a glance at their enemies, to persuade themselves of it, to *convince themselves through lying* (as all men of *ressentiment* usually do)' (Nietzsche 1996: 23). If the noble man ever feels *ressentiment*, it 'exhausts itself in an immediate reaction', and so does not poison (Nietzsche 1996: 24). The person of *ressentiment*, however, 'is neither upright nor naive in his dealings with others, nor is he honest and open with himself. His soul *squints*; his mind loves bolt-holes, secret paths, back doors, he regards all hidden things as *his* world, *his* security, *his* refreshment; he has a perfect understanding of how to keep silent, how not to forget, how to wait, how to make himself provisionally small and submissive. A race of such men of *ressentiment* is bound in the end to become *cleverer* than any noble race' (Nietzsche 1996: 24). The noble person respects his enemy, indeed would only identify someone as an enemy in order to mark that person as worthy of attention. 'In contrast, imagine the "enemy" as conceived by the man of *ressentiment*. This is the very place where his deed, his creation is to be found – he has conceived the "evil enemy", the "*evil man*". Moreover, he has conceived him as a fundamental concept, from which he now derives another as an after-image and counterpart, the "good man" – himself!' (Nietzsche 1996: 25). The person of slave morality therefore creates the evil enemy, and the idea of evil is 'the original, the beginning, the real *deed* in the conception of slave morality' (Nietzsche 1996: 25). And who is the evil enemy of slave morality? – 'the answer is: *none other* than the "good man" of the other morality, none other than the noble, powerful, dominating man, but only once he has been given a new colour, interpretation, and aspect by the poisonous eye of *ressentiment*' (Nietzsche 1996: 25).

And so we emerge with a morality of praise and blame, reward and punishment, in contrast with a morality of character (one cannot be praised or blamed for one's character – one just possesses it through good fortune, or perhaps 'moral luck'; this is an important problem which I will discuss in detail in Chapter 7). 'Only through the transformation of bad into evil, of inferiority into something for which one could be blamed, could the revaluation succeed' (Clark 1998: 854). It is through this transformation of the nobility into 'evil' that the priestly caste can seize power by re-directing the loyalty of the masses to themselves, and it is through the morality of praise and blame, reward and punishment, that they can maintain their power, for their final triumph lies within the notions of sin and guilt. In the second essay of the *Genealogy* Nietzsche traces the development of the idea of guilt from the realm of trade and the notion of debt (Clark 1998: 855). 'It is in this sphere, in legal obligations, then, that the moral conceptual world of "guilt", "conscience", "duty", "sacred duty" originates...' (Nietzsche 1996: 46). Priests exploit the notion of debt as owed to ancestors, gods and so on, and moralise it into guilt which can never be paid off. Eventually it is owed to God conceived of as a purely spiritual being, and what must be sacrificed to God is one's natural, physical existence. The debt is paid to God through self-denial, through the ascetic form of life (Clark 1998: 855). The triumph of the priest class is, therefore, the turning of humanity's natural instincts of freedom and power *inward*. 'Every instinct which does not vent itself externally *turns inwards* – this is what I call the *internalization* of man . . .'; and '. . . *such* is the origin of "bad conscience" ' (Nietzsche 1996: 65). Bad conscience is therefore 'that very same *instinct of freedom* (in my terminology: the will to power): except that the material on which the form-creating and violating nature of this force vents itself is in this case man himself' (Nietzsche 1996: 67). Humanity, therefore, begins to *suffer from itself* (Nietzsche 1996: 65).

This suffering would be self-destructive, but once more the priests learn how to exploit it, and this is perhaps their greatest triumph – they make suffering meaningful. 'The aspect of suffering which actually causes outrage is not suffering itself, but the meaninglessness of suffering . . . So that hidden, undiscovered, and unwitnessed suffering could be banished from the world and honestly negated, mankind was at that time virtually forced to invent gods and supernatural beings of all heights and depths' (Nietzsche 1996: 49–50). This is the meaning of the ascetic ideals that take the forefront of the slave morality and which Nietzsche explores in the third and final essay of the *Genealogy*.

For the masses, ascetic ideals represent 'an attempt to imagine oneself "too good" for this world, a holy form of dissipation, their principal means in the struggle against chronic pain and boredom' (Nietzsche 1996: 77). For the priestly rulers, they represent 'its most effective instrument of power, also the "very highest" licence for power' (Nietzsche 1996: 77). It is by making the suffering of the masses meaningful that the priests both conserve their power over them and give them a reason for continuing that suffering: '*the ascetic life is derived from the protective and healing instincts of a degenerating life*, which seeks to preserve itself and fights for existence with any available means' (Nietzsche 1996: 99). And so 'the ascetic ideal is a trick played in order to *preserve* life' (Nietzsche 1996: 99). The 'master-stroke' of the priest is therefore 'his exploitation of the *sense of guilt*' (Nietzsche 1996: 118). The priest 'engages his cunning in a tough and secret struggle against the anarchy of the herd, the continual threat of its disintegration, the herd in which that most dangerous explosive substance, *ressentiment*, is piled ever higher. To discharge this explosive in such a way as to avoid blowing up either the herd or the shepherd is his greatest master-stroke, and also his supreme usefulness' (Nietzsche 1996: 105). The priest reverses the direction of *ressentiment* so it now turns inwards, so that the suffering masses have no one to blame for their suffering but themselves. 'The suffering are gifted with a horrific readiness and inventiveness in finding pretexts for painful feelings; they even enjoy being suspicious, grumbling over misdeeds and apparent insults, they rummage over the entrails of their past and present in search of dark, questionable stories which allow them to revel in a painful mistrust and to intoxicate themselves on their own malicious poison – they tear open the oldest wounds, they bleed from scars long healed, they make evil-doers out of friends, wives, children, and what-ever else is closest to them. "I am suffering: someone must be to blame" – this is how all sickly sheep think. But their shepherd, the ascetic priest, tells them: "Just so, my sheep! someone must be to blame – *you alone are to blame for yourself!*"' (Nietzsche 1996: 106). The suffering person therefore becomes a sinner, and the cause of his suffering is himself – 'he should understand his suffering itself as a *state of punishment*' (Nietzsche 1996: 118).

Here lies Nietzsche's conclusion to our present condition. Our morality is an expression of *ressentiment* aimed at our selves. We have learned – have been taught – to loathe our physical selves, our natural selves, our desires. We are consumed by guilt. But this suffering does not drive us to nihilistic despair, and for this, as well as for the guilt, we have to thank the priests. Nietzsche concludes the *Genealogy*: 'his problem . . . was *not* suffering itself, but rather the absence of an answer to his questioning cry: "*Why do I suffer?*" Man, the boldest animal and the one most accustomed to pain, does *not* repudiate suffering as such; he *desires* it, he even seeks it out, provided that he has been shown a *meaning* for it, a *reason* for suffering. The meaninglessness of suffering, and *not* suffering as such, has been the curse which has hung over mankind up to now – *and the ascetic ideal offered mankind a meaning!*' (Nietzsche 1996: 136). The ascetic ideal explains our suffering. 'The explanation – there is no doubt – brought new suffering with it, deeper, more internal, more poisonous, gnawing suffering: it brought all suffering under the perspective of *guilt* . . . But in spite of all this – or thanks to it – man was *saved*, he had a meaning' (Nietzsche 1996: 136).

Twisting Nietzsche

What can we learn from Nietzsche about the concept of evil? He is, notoriously, a difficult writer, and one from which we can extract too much or too little. Bernstein identifies a positive project behind Nietzsche's critique of morality. His aim is not a return to the aristocratic morality, but to show a way forward – the project is dialectical (Bernstein 2002: 112–13). The aim 'is to open the possibility of a higher, life-affirming ethic that can grow out of the soul of the morality of good and evil' (Bernstein 2002: 113). On the idea of evil itself, Bernstein points out that it has two meanings in Nietzsche's text: what the priests mean by it, and what Nietzsche means by it when he, for example, describes the priests as the 'most evil enemies' (Bernstein 2002: 119). Nietzsche's own use of evil is directed against *ressentiment*. 'If *ressentiment* is left to fester, it becomes a dangerous poison, and leads to a type of nihilism that undermines *all* valuation' (Bernstein 2002: 121). Nietzsche's own example of contemporary *ressentiment* is anti-Semitism, which he attacks ferociously (see Nietzsche 1996: 103 and 133). 'Nietzsche uses his most barbed rhetorical weapons to condemn this vicious form of *ressentiment*' (Bernstein 2002: 129). As we have seen, Nietzsche thinks the nobility were not poisoned by *ressentiment* even if they occasionally felt it, and that those who move beyond good and evil will not be affected by it at all. But, says Bernstein, 'these possibilities are far less persuasive than Nietzsche's account of the *ever-present* danger of venomous outbursts of this form of evil' (Bernstein 2002: 130). And it is important to remember that for Nietzsche *ressentiment* can be expressed not only individually but also at the social, political and cultural level: 'he is insightful about the explosive dangers of modern nationalisms. He has an acute sense of the dark underside of these processes – where *ressentiment* festers and then bursts forth in an orgy of vicious destruction' (Bernstein 2002: 130). Therefore he is important 'because of his insight into the psychological dynamics of *ressentiment*, the ways in which it is related to envy, jealousy, and hatred; the multifarious individual, social, political, and cultural forms it can take; its poisonous festering, and its *ever-present* dangerous consequences' (Bernstein 2002: 131).

I think Bernstein is correct that Nietzsche is extremely important for our project of understanding the value of the concept of evil, and not merely for directing our attention to the importance of a critique of morality, of embarking on the kind of project

Claudia Card believes is a mistake. Card herself thinks Nietzsche does provide some important insights: 'That judgment of evil comes, basically, from a victim's perspective...'; 'That judgments of evil are often accompanied by a distorting hatred...'; and 'That hatred is often rooted in one's fear of impotence...' (Card 2002: 29). However, she questions the beliefs that accompany these insights: 'that the perspectives of the weak are more distorted and yield more dishonest judgments than those of the powerful'; 'that powerful perpetrators are not likely to hate their victims'; and 'that hatred underlies judgments of evil' (Card 2002: 29). Card's own view is that victims and perpetrators can both have distorted perceptions of each other. 'If victims tend to exaggerate the reprehensibility of the perpetrators' motives, perpetrators tend to underestimate the harm they do' (Card 2002: 29). Also, perpetrators often *do* hate their victims, even though that hatred is triggered in different ways. And 'judgments of evil can often be plausibly evoked to explain hatred, a clue that the judgment underlies the hatred rather than the other way around' (Card 2002: 29–30).

There is something to these criticisms, and rather than a wholehearted acceptance of Nietzsche's critique of morality I want to take elements that help us to understand the concept of evil in a way that requires us to 'twist' his account to make it more plausible. First, while for Nietzsche our conventional moral codes are derived from and benefit the weak at the expense of the strong, it seems clear that it is the powerful, not the weak, who command the discourse of evil and shape it to serve their own interests. Of course Nietzsche recognises this to an extent: the priestly caste within the aristocracy shape the revolt and then become the powerful. We also have to allow to Nietzsche that the contrast between the 'weak' and the 'strong' need not be the same as the contrast between the powerful and the powerless – the 'weak' may well be powerful, and the 'strong' powerless as things now stand. Also, as Brian Leiter points out, 'while "master" and "slave" *begin* as class-specific terms, their ultimate significance is psychological for Nietzsche, not social...' (Leiter 2002: 217). It is therefore a mistake to *now* search for members of the 'slave' class and the 'master' class; rather, these are psychological traits that can exist even within the same person (Leiter 2002: 217). We should also note that 'there is even now no shortage of places where the outcome of the conflict remains undecided' (Nietzsche 1996: 34–5). Finally, we should remember that my aim here is, at least in part, to develop a *political* philosophy of evil, and Nietzsche, as Leiter reminds us, 'has no political philosophy' (Leiter 2002: 296). Again, 'it is individual attitudes not political structures that are Nietzsche's primary object' (Leiter 2002: 295). What Nietzsche has left us with is, therefore, not a 'class' analysis of contemporary morality even if that is the beginning of its genealogical account, but a moral psychology of the individual designed to show those who can understand him and who are strong enough to break free from its confines, how to liberate themselves and move beyond it. This is, of course, in part a devastating critique of contemporary culture *and* politics, especially democratic politics, but Nietzsche's focus is upon those few individuals capable of transcending the contemporary value system, and I want to draw very different political conclusions from his approach.

And so rather than debate the accuracy of Nietzsche's genealogical history and attempt to apply his distinctions in a class-based way to contemporary moral culture, I want to follow his insight that the discourse of morality can be used to control the masses, and argue that the discourse of evil, at least as it is now practised, is a manifestation of the powerful manipulating the masses in order to retain and develop their power. This is not at odds with elements of Nietzsche's genealogy, as the priestly caste manipulate the *ressentiment* of the herd to retain *their* power, but what does move us away from his account is that it does not make much sense to claim that the discourse of evil is directed by the ruling caste against a powerful enemy. Rather, as we shall see in the next chapter, the historical record shows that it has been directed against weak and marginalised groups who present very little danger to those in power. The real threat to the powerful comes from the loss of popular support by the masses, and the way to keep their loyalty is to direct their hostility – or *ressentiment* – towards an 'evil enemy', and convince them that the only way to be safe from this terrible enemy is to remain loyal to the ruling caste, because of their vast experience and expertise in protecting them from this particular threat. The group picked out as the 'evil enemy' can never be that genuinely dangerous, because then, of course, the ruling caste would face a genuine threat to their power. In Nietzsche's favour this is not too far from his understanding, and even the weak 'evil enemy' may be characterised as powerful and superior and therefore extremely dangerous. However, we have to say that the value of the idea of evil cannot be the same as it was within the slave morality, to overthrow and keep down the superior class. And, in another twist, while Nietzsche takes it that the priestly caste turn the *ressentiment* of the masses inwards, directed against themselves, on this account it remains focused outwards, upon the 'evil enemy' – it remains political rather than psychological.

Another twist of the Nietzschean account is to do with the idea of *ressentiment* itself, which for Nietzsche is to do with hatred and revenge. In my account, at the heart of the *ressentiment* which the powerful mobilise among the masses is not hatred, but fear. That fear may well be expressed as a grudge-filled resentment, but the moving force behind it remains primarily fear of the 'evil enemy' – the hatred of them follows. Whether it makes sense to describe this fear as *ressentiment* is questionable, and I do not want to do violence to Nietzsche's core concepts and so I will not continue to use the term. The question now becomes: what are we scared of? It is true that the ruling caste creates an 'evil enemy' out of very little, or even nothing, as the focus of our fear, but the fear they exploit is already there – they do not create the fear itself. Only this can explain why the masses are so easily manipulated and directed against the figures the ruling caste identify as the enemy; we are already scared of something. And this brings us to the final twist of the Nietzschean turn, that the struggle for the masses is not to find a meaning for their *suffering*, but to find a meaning for their *fear*; this is what the ruling caste supply through the discourse of evil. Certainly Nietzsche may be right that the purpose of the discourse of 'good' in Judaeo-Christian ethics is to give meaning to suffering, and that meaningless suffering is unendurable, but the discourse of evil seems to have a different purpose here. Being scared of the dark only makes sense if something evil lurks there, hidden from our eyes. If we realise there is nothing there at all, and yet remain scared of the dark, we have to admit that our fears and panics are irrational and meaningless, but they remain with us, undermining reason itself. The struggle to make fear meaningful has a long and disturbing history which I will examine in the next chapter. There, I focus on 'communities of fear' – the extent to which communities are shaped and held together by irrational fear of imaginary monsters (this perhaps fills a gap in Nietzsche's account, when he identifies the importance of community and the importance for the priestly caste to hold the 'herd' together in a community, and yet seems to believe this can be done by directing *ressentiment* inwards; it surely needs to be directed outwards, at something beyond the boundaries of the community, or at least against an enemy within). In Chapter 5 I will address the question: what are we scared of? I return to these themes – and to Nietzsche – in the closing chapter, when we confront the problem that even though we may illuminate the darkness with the power of reason and make the imaginary monsters disappear, we remain scared and so perhaps remain in need of mythical monsters to make sense of the world and our place within it.

Chapter Four

Communities of Fear

Introduction

In Chapter 2 I looked at the search for Satan as a mythological character, and suggested that there was another way to find him, and I want to pursue that particular method here. We have seen how the idea of Satan and diabolical evil emerge within communities that consider themselves to be under attack, and that the most dangerous enemy is the one who lurks within, who appears to be just like us but is a monster in disguise, plotting to transform the community into something else, and perhaps even plotting our complete destruction. Satan is of course a supernatural force, but he recruits human allies, and so historically the search for Satan becomes the search for those allies. Here we see that the idea of diabolical evil has played an important ideological role. It may be understood, not as a metaphysical presence within the world, but as a regulatory and oppressive discourse used in the pursuit of power. And from Nietzsche in Chapter 3 we learned that one way of approaching the concept is not an 'internal' philosophical critique, but an 'external' historical critique that looks at how the idea has developed and been used. In this chapter I use both these insights – the ideology of evil and the importance of history – and look at two historical examples where this understanding seems plausible, the witch trials in Europe and North America in the sixteenth and seventeenth centuries, and the less well documented vampire epidemics of eastern Europe in the eigthteenth century. The point of studying these historical events is to develop a political philosophy of evil, an awareness of how it has been used to marginalise and oppress. If we can make no philosophical or psychological sense of evil, it may be that this political sense is all there is.

Rousseau and the Vampires

At the same time as the Enlightenment was overthrowing the old order of things in western Europe, reports emerged from the east telling of epidemics of vampirism – the dead were rising from their graves to inflict fear and death upon the living. These epidemics began around 1670, ending around 1770, in Istria, East Prussia, Hungary, Silesia, Russia and Wallachia (Frayling 1991: 19). One such epidemic took place in Moravia, centering around Olomoucs. These stories are told by Dom Augustine Calmet in his *Treatise on the Vampires of Hungary and Surrounding Regions*, which was published in Paris in 1746 and in London in 1759, and re-issued as *The Phantom World* in 1850. This treatise was the first and most thorough vampire anthology and report of the plague of vampires sweeping through eastern Europe, and it gives an account of the problems facing the citizens of Olomoucs in Chapter VII, 'The Revenans or Vampires of Moravia'. Calmet himself was drawing on another source, Charles Ferdinand de Schertz's *Magia Posthuma*, published in Olomoucs in 1706, and dedicated to Prince Charles of Lorraine, Bishop of Olomoucs and Osnaburgh. De Schertz himself was drawing on other sources, perhaps oral reports, but certainly other, older texts, such as one by a monk named Neplach (1332–68), *Summula Chronicae tam Romanae quam Bohemicae*, compiled between 1356 and 1362, again from previous chronicles written by others giving accounts of vampire activity in Bohemia (see Jan Perkowsky's *The Darkling* for these accounts). One problem that becomes apparent here is that these are stories that have been told and retold a great many times, and none of the sources cited are the original telling.

One source that de Schertz and Calmet drew upon was, however, much more contemporary. These were the official reports compiled by the religious and political authorities who sent their representatives into the regions afflicted by the epidemics to discover what was really taking place. In the case of Moravia, it was a Monsieur de Vassimont, sent by Prince Leopold, first duke of Lorraine, to assist his brother, the Bishop, Prince Charles. These reports made sensational and disturbing reading. One especially notorious case was that of Arnold Paole, a peasant who died in 1726 who was the subject of an official report published in 1732 (Frayling 1991: 20–2). According to that report Paole returned from the dead and tormented the people of the village of Medvegia near Belgrade, causing the death of four of them. The villagers decided to disinter his body, which they did forty days after his death. The report reads: 'His flesh had not decomposed, his eyes were filled with fresh blood, which also flowed from his ears and nose . . . His fingernails and toenails had dropped off, as had his skin, and others had grown through in their place, from which it was concluded he was an arch-vampire' (Frayling 1991: 21). The report continues that the villagers decided to drive a stake through his heart. As this was done, Paole 'gave a great shriek, and an enormous quantity of blood spurted from his body' (Frayling 1991: 21). But it didn't stop there, as the victims of vampires were believed to become vampires too. The four people thought to have died from Paole's attacks were disposed of in the same way, as were other people who died from eating the contaminated flesh of animals also thought to have been attacked by him. Those, too, had to be disinterred, staked, and their bodies burned. These included a woman who had died in childbirth three months before who had claimed she washed in the blood of a vampire. The report states: 'She was in an excellent state of preservation. Cutting open her body, we found much fresh blood . . . her stomach and intestines were as fresh as those of a healthy, living person . . . fresh and living skin had grown recently, as had finger and toenails' (Frayling 1991: 21–2). And a sixty-year-old woman who had eaten contaminated meat was, after ninety days of burial, 'much plumper', and 'still had much liquid blood in her breasts' (Frayling 1991: 22).

These reports were received with incredulity in western Europe. This was the time of the Enlightenment, when philosophy and science were supposed to have won the struggle against superstition and dark fantasies – vampires certainly had no place in this world view. Christopher Frayling observes: 'Between the late 1720s and the 1760s learned essays on questions relating to superstition were by no means uncommon, for those philosophers in Europe who were pledged to the idea of progress clearly enjoyed amassing evidence about what they called the "primitive" or "dark" areas . . . one time or another the debate involved such leading figures of the Enlightenment as the Marquis d'Argens, Voltaire, Diderot, Rousseau, Van Swieten . . . and the Chevalier de Jaucourt (a prolific contributor to Diderot's and D'Alembert's great *Encyclopédie*). The era known . . . as the Age of Reason, and recently "called the origin of the modern, urbane, secular mind", was much perplexed by the question of vampirism' (Fraying 1991: 23). The primary concern of these intellectuals was to explain the epidemics in scientific terms or to discredit the reports as the ravings

of primitive peoples. There had to be a natural rather than supernatural explanation. Rousseau, however, stood out from the rest
by taking the reports seriously. In a famous passage he comments:
'No evidence is lacking – depositions, certificates of notables, sur-
geons, priests and magistrates. The proof *in law* is utterly complete' (Frayling 1991: 31, taken from the open letter to Christophe
de Beaumont, Archbishop of Paris). This passage has led some
to suppose that Rousseau believed in the existence of vampires,
but this is doubtful. He took the reports seriously in a different
sense, and whether or not vampires existed in the supernatural
sense was, for him, of no interest. The reports of the epidemics
were important in that they revealed something, not about the nature of the vampire, but 'about the nature of authority in civilized
society' (Frayling 1991: 33).

The explanation Rousseau is concerned to find is not a natural, as opposed to supernatural, one, but a social/political one,
because the epidemics were a social/political phenomenon. First,
we can take the vampire as a metaphor for our social and political
condition. It stands, says Rousseau, for the exploitative relationships that have arisen from the possession of private property.
Frayling summarises Rousseau's position: 'So, with the birth of
property and the growth of agriculture we had transfigured ourselves into masters and slaves in turn, everyone moved by contempt for the person and lust for the goods of the next man, so
that we had finally become a species of animal which in its to-
tality is self-destructive' (Frayling 1991: 34). Second, we can look
for a social/political explanation of the vampire epidemics, one
in which religious and political authorities seek to exercise control over populations by appealing to popular myths and superstitions, to irrational panics. Frayling comments: 'For Rousseau,
both sacred and secular authority derived their strength from popular superstitions, and fear of a miraculous monster such as the
vampire helped to underpin respect for and submission to the
worldly agents of an omnipotent God. In this way the dreaded superhuman force of vampires transforms the divinity of God into
the wretched practice of obedience to his temporal ministers, and
vampires – whether they be real or unreal creatures – wield a
sinister power over men which is plain enough' (Frayling 1991:
33). In the face of supernatural forces of evil, we must submit to
those who can protect us from them, those who understand such
supernatural powers, and, of course, have their own sources of it.
And so, says Frayling, vampires are 'yet another manifestation of

the sombre and nefarious tyranny of opinion exercised by priests over the minds of men' (Frayling 1991: 33).

In this chapter I will explore Rousseau's approach to the vampire epidemics further, because I believe he has provided an insight into the nature of political authority and the ideological role of the discourse of evil. However, I will initially shift attention away from the vampire epidemics to an earlier but similar phenomenon, the witch crazes that swept across western Europe in the sixteenth and seventeeth centuries. Here, the historical research is far more detailed, but we see the same pattern of religious authorities using fear of the supernatural to maintain or seize power. I will suggest that we can draw general patterns about the nature of power in 'civilised' society from these two great panics in European history, and the most important element is the centrality of fear in constituting the identity of political communities. Rather than political communities forming themselves around shared identities, they are formed through the exploitation by political authorities of social fears and insecurities, by focusing those fears upon some threatening 'evil' figure – the vampire, the witch, the Jew, the migrant, the asylum seeker, the Gypsy, the 'Islamicist' terrorist – and claiming to protect the 'genuine' members from these deviant and dangerous threats. Political communities are constituted by an irrational horror of imaginary monsters. In this process, those who seek to hold or gain power do not only create the threatening figure, they also create the community itself, or a particular form of it, with themselves at its centre. The witch craze, the vampire epidemics, and, I will argue in the final chapter of this book, our present panics over such phenomena as immigration and terrorism are exactly parallel. What is especially terrifying about the vampire and the witch is their ambiguity – their ability to be among us without detection, and, in the case of the vampire, their ability to pass across borders undetected. They are the enemy within, and, therefore, a source of intense fear and panic, which can be exploited in the pursuit of political power.

Witchcraft and the End of the World

Although largely immune from the vampire epidemics, western Europe had been engulfed in witch crazes from around 1550 to 1670 (the first vampire epidemic occurs, curiously, around 1670). In contrast, eastern Europe had remained largely immune from the witch crazes. According to Hugh Trevor-Roper, this was because the witch crazes had their theoretical source in a demonology specific to the Catholic Church and which was taken over wholesale by the Protestant reformers (Trevor-Roper 1978: 114). The Greek Orthodox Church did not share that demonology, and so with the Christian schism of 1054 the Slavonic countries escaped with the exception of those parts, such as Poland, where the Catholic Church remained in power (Trevor-Roper 1978: 115). The belief in witches was by no means new anywhere in Europe, but two features of the craze of the fifteenth and sixteenth centuries were new. The first was a distinctive view of what witchcraft signified, and the second was a new legal severity in rooting it out and punishing those who practised it. The second feature arose from the first. Prior to the witch-trial period, the popular view was that there were two types of witchcraft, white and black (Larner 1984: 3 and 80). White witchcraft was the exploitation of magical powers for the benefit of the community; black witchcraft was their exploitation to harm the community. The legal authorities were only concerned with witchcraft where it was used to harm others, and the church authorities were only concerned if it reflected heresy. There were forms of magic which involved neither (Peters 2002: 208). The command in Exodus 12: 18 that 'Thou shalt not suffer a witch to live' was interpreted as demanding excommunication and exile: the witch could not live within the Christian community (Peters 2002: 209). And heretics had the option of repentance to escape punishment – the goal was to save souls.

This view of witchcraft changed radically in Continental Europe, with the exception of Spain (except for the Basque region) and southern Italy (Larner 1984: 4). England was also an exception for various complex reasons. It operated a different system of law and never fully imported the changed picture of witchcraft which emerged on the Continent in the fifteenth century. This was developed by intellectuals in the Church and the universities and saw all forms of magic, with no exception, as evidence of a pact entered into with the Devil. All kinds of magic were diabolical heresy. Edward Peters comments: 'Beginning in the early fifteenth century many of the different kinds of offences that had earlier constituted the separate offences of magic, sorcery, divination, necromancy and even learned natural magic began to be considered in some places by some theologians and magistrates, both ecclesiastical and civil, as a single type of crime whose essence was defined as a conspiratorial alliance with the devil whose purpose was to ruin human society' (Peters 2002: 231). According to this view, individuals signed a compact with Satan with their own blood, rendered homage to him and entered into sexual deviations with him, travelled by flying at night to meetings where they engaged in perverted rituals, often accompanied by their familiar demons in the form of an animal, and they carried a mark on their bodies as a sign of membership (Peters 2002: 231). This picture of witchcraft came to dominate European thought, and had its place within the Christian view of cosmological history. The Christian community was under severe attack by Satan, and the rise of witchcraft and heresy were 'signs indicating the increasing and despairing fury of Satan as the end of the world – and his own final defeat – drew near, doubling his onslaught against the people of God' (Peters 2002: 230–1). This meant that people who would have been seen as individuals exploring magical powers for good or evil on their own initiative were now members of a vast conspiracy aiming to destroy humanity. It followed that where one witch was discovered there would be others, and hence the importance of the witch hunt.

The seriousness of this crisis led to witchcraft being declared a *crimen exceptum*, an excepted crime, in 1468 (Trevor-Roper 1978: 43), for which 'there was to be no possible expiation short of death, since there was no way by which an accused person could adequately repent, and hence no justification for mercy when sentencing' (Peters 2002: 232). Indeed, judges who showed leniency were in danger of being seen as part of the demonic conspiracy: – the Rector of the University at Trier was burnt as a witch after it was felt that he had been lenient, not being convinced by confessions extracted through torture (Trevor-Roper 1978: 76–7). The status of witchcraft as a *crimen exceptum* was also a response to the difficulty in establishing guilt. Larner comments, 'since it was not amenable to the normal principles of proof, normal standards of interrogation and court procedure would not meet the situation. It was necessary to use torture to extract a confession' (Larner 1984: 44). There were therefore no legal limits to the use of torture in cases of suspected witchcraft. Trevor-Roper observes that, 'witches' confessions became more detailed with the intensification of inquisitorial procedure; and that the identity of such confessions is often to be explained by the identity of procedure rather than any identity of experience: identical works of reference, identical instructions to judges, identical leading questions supported by torments too terrible to bear' (Trevor-Roper 1978:

44). And he concludes that: 'It is easy to see that torture lay, directly and indirectly, behind most witch-trials in Europe, creating witches where none were and multiplying both victims and evidence' (Trevor-Roper 1978: 46).

So we can see that the idea of diabolical heresy and the witch craze that followed it arose from a sense of fear and anxiety throughout western Christian Europe. But what gave rise to this general fear and anxiety, such that the Christian community saw itself under a terrifying Satanic assault? Historians have identified a range of causes. Certainly, in the fourteenth and fifteenth centuries Europe had experienced famine, plague, general warfare and financial instability (Peters 2002: 224–5). The Christian Church itself was experiencing crisis and instability, with schisms (there were two popes from 1378 to 1409 and three from 1409 to 1415) and pressure for reform (Peters 2002: 226–7). Peters observes that: 'such a sense of loss and uncertainty complemented a heightened sense that the assaults of Satan were growing more powerful, that defences against them were weaker, and that this awareness was linked to ideas about the end of the world, especially those aspects of it that dealt with the growth in strength of the assaults by Satan and the coming of the Antichrist' (Peters 2002: 226). Trevor-Roper offers an explanation of the witch craze that focuses on struggles for religious authority and power. According to him, the causes lay in the efforts of the Catholic Church to impose its authority upon regions of Europe where older traditions and beliefs were still strong – a clash between feudal Christian Europe and 'social groups which it could not assimilate' (Trevor-Roper 1978: 112). The pattern taken by those who sought to gain authority in these regions was to accuse resistant groups and individuals of heresy, and for heresy eventually to become witchcraft. This was a clash of civilisations, says Trevor-Roper. Feudal civilisation was based in the cultivated lowlands, while the mountain regions contained closed societies, isolated and relatively untouched, and here were 'primitive religious forms and resistance to new orthodoxies' (Trevor-Roper 1978: 31). The Christian missionaries, largely Dominican friars, found that the faith had to be established over and over again in these regions, as 'ancient habits of thought reasserted themselves' (Trevor-Roper 1978: 31). The witchcraft trials died down in the period from 1500 to 1560, perhaps partially under the influence of Renaissance humanism, but flared even more powerfully from 1560 to 1630 with the Reformation and the Counter-Reformation, as both Catholic and Protestant churches had to be militant in establishing their authority. For both sides, the heretic and the witch were identical figures, as each side identified its opponents as entering into the pact with Satan: 'this recrudescence of the witch-craze in the 1560s was directly connected with the return of religious war...' (Trevor-Roper 1978: 70). And: 'Every crucial stage in the ideological struggle of the Reformation was a stage also in the revival and perpetuation of the witch-craze' (Trevor-Roper 1978: 88). These were times of great fear and insecurity, and, says Trevor-Roper, 'When a "great fear" takes hold of a society, that society looks naturally to the stereotype of the enemy in its midst' (Trevor-Roper 1978: 119). And then, 'the stereotype, once established, creates...its own folklore' (Trevor-Roper 1978: 120).

Christina Larner draws two more important developments from the context of religious warfare. The first is the importance of personal religion among the general population. Prior to this period it was not important what the peasantry believed, but the Reformation and Counter-Reformation christianised the peasantry for the first time (Larner 1984: 89). The second development is the rise of the nation state, as new regimes established 'more centralized, more secular governments' (Larner 1984: 89). These new regimes had to 'demonstrate their legitimacy' by appropriating religious authority. 'The rise of rival versions of Christianity, each with exclusive claims, greatly enhanced the political usefulness of religion to the rulers of early modern Europe. Borders were staked out not with fences but with churches' (Larner 1984: 89). Which version of Christianity the state adopted now identified people as members of the community – it became necessary that the population hold the *right* version. This meant that 'Christianity had become a political ideology' (Larner 1984: 89). The witch trials can therefore be seen, in part, as a strategy to enforce a religious/political identity; witchcraft became a 'political and ideological crime', and 'witches represented the most extreme form of deviance' (Larner 1984: 89). Larner concludes: 'The witchcraft prosecutions in Europe were exactly coterminous with the period during which Christianity was a political ideology. When the establishment of the Kingdom of God ceased to be a political objective and was replaced by the pursuit of liberty, the defence of property, the belief in progress, enlightenment, patriotism and other secular alternatives, the courts ceased to convict' (Larner 1984: 90). Christianity lost its status as a political ideology as it lost its political importance. Of course, at particular times and

places, religious identity emerges once more as politically important, but never again on this scale; and also the need for 'ideological deviants' continued (Larner 1984: 91), but they would cease
to be the witch, or even the heretic.

Dissolving into Vampires

We have here, then, one element of Rousseau's approach to the
vampire epidemics. The witch trials give us a social/political explanation in terms of struggles to assert power over resistant communities, and there is evidence that similar forces were at work
during the vampire phenomenon, although historical scholarship
here is much inferior to the work on the witch trials. In fact what
suggests itself is a struggle between local religious and regional
secular authorities for power and influence over communities,
with local religious authorities invoking fear of the diabolical supernatural and the secular regional authorities seeking to control
that fear. But what of the other element Rousseau identifies, of
the vampire as metaphor for social relations? The vampire represents the exploitative relationships created by private property.
This is certainly a metaphor we find elsewhere, including in the
works of Karl Marx. Ken Gelder explores some of these uses of the
vampire figure, such as, from Chapter 10 of *Capital*, 'Capitalism
is dead labour which, vampire-like, lives only by sucking living
labour, and lives the more, the more labour it sucks' (Gelder 1994:
20); and in *Grundrisse*, capital survives 'by constantly sucking in
living labour as its soul, vampire-like' (Gelder 1994: 20). Gelder
comments: 'The representation of capital or the capitalist as a
vampire was . . . common both to Marx and to popular fiction in
the mid-nineteenth century' (Gelder 1994: 22).

However, this particular metaphor is not that helpful here, and
there is another way of taking the vampire figure which helps us
to further understand the epidemics. Gelder identifies an association between the figure of the vampire and the figure of the
Jew, especially the Jews of eastern Europe, who, it was thought,
presented particular problems of assimilation and therefore a particular danger to the identity of the political community. Gelder's
concern here is with the vampire in fiction and specifically the
figure of Count Dracula in Bram Stoker's novel. He points out
that at the end of the nineteenth century there were various and
powerful 'discourses of degeneration' in Britain (Gelder 1994:

14). Maurice Hindle identifies Stoker's novel as part of a late nineteenth-century feeling that 'some gigantic evil was gnawing away at Christian confidence' (Stoker 1993: ix). The unregulated influx of foreigners, especially 'foreign' Jews from eastern Europe, was seen as one important source of degeneration (Gelder 1994: 15). Stoker represents the Count as 'a tall, thin man, with a beaky nose and black moustache and pointed beard' (Gelder 1994: 14), who hoards riches and moves across borders evading regulation and control. The person who helps him escape from England is Immanuel Hildesheim, a Jew who arranges illegal entry and exit, 'a Hebrew of rather the Adelphi Theatre type, with a nose like a sheep, and a fez' (Gelder 1994: 15; Stoker 1993: 448). And so we have here 'the representation of the vampire as "unassimilated" – as a "cosmopolitan" or internationalised character who is excessive to national identities, whose lack of restraint threatens the very *notion* of identity' (Gelder 1994: 23). Failure or refusal to assimilate creates a dangerous diversity of identity. 'Diversity means instability: it invites contestation: identities become confused: one can no longer tell "who was who". In short, diversity means the *loss* of one's nationality – hardly appropriate for an imperialistic ideology which depends upon a stable identification between nation and self. The more diverse a nation, the less claim it has to national identity; and this "weakening" of identity makes it more vulnerable to absorption by imperialistic nations elsewhere' (Gelder 1994: 11–12). Therefore there is fear of loss of national identity through unregulated movement across borders and growing deviance within them, as one's nation 'dissolves', and in Stoker's novel this becomes 'the fear of dissolving into vampires' (Gelder 1994: 12). During the period Larner identifies in early modern Europe, with the rise of new nation states and new political regimes, the fear of absorption was very real, but during Stoker's time of British Empire the fact was that 'even the most apparently stable, imperialistic nations can evoke horror fantasies in which self-identities are invaded and absorbed into the Other' (Gelder 1994: 12). Hindle points out that this, although the 'apogee of imperialism', was a period of uncertainty for Britain as it underwent a fundamental shift from a competitive to a parasitic economy (Stoker 1993: xi; see E. J. Hobsbawm's *Industry and Empire*, 1999: 192). Decline had set in with competition from the United States of America and Germany. Stoker's novel, published in 1897, was just one of a number reflecting this theme, including H. G. Well's *War of the Worlds* published in 1898, in which the alien invaders live off human blood (Gelder 1994: 12). Indeed, colonising nations were particularly vulnerable to this fear, as vampirisation, says Gelder, represented reverse colonisation (Gelder 1994: 12).

This problem of assimilation has already been identified by Trevor-Roper with regard to the witch trials. They arose because of the clash between orthodox Christianity and 'social groups which it could not assimilate' (Trevor-Roper 1978: 113). These groups' defence of their identity became heresy and subsequently witchcraft. During this period of intense persecution the Jew appeared alongside the witch as the victim, the Jew being the predominant target of the Inquisition in Spain, and the witch in the rest of western Europe. Indeed, Christian thought had, from its earliest days, 'portrayed some Jews as magicians', and, says Peters, 'the poisonous image of the Jew as sorcerer survived for a long time in later European thought' (Peters 2002: 178). According to Trevor-Roper: 'The witch and the Jew both represent social nonconformity' (Trevor-Roper 1978: 33); and so, 'Jews and witches were persecuted rather as types of social nonconformity than for doctrinal or other given reasons' (Trevor-Roper 1978: 35). Such unassimilable social groups became 'objects of social fear' (Trevor-Roper 1978: 52). To this extent, 'social fear, the fear of a different kind of society, was given intellectual form as a heretical ideology and suspect individuals were then persecuted by reference to that heresy' (Trevor-Roper 1978: 53–4). The witch trials therefore represent 'political exploitations of a social fear and a social ideology, whose origins were to be found at a deeper level and in another field' (Trevor-Roper 1978: 54). Christina Larner has already identified the importance of the witch as a social and political deviant, enabling authorities to pursue the enforcement of a particular ideology, and using it to identify 'genuine' members of the community. She comments: 'new regimes tend to be repressive, not only in that the new leader or leaders must first extinguish rivals, but they must also establish their own legitimacy. This is done by raising the level of social control and by attacking non-conformity' (Larner 1984: 64). The new leadership achieves this by raising a moral panic over the danger of certain deviants, and then moving to protect the legitimate members of the community from this threat. 'The punitive treatment of deviance not only demonstrates the control of rulers but also asserts the values of conformists. The advantage of witchcraft over other crimes in this context is that it sums up all forms of non-conformity. Witches are evil. The prosecution of witches is a peculiarly economical way of attacking deviance' (Larner 1984: 64–5). This also, to an extent, explains why the victims of the trials were predominantly female (around 80 per cent). The position of women is so crucial to the social order that any deviance is seen as extremely destabilising; men have a much wider range of acceptable behaviours before being labelled as deviant. In times of social crisis, therefore, the woman is the primary problem and it is her role that has to be enforced most strictly. 'There is much to suggest', says Larner, 'that in the law-and-order crises generated by the new regimes of early modern Europe, women were a prime symbol of disorder' (Larner 1984: 86). This, of course, was because they were a prime symbol of order.

We can see, then, that a refusal or inability to assimilate, to adopt the role appropriate to one's identity, can, in times of social and political instability, be seen as the most dangerous threat to the well-being of the community. In one important sense, of course, the vampire epidemics and witch trials are importantly different. In the witch trials it was the living who were the victims, being persecuted, tortured and burnt. In the vampire epidemics it was the dead who were the victims, dug from their graves, dismembered and burnt. However, in another crucial sense they are the same. We can take the vampire epidemics as a similar problem of non-assimilation because the vampire refused to assimilate with the dead. The vampire invades the community by crossing a boundary, from the world of the dead back into the world of the living, and so is a trespasser who transgresses and disrupts one of the most potent and important borders, that between the living and the dead. Here, metaphor and social practice came together, as the localised religious authority figures claimed to protect the community from invaders who refused to assimilate in a radical way.

Conclusion

Rousseau believed that the vampire epidemics could tell us something important about the nature of authority and the pursuit of power. The lesson has been the importance of fear of an evil enemy who threatens the community with destruction, and the extent to which political communities are constituted through that fear of these imaginary monsters. These enemies are so monstrous and evil that our only defence is to grant power to those who have the power to protect us, the capacity to detect this enemy and pursue its destruction as ruthlessly as it pursues ours. Margaret Canovan has described the nation as a 'reservoir of political power' (Canovan 1996: 72), which can be mobilised despite the fact that it has lain dormant over long periods of time. That there is a body of people who can be mobilised in this way proves that a particular nation exists. What people share, what makes them a nation, is 'typically a heritage compounded of ethnic, political, cultural and other elements', a *national* heritage (Canovan 1996: 72). My counter-suggestion is that the 'nation' is re-invented at every mobilisation, and that the national heritage that is appealed to in order to unite the people is similarly a new invention, called into being for the purposes of that mobilisation. It need bear little resemblance and have little connection with other moments of 'national heritage' in the past, to other mobilisations of the same 'nation'; indeed, it would be surprising if it did, as the historical 'memory' of a people can only draw upon what is called into being at any particular moment for some specific purpose – we never *remember* the history of our 'people', we can only be *taught* it (see Jo Littler and Roshi Naidoo's edited collection of essays, *The Politics of Heritage: the Legacies of 'Race'* on how 'heritage' is created for political purposes). The past is not only another country, as L. P. Hartley describes it in his novel *The Go-Between*; it is also another 'nation'. Crucially, what is mobilised at these moments of national 'identity' is not a reservoir of power, but of fear.

What we are confronted with is a figure whose refusal or inability to assimilate threatens our identity and perhaps even our existence, and this gives rise to an irrational horror of the imaginary monster who refuses to be like 'us', and, even worse, has the power to assimilate us. The vampire is a potent figure for this fear, having the capacity to turn us into dead corpses, or living ones like it. Maurice Hindle points out that, 'the menace of the vampire is that . . . it works on us from the *inside*, taking over our bodies, "infecting" our deepest desires with the lust for power and domination' (Stoker 1993: ix). The authorities therefore seize upon these figures or create them through the language of pollution, of sexual perversion, of disease and death – the witch, the vampire, the Jew, or in contemporary times the immigrant, the asylum seeker, the gypsy. Driven by this horror, we join forces with the authorities in hunting down those who have found their way inside our community already, and in erecting more secure fortifications to prevent further invasions. Elsewhere I have argued that the dominant view on immigration found within liberal political theory takes this form (Cole 2000). Broadly there are three strategies through which liberal theory aims to legitimate strategies of exclusive membership. The first is to justify exclusion by appealing to traditional liberal values such as public order, welfare, private property, social justice and democracy, and argue that the damage to these caused by uncontrolled immigration outweigh the liberal commitment to the moral equality of persons. The second is to argue that the principle of moral equality is less important than traditionally thought, and should be translated from a principle of general humanity into a principle of particular community. There is still room for global ethical principles but these are secondary and outweighed by the local ethical principles of our community. Therefore the protection of that community is an ethical commitment that has priority over any concern for 'outsiders'. This is a liberal-communitarian approach found in versions of liberal nationalism developed by, for example, Yael Tamir (1993) and David Miller (1995). The third strategy is to appeal to the moral difference between the 'inside' and the 'outside', such that the inside is a sphere of liberal order and the outside is a state of disorder, a Hobbesian state of nature. The liberal state must therefore protect this moral order from the amoral disorder of the outside, by, for example, controlling migration. All three positions, whatever their differences, see the 'outside', and therefore the 'outsider', as posing some kind of threat which can only be repelled by maintaining strong boundaries of exclusion. The 'traditional' liberal sees the need to protect members from those who want to overconsume liberal resources and so drain the liberal polity of its ability to supply liberal goods to all – the immigrant as resource-sucking vampire figure. The liberal nationalist sees the need to protect the local sense of community and identity from those who are so different that they cannot be assimilated, and indeed may counter-assimilate members and so destroy that community identity – the immigrant as Gelder's vampiric 'reverse-coloniser'. The Hobbesian liberal sees the need to protect members from those who will, by their very nature, bring with them disorder and chaos. The outsider infects the liberal polity with disorder, eventually destroying it – the immigrant as the vampiric disease-carrier.

In examining the witch trials and the vampire epidemics, I am suggesting that we can draw general patterns about the nature of authority in a 'civilised' society from these two great panics in

European history, and the most important element is the importance of fear in constituting the identity of political communities. A specific community and its boundaries only become clear under a perceived threat, from inside or outside, rather than any positive identification between members. There is something that threatens 'people like us', although who people like us actually are remains, for the most part, curiously undefined. The detail of the threat and who 'we' are only become focused when those who are in political authority or who seek it exploit our individual fears and insecurities. An object of fear is created, a specific enemy who will 'dissolve' us. Both the threatening figure and the community the authorities seek to protect from it are new creations – neither existed in this form before, although the fear being exploited had existed at the individual level, lacking any specific focus. Our individual fears and insecurities are given a shape and form by political power seekers who make them into the fears and insecurities of the community or nation. At the same time it begins to matter what individual members of the community believe – there is an ideology, itself a new invention, that identifies us, and one of the major tasks to protect the community from destruction is to seek out those who do not share that ideology. This may entail a 'witch hunt' within the community itself, as the enemy is already within, as well as a 'vampire hunt' at the border, as we seek to ensure that nobody enters who does not already have the required ideology in their political consciousness (see Cole 2000: 123–7).

The power seekers may represent themselves as protecting long-standing communities with old traditions from dissolution by 'invaders' or 'deviants', but they actually seek to create a new unity with themselves at its centre. The threat itself is almost entirely fictional (sometimes entirely so), as the authorities attribute dark practices and powers to the threatening figure, so that they have the capacity to destroy our identity. This identity is, of course, very easily threatened as it lacks specific content, and that content is itself created by those who wish to mobilise fear. The situation is characterised as a crisis of assimilation: there are those who cannot or will not be like us in crucial respects. Even worse, they have the power to take away our identity, to make us less than human. This is why the campaigns to protect the community from these 'threats' have been especially spiteful and, in the past, physically cruel beyond our present understanding of human cruelty – normal rules of justice were suspended for the witch trials (see

Russell Hope Robbins' *The Encyclopaedia of Witchcraft and Demonology* (Robbins 1972) for details of the methods of torture and execution used against those accused of witchcraft).

There is a theme here that has been made familiar by Benedict Anderson (Anderson 1991), that communities are, in important respects, constituted by the imagination. They only exist in the minds of those who believe they are members. The crucial point is that the boundaries of the community are constituted by the imagination also, with the imaginary inside under attack from the imaginary outside. This means they have to be policed more stringently and frantically once they are threatened. The border is constituted through fear of the imaginary enemy, but an imaginary enemy cannot be held at the border and exposes it as a fabrication. The enemy is always within – the vampire and the witch already pass among us. This is not because of the lack of secure borders, but because the enemy is always within *us*, in the form of our deepest fears and insecurities about who we are, fears that are exploited in the struggle for political power and legitimacy. The answer to these fears is not more elaborate rituals, or higher walls or more powerful authorities to protect us. Nor can it be the pre-emptive military attack to destroy what is represented as the source of future fear. What we must find and seize upon and protect is a genuine unity of humanity, one that rules out any category of 'human waste' which we are entitled to trample over for the sake of the fictional identity of our imaginary community. What we see here is the myth of evil in action, and specifically the myth of monstrous evil, that there are monsters in disguise within our community who seek to destroy it. There can be no negotiation and no compromise against such an enemy, and certainly no redemption – they can only be hunted down and destroyed.

But why is this fear so intense? In great wars between nations, where they have faced the real prospect of destruction, the suspension of rules and the use of torture have mostly been resisted – not always with complete success of course (and, as we shall see in Chapter 8, when they take the form of 'race' wars – such as between Germany and Russia on the Eastern Front, and the United States and Japan in the Pacific, during the Second World War – rules of war seldom hold firm, if at all), but the historical movement has been towards the establishment of rules of conduct and the abolition of torture and mistreatment of prisoners. And yet when the enemy is within, such as in civil wars – in recent memory those in Spain and the former Yugoslavia – or pogroms against internal groups, there are few limits to what people will do to others. Why is there such an intense, terrible fear in these situations? It may be something to do with the fact that the evil is precisely ill-formed and ambiguous, or is suspected of already being within the community, eating away at it to destroy it. There is a much deeper horror here than when faced with the armies of an enemy nation marching towards us, really intent upon our destruction. In the next chapter we will examine the sources of horror to seek to understand the intensity of this fear.

Chapter Five

The Enemy Within

Introduction

In his book *A History of Terror: Fear and Dread through the Ages*, Paul Newman describes the deep insecurities that have afflicted humanity through recorded history, and observes: 'No doubt, in this third millennium, mankind will continue to be beset by fears, crazes and swirling panics' (Newman 2000: 223). These, he says, can strike any nation, any profession, any social group at any time. His book is 'a kind of journey through the badlands of history – a narrative of terror, torture and desecration' (Newman 2000: 223). This journey shows how, 'by the political use of fear, the darker side of mankind has so often gained the upper hand; how it can manifest itself in violence against peoples and animals; how men and women down the ages have been oppressed with a nameless dread or ubiquitous "fear of nothing" which has assumed various spectral shapes' (Newman 2000: 223). To deal with this 'primal terror of existence', we have to recognise first that it afflicts us, that it is baseless, and so 'suppress any headlong urge and think long and hard about an issue before embracing it or rejecting it' (Newman 2000: 223). In a time when the political use of fear is particularly intense, Newman's warning is pertinent, but although he presents the historical events to show that fear has been a constant presence, there is little here to explain it other than the 'primal terror' of our own existence. His solution is that we must think more clearly and carefully about issues that may send us into a panic, and this has a resonance with Hannah Arendt's warning against the banality of evil, which she characterises as a problem of thoughtlessness. Her solution is identical to Newman's: 'What I propose, therefore, is very simple: it is nothing more than to think what we are doing' (Arendt 1958: 5).

For Arendt, therefore, thinking clearly can prevent us from falling into the banality of evil itself, and for Newman can prevent us from flying into irrational panic at the thought of evil. There is a faith in the power of reason here which I share, but in order to ground that faith we need to assess the power of un-reason, the power of the fear that must be suppressed. What Newman suggests is that while the apparent source of fear is some external evil that threatens us, its actual source is internal, something to do with our psyches rather than the external world, and it is this internal fear that is politically exploited and mobilised against the myth of evil in the world. And so we must explore our inner psyches to discover the source of fear. One practice that claims to chart this inner life is psychoanalysis, and although it does not have direct access to it, it claims to find it represented symbolically in our dreams, our mistakes, our neuroses, and in a particular kind of dream, the world of fiction such as of literature and cinema. There are two senses here in which evil could be present in our minds: first, that we entertain evil thoughts and desires ourselves; second, that we entertain the belief that evil exists in the world and threatens us. Both these may be true, but my concern in this chapter is with the second aspect – the myth of evil – and my aim is to try to understand the source of that constant and extraordinarily strong belief. The key to this understanding is the discovery of the sources of fear, and the approach I will take is through a particular form of fiction that we find especially frightening, that of horror in literature and film. The hope is that, with the aid of psychoanalytic theory, we can pass through the gateway of fiction, and discover what frightens us so intensely.

Dark Narratives

Gothic literature has a tradition of bringing fear into people's minds and has been closely studied by academics seeking insights into our predilection for terrifying or horrific fictional experiences. Dani Cavallaro argues that Gothic fiction has been so successful precisely because fear is ever present in our lives. She says: 'fear is not a sporadic event but an ongoing condition endowed with eminently ambivalent powers' (Cavallaro 2002: vii). Fear is not caused by occasional disturbances, but is always present as an awareness of ongoing disorder. 'What is aberrant is not the disconcerting sensation of dread but rather the fantasies of order superimposed upon life to make it look seamless and safe' (Cavallaro 2002: vii). She draws attention to the distinction made in academic studies of Gothic fiction between horror and terror, a distinction between the visible and the invisible. At its simplest the distinction is that horror is 'fear occasioned by visible gore' while terror is 'fear triggered by indeterminate agents' (Cavallaro 2002: vii). Horror, then, is a matter of spectacle, while terror is a matter of invisibility. Horror is 'definable by virtue of its material nature'; terror is 'deemed intangible and resistant to definition' (Cavallaro 2002: 2). Terrorism is, then, well named in this respect, in that the terrorist passes unseen through borders, and remains invisible even as bombs explode around us. Horror, says Cavallaro, focuses on the physical and provokes physical reactions: muscular contractions, shuddering, recoiling, vomiting and so on. Terror 'disturbs because of its indeterminateness', such that 'it cannot be connected with an identifiable physical object and the factors that determine it accordingly elude classification and naming' (Cavallaro 2002: 2). Its causes are always 'uncertain and obscure' (Cavallaro 2002: 3), such that 'if horror makes people shiver, terror undermines the foundations of their worlds' (Cavallaro 2002: 2–3). Horror is typified by the macabre, while terror is typified by psychic dread of something unknown but threatening, an unseen enemy intent on harming us.

Because terror is fear of the unseen, academic commentators on the Gothic have argued that it is a superior form of fear to horror, because it stimulates the imagination in ways that horror does not. While horror confronts us with the object of our fear, terror challenges us to imagine it. However, Cavallaro points out that terror and horror are closely related: 'terror may well be incorporeal per se (as intimations of danger and malevolence are often impalpable), but acquires vibrant bodies through the psychological and physical reactions of those exposed to terror and through the material settings of its occurrences. Horror, for its part, may well be tied to corporeal phenomena, yet our inability to classify its sources renders it elusive, as does the sensation that the motives leading to brutal spectacles are ultimately unfathomable' (Cavallaro 2002: 5). And so while horror may be produced by the physical confrontation with the consequences of evil, the inability to understand the motivations of the evil agent who has brought about these macabre effects results in the psychic dread not so much of the unknown, but of the incomprehensible. Horror and terror are therefore intertwined in our experiences of evil.

Gothic fiction, as a form of dark narrative, shows that 'we actually seek fear, consciously or unconsciously', because 'we cannot resist the attraction of an unnameable something that insistently eludes us' (Cavallaro 2002: 6). These dark narratives point to something 'beyond the human, and hence beyond interpretation – a nexus of primeval feelings and apprehensions which rationality can never conclusively eradicate' (Cavallaro 2002: 6). But why should this 'fear of nothing' be so intense, and why should the 'beyond the human' exert such a powerful attraction? Although, in contrast to Newman, Cavallaro seems to take a pessimistic view of the power of reason to control these primeval terrors, she takes a more optimistic view of the power of fear itself – it has positive aspects. In short, fear wakes us up. 'Fear does not anaesthetize consciousness but actually sharpens it. It makes us aware that reality contains many more layers than common sense would have us recognize, and that some of these layers are enticing, though also menacing, precisely because we do not understand them' (Cavallaro 2002: 6–7). Furthermore, 'horrific images have the power to revive consciousness. They are capable of waking us up or at least reminding us that we have been asleep without necessarily knowing that this was the case' (Cavallaro 2002: 14). This means that Gothic narratives have a powerful role to play as an 'alerting fiction' (Cavallaro 2002: 15), which Cavallaro defends against those who dismiss it as 'pop' culture. For example Walter Nash, in *The Language of Popular Fiction*, condemns it as 'committed to the simplest moralities, the crudest psychologies, and has few philosophical pretensions' (Nash 1990: 3; Cavallaro 2002: 15).

But Cavallaro's optimism about the positive role of dark narratives is puzzling. If we stay within the boundaries of fiction, then whether or not Gothic narrative plays an alerting role in reviving our consciousness is going to depend on the quality of the particular work we are reading, and Nash surely has a point that at least some of it is too crude to be helpful. However, if we extend the concept of the dark narrative beyond fiction into political narratives about the world then we can see its negative power. Cavallaro claims that: 'It is by allowing repressed materials to surface, often abruptly, that these stories enable dread to operate as a psychodynamic awakener' (Cavallaro 2002: 16). But the return of the repressed here can produce neuroses rather than alertness – we cannot assume that horror narratives wake us into something we can identify as reality. It is just as plausible to suppose that they could 'wake' us into another dream, or push us deeper into violent and fearful fantasies about the world. Certainly psycho-analytic theory does not take this optimistic view of the return of repressed materials, and does recognise that our grasp on reality can be lost altogether when confronted by these forgotten terrors. And if we look at the effect of the political narratives of global terrorism and migration, it is difficult to argue that people have wo-ken to reality because of them. Rather they have created a fearful fantasy, and have pushed people towards violence against migrant communities and asylum seekers by creating a climate of hatred and fear. The horrific images of torture in Abu Ghraib prison in Iraq may serve Cavallaro's purpose, as they do seem to have acted as 'psychodynamic awakeners', as do many images of the horror of warfare. But we are only alerted to the boundary between the fantastical and the real if the narrative or image that confronts us alerts us to that boundary itself, and there is no reason to suppose that Gothic literature does this, and the evidence presented by the political narratives of global terror and migration surely shows the opposite is all too often true. Cavallaro insists on the truth of the paradox that: 'Darkness can be enlightening' (Cavallaro 2002: 24), because 'what is commonly demonized as evil may actually open our eyes to valuable experiences and submerged levels of reality' (Cavallaro 2002: 24). Part of this process is the embracing of things that have been condemned, the kind of erotic experience we find in the work of George Bataille, for example, where sexual taboos are violated in the extreme. According to Cavallaro, 'the erotic experience epitomizes the spirit of the perverse as a quasi-diabolical urge to violate the most inveterate boundaries: physi-cal, psychological, ethical, aesthetic, philosophical and religious' (Cavallaro 2002: 26). Fear and horror are therefore not bound-aries, but are temptations to transgress boundaries. The problem remains, however, that the boundary we transgress takes us not closer to a true understanding of the world and ourselves, but deeper into dark and fearful fantasies, so that our relations with the world and others are dangerously damaged.

Cavallaro gives a slightly different account of the positive power of the Gothic when she says that if we embrace the darkness we can grapple with the 'limbo to which reason and systematic knowl-edge are so insistently relegated by fear' (Cavallaro 2002: 24). The difference is that here fear is the enemy to be subdued by reason, while before it was the stimulus that awakened reason – we could wonder how both can be true. Still, this is more like Newman's account, and Cavallaro tells us how this is possible. The struggle with the fear inspired by dark narratives can lead us to accept 'the inevitable pervasiveness of dread' (Cavallaro 2002: 24). Through this, we can 'try to localize the experience of fear by associating it with extraordinary entities and phenomena. Creatures of the Beyond such as demons and spooks serve a consolatory purpose, for they enable us to nourish the illusion that the ordinary world, putatively immune to the influence of those entities and occurrences, may not be constitutionally burdened by fear' (Cavallaro 2002: 24). Also, 'By resorting to supernatural threats, human beings seek to exorcize the terrors and horrors of the everyday and the mundane' (Cavallaro 2002: 25). Marina Warner offers a similar argument in her *No Go the Bogeyman*, which is also a book 'about fear' (Warner 1998: 4), this time looking at stories and fables for and around the theme of children. Fear, says Warner, is 'one of the most everyday yet least examined of human feelings', but fear as pleasure is a modern phenomenon, 'the defining flavour of the modern sensibility. . . ' (Warner 1998: 4). Although 'dread was cultivated as an aesthetic thrill' for the first time towards the end of the seventeenth century, it is in the twentieth century that 'the ambiguous satisfactions of scariness have been cultivated more intensely. . . than ever before' (Warner 1998: 4). Warner's explanations for the attractions of fear are similar to Cavallaro's. 'Being scared by a story or an image – scared witless, scared to death – can deliver ecstatic relief from the terror that the thing itself would inspire if it were to appear for real' (Warner 1998: 6). And 'the condition of being scared is becoming sought after not only as a source of pleasure but as a means of strengthening the sense of being alive, of having command over self.' People 'discover that they are still alive, outside the tale' (Warner 1998: 6). Another explanation is that 'the changing features of the bogeyman mirror the insecurities and aggression of those who see him' (Warner 1998: 6). So we have two themes here: first, that knowing these tales are fictional, we use them to hide from the terrors of everyday life, and in doing so we confirm that we are alive; second, that they act as a mirror for our insecurities and aggressions – we are acting out something dark that lies within us, through the story. The first of these is positive – being outside the tale of death confirms that we are alive; the second is less so – that there is a darkness within us which we fear, and which we find reflected in these stories, although this may also have the positive aspect of catharsis.

The first reading suffers the same problems as Cavallaro's account. For Cavallaro, the dark narratives of fiction distract our focus from the fear of the everyday and place it upon imaginary monsters, and this gives us some respite from reality – after all, we do know that the imaginary monsters of fiction are not real and so we do not have to be genuinely scared of them. For Warner, our realisation that we are outside the tale confirms our existence and our freedom from these monsters. But both these accounts assume there is a clear boundary between the tale and our real lives, that there is a distinction which we make between fictional narratives which we *know* are fictional and everyday narratives which we *know* relate to reality in a straightforward way. Things are, of course, more complex than this. First, we are never fully convinced that fictional narratives are purely fictional, and it is this ambiguity that gives them their power over us – the possibility that the monsters they imagine actually do exist in some form, and that the 'real' world may not be so mundane as it appears. We are never sure that we are outside the tale: if we were, how could we really be scared witless? This is clearly a possibility when it comes to fictional representation of real-life monsters. An acquaintance of mine refused to swim in the sea after watching the film *Jaws*, despite being fully aware that great white sharks – indeed sharks of any kind – were absent from the waters in her neighbourhood. No amount of reasoned argument could enable her to overcome her irrational fear. Fictional representations of serial killers are especially chilling in this respect. But I think it is also a possibility when it comes to fictional monsters such as vampires and werewolves and, of course, aliens. We are simply not that confident that they do not exist. If we were, the horror film may scare us through internal structures of shock and surprise, but it would not 'spook' us so effectively. Historically vast numbers of people have been convinced that such monsters really existed, and vast numbers still are convinced, especially now monsters from outer space are thought to be such frequent visitors. In our fully rational moments we know this is not true in the case of werewolves and vampires, and highly unlikely in the case of aliens, and it may well be that some of us have such a complete grasp of our rational powers that we are not susceptible to the thrills of the horror film. But I have to confess that I am not included in that admirable class.

Second, we know that narratives that purport to represent reality are themselves highly constructed, and so there is no clear boundary between the dark narratives of fiction and the dark narratives of the 'real' world, and so no guarantee that the dark narrative will alert us to reality – it may simply create more imaginary terrors, and lead us to mistake those imaginary terrors for real ones. The boundary between fiction and reality is blurred, or rather our awareness of where that boundary lies is blurred, and everyday life itself is framed within the fictional constructs of our imagination or the imagination of our political and cultural leaders. A third problem is that the obsession with being scared to death is read as a rejection of death and an affirmation of life, but it could just as easily be read as an obsession with death itself, a flirtation with self-destruction. Death, rather than life, is the attractive force here. Certainly Cavallaro is right that Gothic fiction and other forms of dark narrative show the pervasiveness of fear in our everyday lives, but her optimism about the positive powers of dark narratives seems to be misplaced. Behind her account, though, lies psychoanalytic theory, and both she and Newman seem to believe that it is through understanding the psychic causes of our fear that we can control it, and it may be that this body of theory can shed light on what scares us so intensely. As Cavallaro rightly observes: 'We cannot begin to know ourselves unless we are prepared to acknowledge the extent to which fear relentlessly shapes us' (Cavallaro 2002: 202–3).

Fear Begins at Home

Sigmund Freud's essay on the uncanny, published in 1919, has had an enormous influence on literary and cinematic studies of horror. In his introduction to the essay, Hugh Haughton describes it as an essay on Gothic (Haughton 2003: xlii), in which Freud looks to develop 'an aesthetics of anxiety' (Haughton 2003: xli), an account of those ambiguous wishful fears (Haughton 2003: xlii) that we experience when reading horror fiction or watching horror films. The essay 'underpins much of the huge modern critical literature on both Gothic and the Sublime' (Haughton 2003: xliii). The subject of Freud's essay is an earlier one by psychologist Ernst Jentsch published in 1906, 'On the Psychology of the Uncanny' (Jentsch 1996), and the subject of Jentsch's essay, and subsequently of Freud's, is E. T. W. Hoffman's Gothic tale, 'The Sand-Man'. In his essay, Jentsch argues that the experience of the uncanny is linked to loss of orientation, with intellectual uncertainty, and he pinpoints key moments in Hoffman's story where the central characters suffer from this intellectual uncertainty. For Jentsch, the central moment concerns a doll which the main character mistakes for a real woman and falls in love with. Jentsch says: 'Among all the psychical uncertainties that can become an original cause of the uncanny feeling, there is one in particular that is able to develop a fairly regular, powerful and very general effect: namely, doubt as to whether an apparently living being is animate, and, conversely, doubt as to whether a lifeless object may not in fact be animate – and more precisely, when this doubt only makes itself felt obscurely in one's consciousness' (Jentsch 1906: 11; taken from Scharpé 2003). Certainly, Jentsch seems to have captured something central about the feeling of the uncanny: recall the fascination of a waxworks exhibition, especially if the proprietor has played the game of asking some people to stand stock still – imagine the terror that occurs when one of the 'waxworks' leaps out at you, or even merely raises an eyebrow. Imagine being in a museum, surrounded by dead, stuffed animals, or statues, and the spooky experience of being there during the night – would there not be the constant underlying terror that one of these figures will move? However, Freud rejects this reading of the uncanny, and reinterprets it in terms of the return of the repressed, and reads 'The Sand-Man' as a return of the castration complex in particular. Many critics have pointed out that Freud is too cavalier here, and that Jentsch's reading of the uncanny has more life in it than he allows; indeed, Jentsch's thesis is Freud's own return of the repressed, as in places his own readings of the uncanny are close to Jentsch's disorientation view. But although Freud interprets his version of 'The Sand-Man' in terms of the castration complex, the essay on the uncanny covers far more territory and is far more subtle and insightful.

For Freud, the uncanny is a particular kind of being frightened. Rather than to be identified with fear as such, it is a particular kind of fear: 'the uncanny is that species of the frightening that goes back to what was once well known and had long been familiar' (Freud 2003: 124). But how can the familiar become uncanny? To show this Freud spends a large part of the essay in etymological analysis of the concept of the *unheimlich*, literally meaning 'unhomely' in English but normally taken to mean uncanny or eery, or in more contemporary language, spooky. If we take *unheimlich* as literally the opposite of *heimlich*, then as the *heimlich* is that which is familiar, then the *unheimlich* becomes frightening simply because it is the unfamiliar (Freud 2003: 124–5). But not everything unfamiliar is frightening: 'All one can say is that what is novel may well prove frightening and uncanny; some things that are novel are indeed frightening, but by no means all. Something must be added to the novel and the unfamiliar if it is to become uncanny' (Freud 2003: 125). Freud, therefore, argues against equating the uncanny simply with what is unfamiliar, and one can see an important political point in doing so – to equate anything that is unfamiliar with fear means that 'strangers' are by definition frightening, and this is by no means our first response to the new and unfamiliar and the 'strange'. Freud's etymological exploration of the meanings of *heimlich* shows that it can mean homely/familiar, but also that which is mysterious and concealed (in the home, for example): 'this word *heimlich* is not unambiguous, but belongs to two sets of ideas which are not mutually contradictory, but very different from each other – the one relating to what is familiar and comfortable, the other to what is concealed and kept hidden' (Freud 2003: 132). And so *unheimlich* is the antonym of the first sense of *heimlich*, but not the second. Freud quotes Schelling approvingly, when he observes that 'the term "uncanny" (*unheimlich*) applies to everything that was intended to remain secret, hidden away, and has come into the open' (Freud 2003: 132). And so the *unheimlich* may be the return of the repressed *heimlich*, something that was familiar but which has been concealed. For Freud, then, the *unheimlich* begins at home. He says: 'the uncanny [the "unhomely"] is what was once familiar ["homely", "homey"]. The negative prefix un- is the indicator of repression' (Freud 2003: 151).

The next part of Freud's essay discusses specific examples of the uncanny, of which manifestations of the castration complex are only a few. First, there is infantile anxiety over damage or losing one's eyes, which is often 'a substitute for the fear of castration' (Freud 2003: 139). But there is also the infantile belief than inanimate dolls can come to life, or the wish that they could; the fear of the double, the doppelganger; and fear of repetition, which under particular conditions can be uncanny. An important example of the uncanny is connected with belief in the omnipotence of thoughts, that by thinking hard enough we can make things happen, and another is 'anything to do with death, dead bodies, revenants, spirits and ghosts' (Freud 2003: 148). This latter Freud identifies as 'perhaps the most potent', and 'in hardly any other sphere has our thinking and feeling changed so little since primitive times or the old been so well preserved, under a thin veneer, as in our relation to death' (Freud 2003: 148). A living person can be uncanny 'when we credit him with evil intent', and if 'this

intent to harm us is realized with the help of special powers'
(Freud 2003: 149). Severed parts of the body that move independently are especially uncanny, but this is another example, perhaps, of the castration complex. And fear of being buried alive,
'the fantasy of living in the womb', is also on Freud's list of uncanny experiences (Freud 2003: 150).

Working from these examples, Freud proceeds to make some
general observations about the uncanny, first noting 'the fact that
an uncanny effect often arises when the boundary between fantasy and reality is blurred, when we are faced with the reality of something that we have until now considered imaginary'
(Freud 2003: 150). Here Freud specifically admits the importance
of intellectual uncertainty 'in relation to the link between the uncanny and death' (Freud 2003: 153). This intellectual uncertainty
arises when boundaries we thought were firmly established are
shown to be fragile or even non-existent. The boundary between
ourselves and the dead is one such potent boundary, such that the
return of the dead through that boundary in the form of ghosts
or revenants, or other kinds of visit, is deeply uncanny. However,
Freud also notes that in some contexts the examples he has given
of the uncanny fail to be so – specifically in certain fictional frameworks. In fairy stories most of these features occur routinely, as
part of the fairy-tale world in which characters act, and so, being
familiar in the first, benign sense of *heimlich*, they are, of course,
not uncanny. This leads Freud to suppose that we have to distinguish between experiences of the uncanny we have in everyday
life and those we encounter in fiction. He observes that he is far
more confident about giving a psychoanalytic account of the former (Freud 2003: 154), but the latter is extremely important and
cannot be ignored. The uncanny of everyday experience arises
from repressed childhood complexes such as the castration complex and the womb fantasies or from what Freud calls surmounted
beliefs (Freud 2003: 154), and in fact most of our everyday experiences of the uncanny are caused by this latter group, in which he
includes the omnipotence of thought, the return of the dead, and
fear of secret harmful forces (Freud 2003: 154). And therefore the
major part of Freud's explanation of our experience of the uncanny
does *not* rest upon the return of repressed childhood complexes
such as the castration complex, but on another kind of return of
the repressed. He says: 'We – or our primitive forebears – once
regarded such things as real possibilities; we were convinced that
they really happened. Today we no longer believe in them, having

surmounted such modes of thought. Yet we do not feel entirely secure in these new convictions; the old ones live on in us, on the look-out for confirmation. Now, as soon as something *happens* in our lives that seems to confirm these old, discarded beliefs, we experience a sense of the uncanny, and this may be reinforced by such judgements like the following: "So it's true, then, that you can kill another man just by wishing him dead, that the dead really do go on living and manifest themselves at the scene of their former activities", and so on' (Freud 2003: 154).

Here, we should note that we have an almost complete theory of evil, that our belief in the myth of evil is an example of the return of primitive beliefs we thought we had overcome, but which, when certain events occur, gain hold on us and threaten to overpower our reason. Earlier in the essay Freud makes the connection between childhood and 'primitive' peoples specifically in the case of the belief in the omnipotence of thought, which he connects with primitive beliefs in animism. 'It appears that we have all, in the course of our individual development, been through a phase corresponding to the animistic phase in the development of primitive peoples, that this phase did not pass without leaving behind in us residual traces that can still make themselves felt, and that everything we now find "uncanny" meets the criterion that it is linked with these remnants of animistic mental activity and prompts them to express themselves' (Freud 2003: 147). And so these primitive beliefs, which our ancestors held, are still present within us, manifested most clearly in childhood, but then repressed.

Finally, Freud notes that the uncanny in literature deserves separate treatment. 'It is above all much richer than what we know from experience; it embraces the whole of this and something else besides, something that is wanting in real life' (Freud 2003: 155). Freud has already noted that many things that would be uncanny experiences in real life are not uncanny in certain literary contexts. So, for example, a writer can choose to set the story in a world that deviates from real life so much that demons and ghosts, although they may be terrifying in form and performance, are not uncanny in their presence – we are not surprised to see them (Freud 2003: 156). However, if the writer sets the story in what seems to be a world of everyday experience, then the sense of the uncanny can be intensified: 'he betrays us to a superstition we thought we had "surmounted"; he tricks us by promising us everyday reality and then going beyond it' (Freud 2003: 157).

Haughton observes that Freud teaches us that 'our most haunting experiences of otherness tell us that the alien begins at home, wherever that may be' (Haughton 2003: xlix), but at the same time it reveals that 'there is no place like home' (Haughton 2003: xlix). Death becomes the key theme for Freud here, and Haughton believes this undermines Freud's analysis and returns us to the intellectual uncertainty that Jentsch identified, about the boundary between life and death. To be fair, Freud does admit this in his essay, but, according to some critics, the return of Freud's own repressed here points to an ambiguity in his essay. Diane Jonte-Pace, for example, observes that in the essay: 'Death, or the theme of the living/dead, animate/inanimate woman, rather than castration, seems to demand centrality' (Jonte-Pace 2001: 65); and 'the priority of death over castration is irrepressibly expressed through textual interruptions and inconsistencies' (Jonte-Pace 2001: 65). However, while Freud's psychoanalytic reading of 'The Sand-Man' does prioritise the castration complex over Jentsch's intellectual uncertainty over the boundary between the living and the dead, the essay as a whole does not, and it would be a mistake to suppose that Freud's description of uncanny experiences rests heavily upon that particular complex, or with any complex, given the important role he gives to 'surmounted' beliefs. His brief reading of 'The Sand-Man' has rightly been criticised on these grounds, but, perhaps oddly, that reading is not central to the essay. Michiel Scharpé is another critic who points out that it is death and our relationship with it that is the central ground of the uncanny – something Freud himself states clearly in the essay – but makes the further, insightful point that perhaps it is not so much our relationship with death that is crucial here, but our relationship with *the dead* (Scharpé 2003). The boundary that is being challenged is not so much that between life and death, but between the living and the dead. These are, of course connected, but not all journeys between life and death and vice versa are uncanny – what strikes us as most uncanny is the return of the dead themselves into the realm of the living.

Our Dead Bodies, Our Selves

Scharpé's comment that the uncanny has more to do with our relationship with the dead than with death is perceptive and important. The fear of vampires, ghosts, zombies, becomes clearer when we see it as a fear not of death as such, but of the dead. What is at stake here is our relationship with the dead and the fear that they are going to return – the vampire and the zombie are very literally the return of the repressed; they are buried deep in the ground, but they dig their way out and return to us again and again. Fear of our own death is, of course, linked with them, because they bring the threat of our destruction with them from beyond the grave. But there is something special about this particular form of death which marks it out. Death is to be feared in many forms: flying, disease and illness, acts of war, road accidents, murder, old age, can all give rise to fear of death. But death can also be welcomed – death holds the prospect of peace. In the television series *Six Feet Under* shown on the American channel HBO, the Fisher family run a funeral home and encounter death and dead people each week. In one episode, David – one of two brothers who run the business after the death of their father – is confronted by the violent prospect of death as he is sadistically robbed at gunpoint. But in the same episode we get a radically different picture, as his art-student sister Claire displays her self-portrait photographs to the rest of the class for comment. One of the students says of them: 'Dead. That's what I like about them. This girl who's, like, dead, and beyond everything – beyond hunger, beyond sex, beyond boredom. And really it's so beautiful to be in that state. Like, nothing can reach her, nothing can get to her.' The dead people in the funeral home have a serenity even where they have met violent ends, and occasionally they return in a benign way to have discussions with family members – quite often these discussions are comforting and revealing, as the dead seem to have acquired a depth and a wisdom lacking in the living. Here, then, both death and the returning dead hold not fear, but an attraction, and in contrast the Fisher family's lives are filled with disappointment and torment. The attraction is, perhaps, that of being absorbed into a greater whole, even if that whole is a complete nothingness, an emptiness. To an extent, the Fishers are already dead in that their lives are empty – the conclusion to the student discussion of Claire's pictures is that they display her as an empty space, although she vehemently denies it. But even in this attractive, beckoning form, death is ambivalent and must be resisted, and the Fishers do resist it, stubbornly sticking to the living despite their seemingly remorseless misery. In *Six Feet Under* existence appears in all its absurdity, and in the end the programme, despite its darkness, is a comedy – albeit without a laughter track – and represents one of the traditional existentialist responses to this absurdity of existence. The Fishers have no clear answer to Albert Camus' challenge: why continue to live? But they do continue to live. This reflects back on David Newman's explanation of our underlying fears and insecurities that lead to social panics, the 'psychic terror' of our existence. The Fishers and the existentialists show that our response to our existence need not be dread but can be amusement at its absurdity.

The point is that, just as existence is not necessarily something to fear, neither is death, and many of the forms in which we *do* fear it are not the material of the uncanny, nor of Gothic horror and terror. So we are left with the question, what is so especially chilling about the dead in the form of vampires and zombies and so on, and what is especially horrifying about the prospect of death they offer? In the first place, perhaps, what they offer – and here they are joined by fictional representations of serial killers – is that motiveless malignity, the evil intent to destroy us for no reason. In the case of serial killers, Freud points out that this evil intent is not enough for the uncanny: 'it must be added that this intent to harm us is realized with the help of special powers' (Freud 2003: 149), and so these killers possess powers beyond the human. For example, Jason in the *Halloween* film series is remorselessly unkillable, and Hannibal Lecter in the trilogy of films based around his character, *Silence of the Lambs*, *Hannibal* and *Red Dragon*, has, for a man of his age, extraordinary physical strength and hypnotic intellectual powers. Vampires and zombies, of course, have supernatural powers of their own. The dead, then, bring with them a supernatural malice towards us, which is inexplicable and irresistible, and which is terrifying.

The uncanny, then, has much to do with our relationship with the dead and our fear that they have passed into the realm of the supernatural, from which they will return to destroy us, a primitive fear which, as Freud's essay asserts, can be surmounted but often returns in uncanny moments. But there is something especially disturbing about the death these creatures offer, in contrast to the death we encounter in *Six Feet Under*. Here, again, there is absorption, but this time it is not a promise but a threat, a violent absorption – we will be consumed. The vampire will drain our blood; the zombie will eat our flesh; the serial killer will, in the case of Hannibal Lecter, dine on us, or in the figure of Buffalo Bill in *Silence of the Lambs*, skin us. We are reduced to blood and flesh and skin in this act of absorption. Here we become nothing not by entering a pool of greater nothingness, but by being sliced and diced and roasted. But what's the difference between this and dying, say, in a traffic accident in which we also end up sliced, diced and roasted? It may seem a nonsensical question, but it has a point – in both cases we are dead, whether we enter the Fishers' funeral home or the serial killer's fridge. Why should the latter be so horrific?

The key, oddly enough, lies in the cartoon series *The Simpsons*, and in the cartoon-within-a-cartoon, *Itchy and Scratchy*. Itchy and Scratchy are cat and mouse, a parody of *Tom and Jerry* and of its extremities of violence. In each episode Itchy the mouse murders Scratchy the cat in an imaginative and shocking act of murder, but the true appalling horror only starts after Scratchy's death. For whatever Itchy then does to Scratchy, always present are Scratchy's eyes, watching the whole process – whether the cat is liquified in a milkshake and then drunk by the mouse, or whatever cannibal or brutal act Itchy perpetrates, Scratchy's eyes blink and widen in shock and horror as he watches. And it is this – that throughout whatever is happening after his death, Scratchy is a witness, conscious and aware of it – that is most deeply and horribly disturbing about this cartoon-within-a-cartoon. And it is this fear that makes horror films and literature quite so disturbing, that as the vampire drains us, or the zombie eats us, or the serial killer skins us – as we are reduced to the blood and flesh and skin that make us – we are aware, we are watching, we are not yet really dead. We saw earlier that Marina Warner and others emphasise the positive aspect of the dark narratives, that they are 'a means of strengthening the sense of being alive, of having command over self' (Warner 2000: 6), that people 'discover that they are still alive, outside the tale' (Warner 2000: 6). In fact the opposite process is in play, perhaps at the same time, that these stories strengthen the sense of being completely helpless and destroyed, that we discover that we are *inside* the tale, being dead – and, worst of all, despite our death we continue to watch, our eyes wide and blinking in horror, as the cannibal eats us and the serial killer skins us; we are dead, but not dead – the undead audience, being violently consumed by our malignantly evil pursuers.

This disturbance can be read in terms of Freud's essay on the uncanny. That we are beings being chopped and diced can be seen as a return of the castration complex. That there are creatures out there with malignant intent combined with supernatural powers is the return of our surmounted, childhood beliefs which reflect more primitive times when humans actually did believe in the existence of the supernatural. We can even draw on Jentsch's thesis of intellectual uncertainty, as boundaries between living and dead and fiction and reality become blurred. Is Jason, the serial killer in the *Halloween* series of films, finally dead, or is he alive somewhere, lurking and ready to kill? Was he ever really alive? In the terrifying and disturbing *Blair Witch Project* we have Freud's uncanny effect of repetition: 'One may... have lost one's way in the woods, perhaps after being overtaken by fog, and, despite all one's efforts to find a marked or familiar path, one comes back again and again to the same spot, which one recognizes by a particular physical feature' (Freud 2003: 144), and through such repetition we build up a sense of helplessness, 'the idea of the fateful and the inescapable' (Freud 2003: 144). And in all sorts of ways in these films, we have a deeply problematic and disturbing relationship with death and with the dead. But at the centre of the disturbance is a problematic relationship, not so much with our own death – although this is ultimately implied – but with our own dead bodies. But this latter point seems strange, as this is fiction and we are the reader and we are not dead; we *are* outside the tale. Undeniably here we have a clear boundary between fiction and reality, between the living and dead – how can it be so easily disrupted?

Fearful Desires

Near the beginning of his essay on the uncanny Freud observes that he is not particularly open to this kind of experience (Freud 2003: 124), perhaps because he has successfully surmounted any primitive beliefs and resolved any repressed childhood complexes. Certainly it would seem that primitive beliefs of the kind he describes should not have any power over someone in whom reason has completely triumphed over superstition, even when it comes to those most powerful primitive beliefs about death. Jeremy Bentham is a good example of someone who seems completely free of such concerns – his emotional relationship with his own dead body seems to have been thoroughly rational. It sits in a wooden cabinet in the cloisters of University College London (UCL) on Gower Street, open to view to anybody who wishes to make the effort to see it, and to those who just happen to stumble across it, a thoroughly uncanny experience. He is sitting there, dressed very smartly, looking out, his stick by his side, as if ready to engage in argument. Both Bentham's life and death are surrounded by myth. One myth about his life is that he was instrumental in founding the University of London in Gower Street, the forerunner of UCL. This is not true – it was founded in 1826 without his help, and yet this untruth is embodied in a mural in the UCL library, which shows Bentham being presented with the architectural plans for the college by its designer, William Wilkins (see www.ucl.ac/Bentham-Project/info/jb.htm). When a myth becomes solidified in a monument such as this, then it is hardly surprising that most people still believe it. Much more fascinating, though, are the untruths that surround his dead body. The story goes that Bentham left it to the college in his will, stipulating that it be preserved and displayed in the cabinet, and that it attend meetings of the college council. He is wheeled into the council room whenever it meets, and his presence recorded. He is, obviously, a non-voting member, unless the council is split, in which case he has the casting vote, and always votes for the motion. None of this is true. What is true, partially, is that the head now displayed in the cabinet is plastic, as the original could not be preserved sufficiently well to be displayed. It used to be kept in a box between his legs but students, especially medics from Kings College, would regularly steal it, sometimes for use in football practice in the front quadrangle, sometimes for other adventures. It was once discovered in a left-luggage locker at Dundee railway station. The head is now kept safe in the college vaults. How much of this is true is impossible to tell. How the body came to be displayed in the college cloisters was told by C. F. A. Marmoy (Marmoy 1958; and see www.ucl.ac.uk/Bentham-Project/info/marmoy.htm).

According to Marmoy, all Bentham left to the college in his will were some of his books for the library. However, he did want his body preserved and left it to his friend Dr Southwood Smith with clear instructions about what should be done. The will stipulated: 'The skeleton he will cause to be put together in such a manner as that the whole figure may be seated in a Chair usually occupied by me when living in the attitude in which I am sitting when engaged in thought', and that 'the skeleton to be clad in one of the suits of black occasionally worn by me,' and placed in 'an appropriate box or case'. Bentham continues: 'If it should so happen that my personal friends and other Disciples should be disposed to meet together on some day or days of the year for the purpose of commemorating the Founder of the greatest happiness system of morals and legislation my executor will from time to time cause to be conveyed to the room in which they meet the said Box or case with the contents there to be stationed in such part of the room as to the assembled company shall seem meet. . . '. Bentham's preserved body was displayed in its cabinet, sitting and clothed, with its wax head, in Southwood Smith's consulting rooms at 36 New Broad Street, and then in his new rooms in 38 Finsbury Square, until he offered it to University College in 1850. Its journeys were not over, however. It resided in the Anatomical Museum until 1906, then in the library, and then the Department of Egyptology. With the outbreak of the Second World War it was among those evacuated to the countryside, and kept in the college's temporary administrative headquarters in Stansted Bury near Ware, returning to the Professors' Common Room at the war's end. Only then did it move to its current position in the college cloisters.

There was an ethical point behind Bentham's desire to become an 'Auto-Icon', as he put it, after his death. One's body is of no use to one after death. The dead person can't enter Bentham's 'felicific calculus' to work out which course of action will bring about the greatest happiness. But the body can be useful to others, who can use it to bring about the greater happiness of the living, for example by using it to educate medical students through dissection. Such use of the dead was illegal until the Warburton Anatomy Act 1832, and Bentham was among those campaigning for the change in the law. But, of course, a change in the law doesn't necessarily lead to a change in social attitudes, and Bentham's display was supposed to show how irrational it was to be at all concerned about one's corpse. This is not to say that one should be deprived of the right to say what should happen to it – Bentham stipulated very carefully what should happen to his own body, and his wishes were carried through scrupulously by Southwood Smith. But to wish for it to be interred in the earth to rot should not be the choice of the educated utilitarian. However, Bentham remains the exception. Most people are deeply concerned about what happens to their dead body, and a great many have a fearful relationship with it.

Here, another psychoanalytic narrative, that of Julia Kristeva and abjection, can help us to understand the forces at work. Kristeva uses the idea of the abject to explain the power of horror in fiction (Kristeva 1982), and Barbara Creed applies it to the horror film (Creed 1993). The idea of the abject has its source in Jacques Lacan's psychoanalytic account of the separation of the infant from the mother and its entry into the symbolic world as an individual (Lacan 1977). For Kristeva this move has to have a motivating force that drives it – the infant has to be pushed from the world of the mother into the symbolic world of identity, and this force is the abject. The abject is therefore to do with the fragility of boundaries, here the boundary between the infant and the maternal body. The infant experiences horror at its dependence on the mother's body, and at the way in which its identity is consumed by that body, but it is also fascinated by it (Oliver 2002: 226). The maternal body becomes associated with what the drives seek to expel, and so: 'With the various little rituals tied to cleanliness, toilet training, eating habits, etc., the "mother" is gradually rejected' (Lechte 1990: 159). But after this process the abject remains with us as both a source of horror and fascination, as 'the ambiguous, the in-between, what defies boundaries, a composite resistant to unity' (Lechte 1990: 160).

The focus of the abject is the material body, and it gives rise to instability and fear because it disrupts the boundaries of that body. It has this power because it is both inside and outside of that boundary, however much we try to expel it and keep our borders secure – the abject undermines all such attempts. The abject is precisely that which connects us with death, and shows us that death is already within the boundary, however much we try to expel it. Our physical bodies embody death. Barbara Creed comments that the sources of the abject are represented in ancient religious and historical notions, religious abominations such as 'sexual immorality and perversion; corporeal alteration, decay and death; human sacrifice; murder; the corpse; bodily wastes; the feminine body and incest' (Creed 1993: 9). These are things that 'highlight the "fragility of the law" and that exist on the other side of the border which separates out the living subject from that which threatens its extinction' (Creed 1993: 10). While these are all things that threaten our identity as a member of humanity, so that we wish to expel them behind a border which will protect us from them, they are all part of who we are such that the expulsion has to be constant and the border remains constantly threatened: perverse sexual desires, our bodies themselves and their waste products, our violence and ferocity, are all things we place beyond a border in order to preserve our selves as members of humanity, but are constantly erupting inside that border. Because of this constant need to repel, ritual becomes centrally important to maintaining the boundary between the human subject and the non-human abject, and that ritual has to become ever more detailed and complex and intense: 'Through ritual, the demarcation lines between the human and non-human are drawn up anew' (Creed 1993: 8). The abject has to be radically excluded and 'deposited on the other side of an imaginary border which separates the self from that which threatens the self' (Creed 1993: 9).

But as well as horror of the abject there is also fascination: 'the subject is constantly beset by abjection which fascinates desire but which must be repelled for fear of self-annihilation' (Creed 1993: 10) – all these threats to our humanity are ambiguous, repelling us and attracting us. They destroy our membership of the moral order of humanity so that we find ourselves beyond the boundary of the human, but they also offer a radical freedom from the limits of the human and so offer extraordinary empowerment – we become more than human. These encounters with abjection are explored in horror fiction and film, and, says Creed, 'the concept of a border is central to the construction of the monstrous in the horror film; that which crosses or threatens to cross the "border" is abject' (Creed 1993: 10–11). They were also expressed in the phenomena of the witch trials and vampire epidemics. The woman as witch is abject in that she embodies much that is threatening – human sacrifice, sexual perversions, perverted sexual relationships with animals, and cannibalism (Creed 1993: 74–6). Indeed, any 'demonised' social group is usually accused of the identical list of crimes against humanity, for example early Christians in the Roman Empire were thought to carry out much the same activities. The vampire holds great powers of abjection because the corpse is the 'ultimate in abjection' (Creed 1993: 9). The physical body is the site of the struggle between the subject and the abject, and the dead body is the ultimate representation of defeat. Kristeva says, 'the corpse, the most sickening of wastes, is a border that has encroached upon everything' (Kristeva 1982: 3). In a biblical context, says Creed, 'the corpse is ... utterly abject. It signifies one of the most basic forms of pollution – the body without a soul' (Creed 1993: 10). The vampire is the ultimate form of a body without a soul, and Creed finds it interesting 'that such ancient figures of abjection as the vampire, the ghoul, the zombie and the witch ... continue to provide some of the most compelling images of horror in the modern cinema' (Creed 1993: 10).

The corpse, then, is the most powerful symbol of the abject, signifying the border between life and death. 'The corpse... is cesspool, and death' (Kristeva 1982: 3), such that: 'corpses *show me* what I permanently thrust aside in order to live. These body fluids, this defilement, this shit are what life withstands, hardly and with difficulty, on the part of death. There, I am at the border of my condition as a living being. My body extricates itself, as being alive, from that border' (Kristeva 1982: 3). And 'In that compelling, raw, insolent thing in the morgue's full sunlight, in that thing that no longer matches and therefore no longer signifies anything, I behold the breaking down of a world that has erased its borders' (Kristeva 1982: 4). But still, even in the extreme form of the corpse the abject both horrifies and fascinates. Emile Zola captures this ambiguity in *Thérèse Raquin*, in Laurent's visits to the morgue to seek the corpse of Thérèse's husband, Camille, whom they plotted to murder and whom Laurent pushed from a boat into the Seine and drowned. When there are no drowned corpses to see, 'He then became a mere sightseer, and found a strange pleasure in looking violent death in the face, with its lugubriously weird and grotesque attitudes' (Zola 1962: 109). He sees the body of a young woman who had hanged herself. 'He lingered over her for a long time, running his eyes up and down her body, lost in a sort of fearful desire' (Zola 1962: 109). He is not the only sightseer in the morgue. 'The door is open, anyone can enter. Some connoisseurs make a special detour so as not to miss one of these displays of death, and when the slabs are bare people go out muttering, feeling let down and swindled. When the slabs are occupied and there is a nice show of human flesh, the visitors jostle each other and indulge in cheap thrills, shudder with horror, crack jokes, applaud or whistle just as they would at the theatre, and finally go away satisfied, declaring that the Morgue has been a good show today' (Zola 1962: 110–11). But the two lovers are doomed by the horror of Camille's corpse, which is with them, haunting them, constituting an impossible boundary between them. 'When the two murderers were lying under the same sheet, with eyes closed, they seemed to feel the slimy body of their victim lying in the middle of the bed, and it turned their flesh to ice. It was like a loathsome obstacle, separating them. A feverish delusion came over them in which this obstacle turned into solid matter – they could touch the body, see it spread out like a greenish, putrefying lump of meat, breathe the horrible stench of this mass of human decomposition' (Zola 1962: 175–6).

We can now see the special horror that the vampire epidemics represented, as corpses rose from their graves to destroy the living, transgressing the boundary between the human and the non-human, the living and the dead. But we misunderstand the power of the abject if we associated it merely with filth and defilement: this is not what the vampire represents. The source of horror lies not there, but in fundamental ambiguity. Kristeva makes this clear: 'It is ... not lack of cleanliness or health that causes abjection but what disturbs identity, system, order. What does not respect borders, positions, rules. The in-between, the ambiguous, the composite' (Kristeva 1982: 4). Kelly Oliver confirms that the abject is not what is grotesque and unclean: 'rather it is what calls into question borders and threatens identity' (Oliver 2002: 225). What is fundamentally disturbing about the vampire, the witch, the migrant, is not their supposed depravity, but their ambiguity, and they are at their most threatening when they refuse to assimilate.

In the end, then, our material bodies are our source of fear because they are the site of a struggle between life and death, humanity and inhumanity, and although we may like to imagine our physical bodies as lying clearly within a firm boundary, in fact they are themselves ambiguous, undermining that boundary, in that our bodies are constantly dying and our minds are constantly filled with inhuman desires and motivations. This connection with death and with the inhuman is a source of horror and fascination, for both inhumanity and death offer different forms of freedom – inhumanity offers freedom from the mundane moral constraints of everyday life, so that we can be powerful and ferocious monsters, while death offers freedom from everyday life in the sense of peace. The monster and the corpse are both powerfully abject, and the vampire combines both. If Kristeva is right, then what is both horrifying and fascinating is precisely the threat of being consumed, and this can be traced back to the infant's desire for the maternal body and the constant infant fear of being overwhelmed by that body, of losing one's identity within it – the initial struggle for self-identity is precisely that against the maternal body. Here we have the source of the psychic dread that haunts us.

Conclusion – Towards a Philosophy of Monsters

One problem with psychoanalytic accounts of fictional stories and what they represent is that they appear to be stories themselves, only at a 'deeper' level. Rather than learning anything profound about the human condition, we may have simply substituted one set of stories for another more complex and obscure set. Earlier in this chapter I objected to the view that Gothic horror narratives always operated as psychodynamic awakeners, alerting people to levels of reality they had not noticed before; they could, I argued, have the opposite effect of taking people deeper into disturbing and violent fantasies, damaging their relationship with 'reality' rather than repairing it. I have assumed, in looking at psychoanalytic narratives, that they will bring us closer to understanding the fears that dominate everyday life and play such a central role in contemporary politics; but I have to allow the possibility that they, like Gothic horror tales, could take us in the opposite direction, and make these matters harder to understand. Still, having examined them we could draw a number of different conclusions. The first and simplest is that we are just plain scared; fear is part of our nature, and if we were not scared of one thing we would be scared of another. It is this ever-present capacity for fear that political authorities exploit as they mobilise prejudice against particular groups. A second and more complex conclusion is that we are scared of something in particular, and psychoanalytic theory can tell us what this is. In the end, the answer is that we must look deep within our own psyches and discover that *we* are the source of our fear; we are, in some sense, scared of our selves. The story we have developed in this chapter is that this fear has something to do with our death, our awareness that our own physicality connects us closely with death; our physical bodies are already dying. Or it may be that a particular kind of death disturbs us most deeply – being consumed alive by a malignant enemy. This particular fear seems to be one appealed to by political authorities as they portray others as an evil enemy intent on consuming our territory, our culture, our identity, our freedom.

But there is another answer we should consider – that we are scared of our selves not because of our connection with death, but because we recognise our own capacity for evil. What frightens us is not the fragility of the boundary between life and death, but of the boundary between our 'civilised' self and our 'evil' self. We may well project that capacity on to others and into fictional representatives, but it is profoundly *our* capacity, and this is why we find such projections and representations so disturbing – they threaten to destabilise our conception of our selves as human beings, indeed our conception of humanity itself. This answer is especially important because it rests on the possibility of human evil. If we truly each have such a capacity then our critique of the myth of evil has to change from the universal – that the concept has no place in any description of the human – to the particular – that it may be a valid description in some cases, but in others our criticism of it holds good. Whether the myth of evil is universal or particular is a central problem, and of course pointing out that specific narratives of evil have little truth in them is not enough to establish the universal argument. However, the universal argument is the one I favour, and it is worth noting that particular accounts of human evil do not necessarily undermine it, because those particular accounts may be misleadingly framed within the overall narrative I am criticising. What I propose is that we focus on human psychology and ask whether we have the capacity for something that can genuinely and usefully be described as evil. And so, in the next chapter, we move away from psychoanalytic theory into psychology.

Meanwhile, though, Freud has provided an important insight, that we construct monsters, fictional or 'real', from familiar materials. They represent our fears and insecurities around death or other repressed complexes and beliefs, or they represent our own monstrosity, our capacity for destructive evil intent. Monsters mark out the boundary of the familiar, but also, if Freud is right, mark out what is hidden at its centre. In his book *American Monster*, Paul Semonin tells the story of the discovery of fossils of primeval creatures such as the Mastodon and their importance in American history (Semonin 2000). Such monsters marked the boundary of scientific knowledge and of the known world, in the sense that at the time they were discovered the notion of extinction was not widely accepted, and it was supposed that these monsters still roamed the American wilderness. But they also identified the uniqueness and superiority of the new American nation. When Thomas Jefferson sent Meriwether Lewis and William Clark on their expedition to find a passage to the Pacific coast in 1803, he also instructed them to find living examples of the Mastodon, described as the Great *Incognitum* and thought to be a ferocious flesh-eating monster, and the Megalonyx, supposed to be a large lion-like creature but now known to be a giant land sloth. There was much at stake here for the American mind, because, as Americans, the settlers had no history of great civilisation or achievement. It was inconceivable to them that the original Americans possessed a civilisation worth studying or preserving, and even if they had, it contributed nothing to the psychology of the new American natives. The bones of these monsters represented the possibility of a glorious past that they could take great pride in. Jefferson thought the Mastodon to be six times the size of living elephants, and it was supposed to have hidden deep in the forests to pounce upon its victims and tear them to pieces with an enormous set of claws, which, it turned out, belonged to the ground sloth. Those who assembled the first skeletons of the Mastodon placed the tusks so that they curved downwards like giant sabre teeth. Jefferson was engaged in a debate started by the French naturalist George Louis Leclerc de Buffon who had outlined a theory of American degeneracy (Semonin 2000: 6). The New World was inferior to Europe in terms of soil and climate and so gave rise to inferior life forms, including people. The Great *Incognitum* and the other fossil bones being discovered allowed Jefferson to put forward a counter-thesis, that American monsters were vastly more ferocious and dangerous than anything that had existed in Europe. And so the *Incognitum* became 'a symbol of both the violence of the newly discovered prehistoric world and the emerging nation's own dreams of an empire in the western wilderness' (Semonin 2000: 3). These monsters marked the boundary of what the Americans knew about themselves, but they also revealed the true nature of the American nation.

This reading sees the monster as revealing something positive about the self in terms of its ferocity, danger and power, but this representation is of course profoundly ambiguous. The thought that we are ferocious, dangerous monsters can be both comforting and disturbing at the same time. It depends whether we believe we can control that monstrous aspect of our selves and use it positively, or whether, in monstrous form, we have no control over what we do, and therefore defy the limits of humanity in horrible ways. The super heroes of Marvel comics and other narratives are usually able to control their monstrosity and use it for the power of good – for example the X-men, a band of mutants, are, for the most part, in control and focus their power on opposing evil. Admittedly the evil they oppose is that of another band of mutants who focus their power on opposing good, but both bands know what they are doing and have made a free and rational choice on how to focus their powers. The figure of the Incredible Hulk in the Marvel comics is an exception in that Bruce Banner has no control over his monstrous form. In the television series that ran from 1978 to 1983 the monstrous power of the Hulk – by lucky coincidence one assumes – always seemed to work for the cause of good, but other monstrous transformations are less fortunate, such as Dr Jekyll's when he becomes Mr Hyde.

Even where the monster is not a direct transformation of the self, Freud's observation holds: the alien monsters who assault us through film and fiction, although they are visitors from outer space, are also constructed from familiar materials. This is at its most explicit in Nigel Kneale's classic science-fiction tale, *Quatermass and the Pit*, screened as a series by the BBC in 1957. Professor Quatermass investigates a strange object discovered during excavations of Hob's Lane in London, concluding that it is millions of years old and is a spacecraft from Mars, still containing the preserved bodies of the monstrous Martians. However, the craft emits a strange energy over people who come into contact with it, directing them towards a race purge, a ritual slaughter that took place on Mars to exterminate mutations, and Quatermass realises that humanity has descended from colonisers from the red planet and is still capable of the ancient destructive urges that the spacecraft catastrophically awakes. Once the crisis is over, Quatermass warns that it is only self-knowledge that can protect us from those irrational urges towards violence against strangers, and the key to that self-knowledge is the realisation that: 'We are the Martians.' In the next chapter we will examine the extent to which, to slightly twist Quatermass' observation, we are the monsters.

Chapter Six

Bad Seeds

Introduction

'Won't someone think of the children?' is the constant refrain of Reverend Lovejoy's wife in the cartoon series *The Simpsons*. Whatever crisis or panic grips the citizens of Springfield, she places the children at the centre of attention. The child, for her, is an innocent and helpless victim in constant need of protection. But in the character of Bart Simpson – one of the children she must be thinking of – we see someone who is far from helpless and certainly no innocent, as he pursues mischief for its own sake and constantly rebels against any form of rules and order. Bart is the mischief maker, the chaos bringer, and as such occupies a central position in the symbolic order of *The Simpson*, and in doing so reflects that childish element in us that takes delight from disorder – not so much a childish innocence as a childish malevolence. Here we see the ambiguity of children, as innocent victims and as untrustworthy mischief makers. Indeed, in horror fiction they often go beyond mere mischief and become fully developed little monsters. Sabine Büssing points out that the presence of children in literature in this form is relatively recent. Up until the end of the eighteenth century they were largely absent. 'The child was mainly an emblem, a symbol of innocence, an object of compassion – functions that are especially rooted in the Christian tradition' (Büssing 1987: xiii). This changed with the Romantics in the nineteenth century when 'childhood came to be treasured as a metaphor for the ideal human condition' (Büssing 1987: xiii), and this evolved into the Victorian cult of childhood towards the end of that century (Navarette 1999: 187). According to this cult, 'both child and mother were thought of as mediating figures retaining intuitive powers as well as a natural vitality and a natural (if untutored) piety' (Navarette 1999: 187). The child represented the future of humanity, and so did childhood itself, but it also represented the primitive past – adulthood was a fall from grace. For the Victorians, the dead child was 'twice blessed' (Navarette 1999: 188); according to Susan J. Navarette: 'Children are memorable figures in death not only because they show pietistic fortitude in extremis . . . but also because they have not yet "fallen" into adulthood, and so retain visions of preexistence . . .' (Navarette 1999: 191).

But it is precisely through this other-worldliness that children become sinister, and this is perhaps why they find their way into horror narratives around this period. In its early form, as Romantic Gothic, they remain absent, but from the early nineteenth century to the present, argues Büssing, the role of the child changes dramatically. 'It has displayed more and more activity, developing from a mere victim into a frequent aggressor, killer, a veritable monster' (Büssing 1987: xiv). She identifies two basic roles for children in the horror genre: the victim and the victimiser. The child's traditional role 'of innocence and vulnerability' make it the ideal victim, playing a very different role to adult victims (Büssing 1987: xvi). For the reader/viewer, 'it is not only the respective child he fears for, but his whole deep-rooted *concept* of purity, incarnate in this small human being, which is exposed to evil and danger' (Büssing 1987: xvi). Paradoxically it is precisely this traditional concept of purity that makes the child such a potent victimiser. The notion of the child as 'monstrous killer' is especially shocking and perverse. Here is a monster that 'looks sweet, harmless, and, in a word, angelic' (Büssing 1987: xvii). And so: 'The possibility that such a creature could harbour the most hideous intentions, that it could turn on its own loving parents and kill them (which it frequently does), seems to be against the very laws of nature' (Büssing 1987: xvii). What we have here, says Büssing, is a generational conflict: 'The individual child represents an entire generation. Between its own generation and that of its parents there exists an insurmountable gap. Both groups regard each other as perfect strangers, and a true reconciliation is virtually impossible' (Büssing 1987: xix). In fiction, this conflict can become a matter of life and death.

The child, then, remains a deeply ambiguous figure – a helpless and innocent empty space, a 'tabula rasa' which we, as adults, can shape as we please; or a mysterious and mischievous rebel, who rarely confronts us directly and honestly, but works behind the scenes to undermine our power in hidden ways. Cavallaro describes children as 'strangers' in the adult world (Cavallaro 2002: 152), who are 'essentially untrustworthy due to their connection with alternative fantasy worlds' (Cavallaro 2002: 151). They are 'tainted by their proximity to prenatal darkness and, by implication, primordial chaos' (Cavallaro 2002: 151). Children are aliens, migrants from another world, and, as in other forms of migration, threaten disorder, instability and chaos, and so must be closely controlled and supervised. Indeed, Büssing cites science-fiction literature as a useful model, for although children do not feature all that often in science-fiction narratives, 'their statements about the confrontation between two cultures, about adult man's being endangered by aliens and monsters, can be applied to the child with almost no reservation' (Büssing 1987: xx).

Little Monsters

On 31 May 2005, a story broke over the British television media that a five-year-old boy had been 'lynched' by a gang of children, themselves aged between eleven and twelve. The boy had been found, deeply distressed, with rope marks around his neck, and arrests were being made on charges of attempted murder. I first heard the news on the radio as I sat having my hair cut, and the person cutting it said, 'Oh, my god, I can't listen to this – what's wrong with children these days?', and turned the radio off. The next day the newspapers carried the story, and the *Sun* published the headline 'Monsters of Devil's Ditch', supposedly the name of the area where the attack had taken place. All papers published the details, and the *Daily Mail* gave it extensive coverage, drawing parallels with another notorious case, that of the murder of James Bulger twelve years before. That killing had radically disturbed people's perceptions of children, and here once more we had the same narrative, the children who carried out this latest attack were not 'real' children, but evil monsters; thus the boundary between evil and innocence could be maintained, even though in our more rational moments we would have to face the truth that there is no such boundary. A few days later this particular story had run its course. Instead of a gang of evil monsters charged with attempted murder, one twelve-year-old girl was charged with causing grievous bodily harm, and it was unclear whether there was any such place as the Devil's Ditch at all. The James Bulger story, though, has never really ended, and the fact that all newspapers covering this latest attack referred to it shows that the trauma it caused is still with us.

On 12 February in 1993, two boys, both aged ten, killed a two-year-old boy in the city of Liverpool in the United Kingdom. The boys were Robert Thompson and Jon Venables, and their victim was James Bulger. They were charged with murder, and tried as adults, although they were eleven at the time of their trial. Found guilty, they were given a minimum sentence of eight years in secure detention. The trial judge, Sir Michael Morland, in sentencing them, told them: 'The killing of James Bulger was an act of unparalleled evil and barbarity', and that: 'In my judgement your conduct was both cunning and very wicked' (Thomas 1993: 271). The crime and trial dominated the British media and shaped political and social attitudes to youth crime. In an unprecedented move, the Home Secretary Michael Howard intervened in 1994 to set their minimum detention to fifteen years, but this was overturned by the House of Lords, and Venables and Thompson were released on parole in 2001. The media have been forbidden from revealing their identities or location, and, at the time of writing, this has been respected, albeit reluctantly.

Was it an act of unparalleled evil and barbarity? The killing of James Bulger was brutal and cruel, but in the history of inhumanity it was by no means unparalleled as an act. What Justice Morland was capturing was the sense of horror that this crime was carried out by children, but even then examples of children killing other children, while extremely rare, are not unknown. David James Smith begins his book on the Bulger killing by setting it in a historical context of such crimes (Smith 1994: 2–7), to point out that Venables and Thompson were, unfortunately, not unique. The British media also used the language of evil to describe the murder. Meg Barker describes the media coverage: 'Images of Venables and Thompson are reproduced, with labels of "evil", "freaks of nature" (*Daily Mirror*, 1993) and "products of the devil" (*Sun*, 1993). One journalist stated that "they did not look like ordinary boys, even before the murder" (*Independent on Sunday*, 28 November 1993)' (Barker 2001). Blake Morrison, writing in *The Guardian* newspaper ten years after he witnessed the trial, comments on the media frenzy and demonisation of Thompson and Venables (*The Guardian*, 6 February 2003). He says: 'Amid the hysteria in 1993, Thompson and Venables lost the right to be seen as children, or even as human. The kids who had killed the kid had to be killed, or at any rate locked up for life. The word used about them stopped all arguments. They were evil'. But, he says: 'Evil is no answer', and that instead of cunning adults, he saw at the trial two 'damaged children'. But it was not only the media who pursued this. While the trial judge stopped short of describing Thompson and Venables as evil themselves, describing the act not the agents, others went that step further. Albert Kirby, who led the police investigation, said: 'I truly believe they are just evil, and there is nothing to provide any excuse for them.' And Phil Roberts, a police officer who interviewed one of the boys, said: 'They were evil. I think they would have killed again' (Morrison 1997: 230–1). Sean Sexton, the solicitor who represented the Bulger family, said after the trial: 'It has made me think about whether there is such a thing as evil and there are some things you can't explain except by accepting that there is evil in the world. Once I would have been talking about boys like this needing a lot of work and counselling but that nobody is irredeemable. Now I would take an awful lot of persuasion that they could ever be released' (Thomas 1993: 290). Nick Cohen, writing in *The Observer* newspaper on 18 January 2004, endorses what he called the public's conception of evil: 'If its concept of evil did not exist, it would have to be invented to cover the gaps in all great crimes between understandable causes and inexplicable consequences.' On Venables and Thompson he writes: 'There is a gap between causes and effect, and if you don't use the concept of evil to bridge it, you'll have to find another word with the same meaning.' And so the 'little monsters' thesis was not only played out in the 'tabloid' media, but had a more intellectual appeal, in that, as Cohen points out, it can fill the 'black hole' between what we can understand and what we cannot understand – we can understand that two ten-year-old boys can be socially deprived and psychologically disturbed, but we cannot understand why they would abduct a two-year-old boy and brutally murder him.

Alison Young comments on the lack of vocabulary to talk about the case, and echoes my own experience of it being raised at a family function where the strongest view was that Venables and Thompson were evil monsters – I was confronted by someone who declared they were prepared to kill them with his own hands. Young also tried to use it in a class to discuss juvenile delinquency with students, a discussion 'which was not forthcoming since the students seemed entirely comfortable with the idea that the two boys were "evil" – a word which ended all discussions before they began' (Young 1996: 111). It was the severity of the event itself that compelled us into silence in the face of the diatribe of evil. She says: 'It is an event which *demands* interpretation. Its paradox, however, is that something about the event itself *prohibits* its interpretation. As an event, then, it both calls for and prohibits interpretation' (Young 1996: 112). We respond to the call for interpretation, but, she says, we are haunted by our failure. And the space of that failure, I argue, is taken up by the discourse of evil. The media discourse about the Bulger murder, says Young, created an imagined crime, falling into an imagined binary between the victim and the victimiser. Here, the victim, James Bulger, embodies the 'representative ideals of childhood', is 'an allegory of the innocence of childhood' (Young 1996: 115). On the other hand, Thompson and Venables represent the opposite: 'They are portrayed as aberrations of children, approximations of what a child might be, or fraudulent impostors. Venables and Thompson *appear* to be children but are not: they are more like evil adults or monsters in disguise' (Young 1996: 115). Part of the problem, then, is one we noted in the previous chapter, that the enemy who threatens us is imagined using resources that belong in the world of fiction, such that the boundary between fiction and reality becomes blurred. In section one of this chapter we saw how children came to represent both innocence and evil in horror narratives, and what we see played out in the media around the killing of James Bulger takes the form of a horror narrative. We also saw Julia Kristeva's argument that the source of our horror lies in being confronted by dissemblance and ambiguity – monsters who appear to us as human. According to the media, 'Thompson and Venables *appear* to be children but *are not*'. They are, therefore, profoundly disturbing figures.

This discourse of evil permeated its way into government policy on youth justice. In the wake of the murder there was, comments John Pitts, an extraordinary preoccupation with young offenders, generated by 'the terror in the face of indiscipline from below which lies at the heart of our culture' (Pitts 2003: 3). Both the media and government focused on the idea of the 'pre-pubescent "super-predator"', who was holding society to ransom (Pitts 2003: 13). In 1997, the Home Secretary Jack Straw abolished *doli incapax*, claiming that its central principle that children between the ages of ten and fourteen could not tell the difference between right and wrong was plainly false. Pitts points out that this was in fact a misinterpretation of what *doli incapax* embodied: '... it holds that in its dealings with children below the age of 14 who have broken the law, the courts must proceed from the assumption that, by dint of their immaturity, and even though they may have known that they were doing wrong, the child does not have criminal intent and does not fully understand the consequences of their actions for themselves or for their victim(s). As a result, the onus is upon the prosecution to demonstrate criminal intent' (Pitts 2001: 176). Between the ages of fourteen to seventeen the onus was on the defence to show a lack of criminal intent. Although Venables and Thompson were both only ten years old at the time of their of-fence, the court decided that *doli incapax* did not hold in their case and so they were tried as adults. Another step taken by the government in 1997 was the overturning of the principle that the identity of juvenile defendants should not be revealed to the pub-lic; youth courts were given the power to 'name and shame' if they wished. Again, the Bulger trial judge had decided that it was in the public interest to name Venables and Thompson. We can see, then, the impact the case had on the treatment of juveniles in the criminal law. Pitts describes this as 'dejuvenilisation' (Pitts 2001: 176). He says: 'considerations of responsibility, culpability and retribution were henceforth to be a legitimate concern of the youth justice system and its agents' (Pitts 2001: 176).

Damaged Goods

But Blake Morrison saw damaged children, not little monsters, and there was plenty of evidence for his view although little or none of it was presented to the court. Morrison observes that the only question addressed in the trial was whether the boys knew that whether what they were doing was seriously wrong: 'The psy-chiatrists are here to give evidence about intellectual maturity, not mental disturbance' (Morrison 1997: 88). There was no informa-tion submitted on 'the boys' family backgrounds, their relations with teachers and peers, their psycho-socio-sexual make up . . .' (Morrison 1997: 94). He complains: 'The law is arranged so that this knowledge, this Why, must be repressed. A child has died and become an icon. A nation's conscience must be appeased. The in-tricacies of responsibility are not at issue' (Morrison 1997: 169). Mark Thomas was a journalist in Liverpool who covered the mur-der and subsequent trial, and gave his account in *Every Mother's Nightmare: The Killing of James Bulger*, published in 1993. He

is open to the suggestion that the two boys were evil: 'Deprivation is no excuse for evil. Nor does it begin to explain how a
child could turn bad, so early' (Thomas 1993: 15). But he also describes what is known of the social background of the two boys.
Robert Thompson was the fifth of six sons. His father left the family suddenly in 1988, when Robert was five, and there is evidence
that the relationship between his parents had been a violent one
(Smith 1994: 156). After he left the family, Ann Thompson 'turned
to drink, and would go out regularly, leaving her six sons pretty
much to their own devices. The oldest brother, then seventeen,
was regularly left in charge, and would hit the other boys if they
did anything wrong' (Thomas 1993: 37). The relationship between
the brothers was itself violent, with each brother bullying the one
younger. Robert regularly bullied the youngest, Simon. 'With their
mother seeming to pay little attention, the boys began playing truant from school on a regular basis. The Thompsons gained minor
notoriety in the area as a problem family, the boys unkempt and
running wild, their mother hitting the bottle...' (Thomas 1993:
37). Eventually the two eldest boys were taken into care and the
next oldest, Arnold, became the primary carer. The next brother
in age was taken into care, and Robert played truant from school,
'spending his days stealing from shops and getting up to mischief.
Robert would also bully little Simon, a pleasant child trying his
best at school, forcing him to play truant too' (Thomas 1993: 37).
Eventually Arnold went into voluntary care. However, neighbours
reported the family as unexceptional, and after having her seventh
son to a different father in May 1992, Ann Roberts seemed to re-
cover and what was left of the family became more stable, at least
for a moment.

   Jon Venables was 'another product of a broken home' and had
'an unhappy childhood' (Thomas 1993: 40). He was born in 1982
and his parents divorced in 1985. His elder brother and younger
sister had learning difficulties and attended a special school, and
he 'was given a difficult time by his contemporaries both in his
home street and at his school because his brother and sister were
"backward". He became a deeply unhappy young boy' (Thomas
1993: 40). By 1991 his behaviour at school was a serious concern
and the school's psychology service report on what was bizarre
conduct. 'Jon's class teacher at the time recalled that after the
Christmas break his behaviour became very strange. She told police: "He would sit on his chair and hold his desk with his hands
and rock backwards and forwards and start moaning and making

strange noises"... Sometimes he would bang his head on the furniture until it must have hurt. He would cry and complain that other children were picking on him outside class' (Thomas 1993: 41). After being banned from a school trip, his behaviour worsened. 'He would go round the room revolving along the walls, pulling off pictures and displays. He would lie inside a group of desks, lodging himself so that his teacher had trouble moving him. Occasionally he would cut himself deliberately with scissors, or cut holes in his socks. He would stick paper over his face and grab anything near him to throw across the room at other children. Once, when he was made to stand outside because of his behaviour, he simply started throwing things down the corridor' (Thomas 1993: 41–2). Eventually he attacked another boy with a twelve-inch ruler, trying to choke him (Thomas 1993: 42). He was suspended from school, and moved to another school in a class a year below his age. Thompson had been attending that school since 1989, and in September 1991 they were both put in the same class, both with children a year younger than themselves (Thomas 1993: 43).

At the new school Jon's behaviour improved and neither he nor Robert Thompson stood out as troublemakers (Thomas 1993: 44). Their teacher was a 53-year-old man who had sixteen years experience with 'maladjusted' children at special schools and who gave Jon special attention (Thomas 1993: 43). The next year their teacher was a woman who found Jon 'disruptive and awkward', but 'no more trouble than many of the other pupils' (Thomas 1993: 45). However, we have to remember that at his previous school Jon did stand out. David James Smith points out that his class teacher there, in fourteen years of teaching, 'had never come across a pupil like Jon' (Smith 1994: 146). What did become worse at the new school, however, was truanting. By November 1992 both boys were kept under supervision at breaks and lunchtimes, and even when they went to the toilet. Robert Thompson responded by not coming to school at all, and by now was severely bullying his younger brother Simon (Thomas 1993: 48). Thomas observes: 'It is extremely unusual to find children of quite such tender years capable of killing another human being. Yet much of their behaviour conforms to patterns familiar to those who have studied such crimes in older children and in adults' (Thomas 1993: 161).

Two questions about the murder have never been satisfactorily answered. The first is whether the two boys set out that day with a plan to kill. There is evidence that they tried to abduct other small children on the day they murdered James Bulger, and earlier Robert Thompson and another boy had taken his younger brother Simon alongside a canal, beaten him and then abandoned him (Thomas 1993: 164–5). Thomas reports that their teacher had noted Jon Venables' particularly agitated behaviour the day before the murder, and speculates: 'Was this evidence of a child excited at the prospect of carrying out a wicked plan?' (Thomas 1993: 165). The other unanswered question is whether the crime had a sexual motive. James' lower clothing had been removed but there was no evidence of sexual interference. After the murder but before the trial Thomas interviewed David Glasgow, lecturer in forensic clinical psychology at Liverpool University, who practised at a secure unit which housed some of the country's most dangerous psychopaths, including Ian Brady (Thomas 1993: 165). He reports Glasgow as suspecting there was a sexual motive (Thomas 1993: 174–5), and that death need not have been the primary aim. 'The process of abuse, humiliation or sex abuse may be what they want to do for various reasons. The difficulty is that they get trapped into escalation' (Thomas 1993: 176). Glasgow also points out that where people act together the abnormality of the individuals involved is reduced. 'When you get children acting together, particularly pre-adolescent and adolescent, they often do quite serious things, including killing people, that to an adult would be horrifying . . . Often their psychopathology as individuals isn't so great' (Thomas 1993: 165). The fact remains, though, that no one suspected that Thompson and Venables, whatever their problems, would commit murder. One reason for this, of course, is that children very rarely commit murder, but another important reason was that the authorities had little information to go on. The two families were reluctant to take up offers of support and assistance, and for much of the time the boys did not display any behavioural problems to make them stand out as potentially dangerous delinquents. Even after the murder, the two boys revealed little about what happened or about their motivation, each generally blaming the other for the killing, and refusing to accept responsibility for it. They certainly never admitted to any sexual motivation, but then it is unlikely that they would, or that they could have understood any such motivation well enough to articulate it.

The fact is that Venables and Thompson fit patterns indicated by research that identify factors to do with psychological, cultural and social damage that contribute to putting children at risk of committing extremely violent acts. David James Smith observes in his book about the murder: 'Such limited research as exists in this area suggests that most young people who commit serious crimes – murder, manslaughter, rape, arson – have one thing in common. They have been abused physically or sexually, or both, and emotionally, in childhood. Not all young people who commit serious crimes have been abused. And not all young people who have been abused commit serious crimes. But the problem is there' (Smith 1994: 1). And so one thesis to counter that of 'a genetic or unborn propensity for evil and hence murder' (Heckel and Shumaker 2001: xx) is that these are socially, culturally and psychologically damaged goods. This is the thesis pursued by Robert Heckel and David Shumaker in their American study of pre-teens who kill. The question is whether such children are psychotic (Heckel and Shumaker 2001: 32–3). A 1990 study found that the majority of such offenders were not psychotic, while other such studies confirmed 'a very low rate of psychotic symptomatology' (Heckel and Shumaker 2001: 33). But a 1995 study found high levels of psychotic and schizophrenic symptoms in thirty-five homicidal youths. Heckel and Shumaker argue that this means that although a minority of them are actually diagnosed, a great many may have a history of symptoms – the pattern is for a 'high rate of psychotic thinking' even though not many meet criteria for diagnosing psychotic disorder. One reason for problems in diagnosing children as psychotic is 'the range of permissible thought, which in adults would be regarded as delusional or at least disordered. For example, precausal thinking, animism, fantasy, and some hallucinatory experiences that are diagnostic signs in adults are often observed in normal children' (Heckel and Shumaker 2001: 33). As well as these symptoms of schizophrenic and psychotic disorder, other factors found in the 1995 study were high levels of substance abuse, conduct disorder, depression, separation anxiety disorder, and lower than normal IQ scores and learning difficulties (Heckel and Shumaker 2001: 34–6). There were also significant neurological abnormalities, such as epilepsy, serious head traumas, abnormal EEG readings and 'other neurological difficulties' (Heckel and Shumaker 2001: 36). Heckel and Shumaker suggest that although psychologists may not be in a position to predict homicidal behaviour, 'there are likely important measurable differences in the personality formation, perceptual processing, and coping mechanisms of children who are at risk for committing murderous acts versus those who are not' (Heckel and Shumaker 2001: 39).

As well as the evidence for psychotic disturbance, there were also factors to do with social and family background that emerged as significant. The first of these was to do with family problems: 'One of the most consistent findings in the literature is that the majority of youthful homicide perpetrators present with a history of adverse family factors' (Heckel and Shumaker 2001: 40). Eight such factors featured heavily: 'physical abuse, sexual abuse, instability of caretaker situation and/or residency, absence of a father, parental alcohol or drug abuse, parental psychiatric history, parental criminal background, and violence in the home' (Heckel and Shumaker 2001: 40). Physical abuse was the major variable, followed by violence in the home. Heckel and Shumaker describe two general theories about the connection between these factors and youth homicide. The first focuses on the failure to experience adequate socialisation through nurturing and training over the years, and a 'need for immediate gratification resulting in periodic aggressive outbursts that may lead to murder in extreme cases' (Heckel and Shumaker 2001: 40). The second argues that children model what they see: 'if a child is abused and witnesses violence, he or she will learn that acting in an out-of-control, violent manner is to be expected' (Heckel and Shumaker 2001: 40). This learned behaviour, along with neurological vulnerabilities in the child, 'increases the risk of murder in cases where that child becomes overwhelmed with the frustration of witnessing repeated violence in the household' (Heckel and Shumaker 2001: 40).

Heckel and Schumaker take a sample of eleven pre-teens, ten of whom committed homicide and one a homicidally aggressive act (Heckel and Shumaker 2001: 42–6). 'Perhaps the most intriguing finding concerned the especially high frequency in which preteens had engaged in cruel behaviour towards other children' (Heckel and Shumaker 2001: 44); this stood at 82 per cent. Heckel and Shumaker comment: 'Homicidal behaviour in young children does not appear to occur "out of the blue"; rather, there seems to be a history of cruel and aggressive behaviour that precedes these horrific actions' (Heckel and Shumaker 2001: 45). Alongside this, 91 per cent of the sample had a negative relationship with a male carer, and 82 per cent had suffered physical and emotional abuse. Heckel and Shumaker report: 'the majority of the preteens' households can best be described as unpredictable, nonempathic environments where the child was consistently at risk for witnessing or experiencing violence, usually at the hand

of the primary male caretaker' (Heckel and Shumaker 2001: 45).
A third theory can explain this correlation: 'children growing up
in abusive family environments experience intense psychological pressure with little opportunity to release such pressure constructively, resulting in highly aggressive behaviour under certain
conditions.' Heckel and Shumaker suggest 'this pressure is an instrumental factor in intrafamilial murder' (Heckel and Shumaker
2001: 45). In other words, children who witness or suffer abuse
reach a saturation point, a breaking point.

Other environmental factors come into play (Heckel and
Shumaker 2001: 46–50). One is access to handguns and gang
membership. Another is exposure to media violence. On the latter
Heckel and Shumaker conclude that: 'substantial data indicates
that exposure to media violence can have a causal effect on aggression in children under specific conditions and may correlate
with criminal behaviour in adulthood' (Heckel and Shumaker
2001: 49). But 'what has been more difficult to prove . . . is a causal
connection between television violence and real-world, violent
criminal behaviour in children' (Heckel and Shumaker 2001:
49). While the results show some connection between exposure
to television violence and 'simulated aggressive behaviour'
(behaviour in the laboratory situation), and 'minor [non-criminal]
aggressive behaviour', there is a minimal connection with 'illegal
activities', including criminal violence (Heckel and Shumaker
2001: 49). The research suggests 'a lack of a substantial relationship between exposure to media violence and real-world,
violent behaviour in children' (Heckel and Shumaker 2001: 49).
It remains possible, though, say Heckel and Schumaker, that it
may have an effect 'on the violent behaviour of children already
suffering from emotional, aggressive, and/or cognitive problems'
(Heckel and Shumaker 2001: 50). But there is a lack of evidence
here. However, in one experiment researchers demonstrated that
'in comparison with a control group of nonemotionally disturbed
children, emotionally disturbed children watched more hours
of aggressive television, were more likely to prefer aggressive
characters, had more difficulty in comprehending the unreality
of the television portrayal of violence [note that Jon Venables
watched Kung fu videos brought home by his father and 'when
he saw them he thought they were real, and he would cry'
(Smith 1994: 176)], and were more willing to hurt other children
following exposure to aggressive content in laboratory situations.'
But still, they found that 'in real-world settings, both violent and

nonviolent television were equally likely to induce antisocial behaviour in the subjects as compared to no television at all' (Heckel
and Shumaker 2001: 50). Heckel and Shumaker say: 'perhaps the
safest conclusion is that no demonstrable connection between exposure to television violence and homicidal behaviour in preteens
has been demonstrated to date' (Heckel and Shumaker 2001: 50).

Overall, Heckel and Shumaker point out that while research has
identified factors that *contribute* to acts of murder, the *causality*
is less clear. However, 'it does appear certain that acts of extreme
violence occur only in children who possess some or many of the
identified problems presented in our review of research' (Heckel
and Shumaker 2001: 158). Those factors that stand out for pre-
teen killers are 'physical and emotional abuse, negative relationship with father or male caretaker, rebellious and oppositional
behaviour, unstable environment, cruelty to other children, iso-
lation, and family psychiatric problems' (Heckel and Shumaker
2001: 158). Research by Garbarino and Eckenrode have identified
three mandates for the universal care of all children (Heckel and
Shumaker 2001: 159): access to preventative health care, education, clothing, immunisation and dental care; appropriate adult
care and supervision; and an enduring relationship with a car-
ing adult. Heckel and Shumaker say: 'These requirements are a
triad for the prevention of abuse. They are no less appropriate as
goals for the prevention of violence and its ultimate consequence –
murder' (Heckel and Shumaker 2001: 159). The two major general factors of negative family dynamics and lack of support in
the community have to be addressed. They cite successful programmes sponsored by the Centre for the Study and Prevention
of Violence at the University of Colorado at Boulder and the
Office of Juvenile Justice and Delinquency Prevention (Heckel and
Shumaker 2001: 145); these include a bullying prevention programme, a mentoring programme for six- to eighteen-year-olds,
and a family therapy programme. 'The implementation of the
techniques and lessons of these efforts by states and communities would represent a major step in the prevention of violence'
(Heckel and Shumaker 2001: 159).

Katharine D. Kelly and Mark Totten have conducted similar research in Canada, published in 2002, a study of nineteen young
people convicted of homicide. Kelly and Totten remark: 'Although
their lives and experiences were diverse, they have one thing in
common: they were all victims of harm' – child abuse, neglect, exposure to parental violence, parents who were addicts, mentally

ill, or themselves involved in crime. Another feature was learning disabilities, and 'Bullying, too, long considered as only teasing, also harmed many of our young people. Victims of bullying were socially marginal – they were unattractive, less intelligent, from visible minority groups, or failed to meet gender standards for either males or females' (Kelly and Totten 2002: 247). A situation of family breakdown – divorce, abandonment by parents, the failure of parents to visit – and negative community environments – poverty, community-based violence, exposure to drug use and harm – provided the context for social, cultural and psychological damage. 'Trauma left them with a terrible emotional legacy. Feelings of shame, anger, fear, frustration, hatred, and powerlessness were shared by our offenders' (Kelly and Totten 2002: 248). These young people turned these negative feelings into a variety of behaviour responses, 'to protect themselves, to increase their social status, to improve self-esteem, to feel powerful, to escape horrible situations, to make sense of their worlds – all through the use of violence to one degree or another' (Kelly and Totten 2002: 248).

It is important to acknowledge that these young people *chose* anti-social behaviour as a response to their frustrations, but it is equally important to acknowledge that 'their choices were constrained. Some modelled the behaviours of people around them – family members, community members, peers – others emulated masculine ideals or the social value placed on violence. Others had limited ability to make pro-social or positive decisions because of mental illness, brain injury, and low intellectual capacity' (Kelly and Totten 2002: 248). Kelly and Totten continue: 'Most participants developed antisocial reactions to their troubles. Most were bullied and some were bullies; many demonstrated self-hatred and routinely engaged in self-destructive behaviours; and many defied authority, unable to trust or bond with adults. Others withdrew into themselves. They exhibited few problems and were generally in school and not in conflict with the law' (Kelly and Totten 2002: 248). This latter aspect made it difficult for the authorities to respond effectively, as some 'did not seem to have many, or indeed any, serious problems' (Kelly and Totten 2002: 249). Where interventions did take place they were often ineffective because those the interventions aimed to assist would not cooperate. 'Some refused to disclose what had or was happening to them. They feared being taken into care or getting into trouble. Some had multiple diagnoses and treatments that were ineffective.

Parents or legal guardians often failed to seek support and failed to follow through with appropriate interventions. Participants were also resistant to getting help. They did not want to be treated – to be viewed as "problems" ' (Kelly and Totten 2002: 249).

Kelly and Totten took a 'life-course' approach their subjects, and conclude that their work 'challenges the stereotype of "the" murderer and replaces it with an understanding of the factors that harmed or helped our participants' (Kelly and Totten 2002: 252). Their findings show 'how constrained choices are made by children who kill and how their adolescence, their personal histories, and immediate circumstances contributed to what they did' (Kelly and Totten 2002: 252). These young people, 'in response to emotional, physical, and sexual harm, adopted behaviour patterns that put them at risk to commit murder' (Kelly and Totten 2002: xi). They killed because of their own choices, choosing to respond to their condition through violence, but those choices have to be understood as severely constrained: 'young people are not born killers. Rather, over their life course, their experiences, their emotional responses to them, and their behavioural choices come together to place them in situations where homicides are likely to occur' (Kelly and Totten 2002: 5). And this is perhaps the crucial point that the 'moral monsters' thesis overlooks, or prefers to ignore. Thompson and Venables, as with other children who kill, were not born killers. They became killers. And the fact that they became killers shows that there are processes and experiences and conditions that can be identified, described and understood as the background which places children at risk of committing acts of extreme violence. The major studies identify the same major factors. Poverty 'creates conditions conducive to extreme youth violence' (Kelly and Totten 2002: 6–7). Gender role socialisation around ideals of masculinity emphasise 'power, independence, aggression, dominance, heterosexuality, and violence' (Kelly and Totten 2002: 9). The research suggests that 'it is how we socialize boys to be male that leads to this increased risk of engaging in violent behaviour' (Kelly and Totten 2002: 9). A combination of rigid, traditional gender beliefs combined with factors that disempower increase the risk of violence. 'These young men often report feelings of being "disrespected", shamed, and humiliated by others and their circumstances' (Kelly and Totten 2002: 10). And negative family contexts are always present: 'Exposure to family violence, child abuse, and neglect are all correlated with an individual's use of violence as a teenager and as an adult. Neglect, deprivation, and witnessing violence... all contribute to the risk that young people will become involved in murder' (Kelly and Totten 2002: 12).

Similar studies have been carried out in the United Kingdom in relation to juvenile delinquency in general. In 1993 David Utting, Jon Bright and Clem Henricson wrote a report called *Crime and the Family: Improving Child-Rearing and Preventing Delinquency*, in which they surveyed the important 'longitudinal' studies that were available (Utting et al. 1993: 11–13). These identified five important predictors of delinquency: bad behaviour by boys aged between eight and ten; economic deprivation; family criminality; parental mishandling; and failure in school (Utting et al. 1993: 12–13). When it came to the family, it was not structure that was crucial, and there was no evidence that single parenting or divorce was a factor. Rather it was the quality of the parenting, and problems caused by inadequate supervision, indifference and neglect, conflict between parents, and the presence of parents with criminal behaviour (Utting et al. 1993: 19–22). They emphasise that this does not mean 'individual infants and families should – or even could – be singled-out and labelled as potentially delinquent' (Utting et al. 1993: 17). On the one hand, all the evidence provides 'an understanding that family and social factors are of special importance in the context of delinquency', but on the other hand they warn against 'the dangers that would surround an over-zealous crime prevention programme that set about stigmatising individual children and their parents known to be statistically "at risk"' (Utting et al. 1993: 18). There is evidence that the effect of a more coercive approach to youth crime 'could exacerbate already difficult relations between parents and adolescents. It could also increase family tensions and lead to a higher incidence of family break-up' (Utting et al. 1993: 62). They recommend a prevention programme with the following elements (Utting et al. 1993: 74): universal – family planning and preparation for family life education in schools; ante and post-natal care networks of support and advice; national, mass-media campaigns on parent education; access to parental skills training courses; good-quality and affordable childcare available to all parents who choose to work; high-quality pre-school education; effective programmes in primary and secondary schools ensuring minimum readings/maths skills; strategies to prevent bullying in schools. Neighbourhood – open-access family centres offering services such as parent and toddler clubs, play groups, toy libraries, parent training, financial advice, after-school clubs, family therapy, special group work on specific issues such as domestic violence; remedial design work and improved management of high-crime estates; community policing; clubs and holiday activities for children and young people; participation of parents in management of family centres, schools and community projects. Home – extension of health visits to parents of young children as well as infants; befriending, babysitting and other outreach services; family support volunteers, family preservation services.

However, government policy did not take the direction suggested by the report, and instead responded to the levels of public disturbance over youth crime following the murder of James Bulger. The main problem was not the effects of social deprivation, but the growth in numbers of 'little monsters'. Under the Crime and Disorder Act 1998 the Labour government took the powers Utting and his fellow authors had warned against. The Act 'allows pre-emptive formal intervention with children and young people below the age of criminal responsibility (10 years), including those who have committed no offence but are deemed likely to do so' (Pitts 2001: 169). These interventions are civil measures but breach of them can bring criminal sanctions. For example, failure to comply with a Parenting Order can bring a fine of £1,000 or six months' imprisonment. Pitts agrees with the authors of *Crime and the Family* that such an aggressive approach can make the situation worse. 'The judicial and administrative arrangements brought into being by the Crime and Disorder Act (1998) threaten to draw greater numbers of younger, less problematic, children and young people into the youth justice system, to subject them to modes of correctional intervention which have not been shown to be particularly effective and, in consequence, to propel many more of them into the custodial institutions from which, Sir David Rowbotham the Chief Inspector of Prisons believes, anybody under 18 should be immediately removed' (Pitts 2001: 188–9).

Although government policy does focus on the family, as suggested in the *Crime and the Family* report, that focus has taken the form of demonisation of 'problem' families. Pitts argues that while research does point to the family as a factor, it has to been seen in the context of other important factors, and yet the family has become the predominant cause of youth crime in the eyes of government. Pitts warns that we cannot ascribe 'causal primacy . . . to the "criminogenic" lower-class family' (Pitts 2001: 178–9). To do so 'denies or ignores the relationship between socio-economic stress, neighbourhood poverty and the biographies of young offenders, the peculiar, mutually-reinforcing, negative contingencies set in train by socially deviant acts perpetrated by lower-class children and young people, and the role of state agencies in the construction and amplification of their "deviant careers"' (Pitts 2001: 179). There can be little doubt that parenting – or lack of it – plays a significant role in a great many cases, but the demonisation of particular parents is questionable, and Young notes the way in which the parents of Venables and Thompson were assigned a sinister role by the media and by commentators (Young 1996: 121–5). A 'joined-up' approach to the problem of youth crime would have a much broader focus than present government policy, argues Pitts. Together with Roger Matthews, he writes: 'It has . . . been evident for some time that crime is related to almost every other negative indicator in society – poor health, limited educational facilities, unreliable transport, bad housing and the more serious environmental problems' (Matthews and Pitts 2001: 5). They argue for social-support theory, which proposes that 'the best predictor of the areas and households with high levels of multiple victimisation are not those with low levels of social control, as conservative criminologists have argued, but rather those with low levels of social support' (Matthews and Pitts 2001: 5). According to Pitts, the research data identifies not so much problem people, as problem processes, namely a process 'in which an initial social or developmental disadvantage, a lack of "social capital", is gradually and cumulatively compounded and amplified, "embedded", through interaction with peers, other adults and defining agencies' (Pitts 2003: 83). This, he says, is a story about 'a complex interaction of social, economic, cultural and developmental factors and burgeoning negative stereotyping. For the people caught up in this spiral, their worsening predicament is paralleled by the progressive erosion of their capacity to make any impact upon that predicament' (Pitts 2003: 84). The question, then, is how particular people become embedded within this kind of negative process, and how they can be assisted to escape it. The fact is that this negative embeddedness is 'likely to be far more prevalent in neighbourhoods characterised by low socio-economic status' (Pitts 2003: 84). There therefore needs to be an emphasis on 'background' socio-structural factors. 'A genuinely joined-up or holistic analysis of the disparate phenomena lumped under the heading "youth crime" – poor parenting, shoplifting, bullying, school exclusion, mugging, etc. – will tend to focus upon the historical, political, social and economic circumstances which precipitate and sustain them' (Pitts 2003: 135).

What is disturbing is the extent to which the 'little monsters' horror narrative – an imagined, fictional world of monsters in disguise – has, at least since the trial of Venables and Thompson, permeated and shaped not only popular cultural and media representations of children who kill, but also government policy towards juvenile delinquency in general. There are strong parallels here with the other 'horror' narratives that I identified in previous chapters – about mass migration and global terrorism – which shows that the myth of evil exerts an extremely powerful hold on how we imagine the world to be. The counter-narratives – in the case of children, those coming out of psychology and criminology – take place in a highly marginalised space, populated by academics, who are largely talking to each other. Most significant social agencies, such as the media and the government, are dominated by the myth of evil little monsters.

The 'Black-Hole' Problem

The argument is not, of course, that any of the factors we have described here *caused* Thompson and Venables to kill James Bulger; this they chose to do, for reasons we may never know. However, the evidence does show that these factors *contributed* to their act. The question is what we do with this information? And this isn't at all obvious, because the immediate rejoinder to anybody who tables this research and reaches this conclusion is that there are many boys who live under the same conditions and suffer the same experiences and who do not commit extreme acts of violence, and therefore there is something missing from the account. This is the 'black-hole' problem I described in Chapter 1, identified by Richard Bernstein: 'The social disciplines and psychology all contribute to this understanding [of a person's background, training, education, character, circumstances, etc.]. But it never adds up to a *complete* explanation of why individuals make the choices they do. There is always a gap, a "black hole", in our accounts' (Bernstein 2002: 235). Mark Thomas says: 'many thousands of children today go through the trauma of broken homes, poor parenting and even outright abuse, without turning into fully fledged killers' (Thomas 1993: 173). And as we saw from Nick Cohen earlier in this section, the only thing that can fill this hole is the idea of evil. What separates Venables and Thompson from others in the same situation is that they were evil little monsters.

There are two immediate responses we can make to the 'black-hole' objection to the psychological account. The first is to argue that evil itself is a 'black-hole' concept; it does not so much close the gap in our account as make it more apparent. What we have here is the illusion of closure. The gap is only closed if we have a theory of evil which involves explanation, and this is what Gordon Graham sought to supply in Chapter 2 by arguing for the existence of Satan as a causal force. Without that explanatory structure behind it, the concept of evil adds nothing to the account. However, any *structured* theory of evil is mythological. The second response to the 'black-hole' objection is to make clear what the psychological account is saying here. The claim has not been that these factors caused Venables and Thompson to kill James Bulger, but that together they contributed to creating a context which heightened the risk that they would respond to situations with extreme violence. The objection seems to be that because other people in the same context did not respond in the way Venables and Thompson and others did, then we have to treat the claim that the context significantly contributed to their actions with scepticism, and look for some other explanation. But this seems to miss the point of the account altogether. We have enough evidence to know that certain contexts increase the risk of children, and others, making such drastic choices. We don't have a strict causal connection here, so that we can say if P then Q, where P is made up of the background factors and Q is the choice to use extreme violence, such that wherever we have P we must get Q. Nor do we have a regular conjunction of events such that where we have P we can say we will probably also have Q as a consequence. What we do have is a number of comparatively rare events which all seem to share the same background factors, such that although those factors remain in place for all too many people in our society, we can say that one comparatively rare consequence of them is the choice of extreme violence by an extremely small number of those people. The fact that the vast majority of people who live in those conditions do not make that choice does not demonstrate that there is no connection between those conditions and the people who do make that choice. And although occurrences of murder by pre-teens may be extremely rare, the connection between these background conditions and general criminality in young people is much more pronounced, with much stronger statistical evidence. Acts of violence resulting in death are at the extreme end of a range of delinquent behaviour which all has its source in the same social, cultural and psychological contexts.

To see the weakness of the black-hole objection we need only construct some analogous objections. Suppose one afternoon there a public event in the neighbourhood, but there is a light rain, such that a small number of people decide not to venture outside, while the vast majority are not discouraged. The argument seems to be that because the majority were not deterred by the rain, those who stayed at home could not have been deterred by it either, and must have stayed at home for some other reason. But this is an obvious nonsense. In other words, there is no black hole here, no gap in our explanation. Or at least there is no gap in terms of looking for some *active* cause for what these children do. The temptation of the black hole is to suppose that, because the majority of children living within this context do not choose to murder, then there must have been some other active factor pushing those who did choose to murder – and this active force is evil, however we articulate it. But when we looked at the evidence presented by Heckel and Shumaker we came across what I described as the 'saturation point' argument, that 'children growing up in abusive family environments experience intense psychological pressure with little opportunity to release such pressure constructively, resulting in highly aggressive behaviour under certain conditions' (Heckel and Shumaker 2001: 45). What this indicates is that if anything *is* missing from our psychological account, it is not some extra *active* force, but something passive. These children do not have something added on, but have something subtracted. And what they lack does not have to be psychologically complex, such that we have to argue that all such children are psychopathic – rather, what they lack may simply be a level of ability to resist responding violently to their situation. Again, an analogy may help make sense of the idea of a passive causal factor. Suppose there is a wall built to resist flood water, but suppose certain areas of the wall have internal structural weaknesses, such that when the flood water comes parts of the wall stay in place and resist, but other parts collapse. There is only one active cause here, the flood water, and we do not have to suppose there was some other active cause at work to make the walls collapse, such as evil saboteurs – the only other causal factor we need for a complete explanation is that there were structural weaknesses within the structure of parts of the wall. We can of course ask how those structural weaknesses came about, and in the case of children this is the information supplied by the psychological and social evidence.

A final analogy – imagine a bucket balanced on a stool which is balanced delicately on a ladder balanced precariously against a wall, and above the bucket is leaking water which is dripping slowly into it, one tiny drop once a day. This goes on for a thousand, two thousand, three thousand days and nothing changes. There comes a day, however, when the bucket is full and can't take another drop, but another drop comes and the bucket overbalances and water falls everywhere and the stool tumbles from the ladder, which clatters from the wall and everything comes crashing to the ground. After an extremely long period of steady, unchanging behaviour, there comes a moment of extreme violence, but the processes leading up to that moment have been going on for a long period. Although the change in behaviour is sudden and dramatic, its causes are not, and just because the drops of water on previous days did not lead to this catastrophic outburst of destructive violence, this does not show that they were not part of the causal process leading up to it – they were contributing factors. By analogy, a child could be on the receiving end of abuse and other kinds of negative experience until he or she reaches a saturation point which triggers a radical change of behaviour, perhaps extreme and catastrophic violence. The cause of the radical change of behaviour does not come suddenly out of the blue, but was a drip-drip-drip process, until the child reaches his or her saturation, or breaking, point.

The crucial point is that it is extremely implausible to suppose that all children have the same saturation point – our experience is that people have different breaking points to different stimuli. And so if two children are subject to the same negative stimuli, and the first child reaches a point where he or she responds violently and the second child does not, it does not follow at all that the cause of the first child's violent response could not have been the negative stimuli; it is simply that the two children had different breaking points. The negative stimuli act as a complete explanation of the first child's violent response, or at least a complete explanation in terms of *active* causes. We do not need another, sinister active cause here to explain why the first child reacts and the second does not. The additional information we need is about passive causal factors, that the first child had lower levels of resistance to the negative stimuli than the second child. This is not to see that first child as psychopathic, but simply, in certain respects, lacking the resources of the second child. The difference in where their saturation points lie plays a role in the complete explanation of the violent behaviour of the first child, but it is not an active causal feature, and it is in the supposed need for an extra active causal factor to make the difference between them that evil gains a foothold in the explanation. If this argument is at all convincing then there is no need for this additional active factor. The levels of abuse these children suffer is sufficient, along with the negative factor in the different saturation points – how much abuse they can 'soak up' until they break. As Blake Morrison observed, Venables and Thompson were damaged children, not evil monsters – they were already broken.

What is perhaps surprising about this way of closing the explanatory gap and squeezing out any space for the concept of evil is how simple it is. That people have different breaking points is surely uncontroversial. We can ask why particular people have different breaking points, and we can acknowledge that this is a highly complex question requiring an intimate knowledge of their psychological history, something we may never be in a position to know. But this is to acknowledge that there will be gaps in any explanation of a particular action; we never have enough information to close all such gaps. These gaps, however, are not mysterious – they are not 'black holes': we do, in fact, know what is within them, the general kind of information that would make sense of them. We do not need any mysterious force to close them in order for us to make sense of a particular human action. To that extent, then, of course we do not have a complete explanation of the action, but we do have as complete an explanation as we need in order to understand it, and, where there is a gap, we do know the sort of information that would fill it. We can speculate about what it might be, but even this is not necessary for understanding. These are comprehensible gaps, not incomprehensible ones. The only real objection to this psychological account would be if some of the children who kill were free from any kind of the negative factors that have been identified, but the balance of evidence here is in favour of the psychological account.

There are a number of important themes at stake here. One is that of understanding, whether we can understand why these children resort to violence; the question here is not only seeing that the kind of negative factors we have described correlate with the choice of some children to use extreme violence, but also seeing how those factors contribute to that particular choice: does the experience of these conditions make the choice of violence a comprehensible one? I suggest that the psychological evidence does show that the choice of violence is comprehensible: much of the negative experience we are discussing is itself experience of violence, and it is also understandable how the frustration of powerlessness can lead to a violent response. The second theme is that of responsibility, and in the case of children who kill who have suffered high levels of abuse and other forms of negative experience my inclination is to say that this context is an overriding contributing factor in shaping their choice, and this has obvious implications for the extent to which we can hold them responsible for their actions. Ten years after the trial of Venables and Thompson, the foreman of the jury who found them guilty of murder said: 'I am ashamed that I allowed myself to be coerced by the judge and the prosecution to agree to a verdict of guilty of murder. A proper judgment would have been that they had behaved like confused, frightened and stupid children caught up in a situation they had created but could not deal with' (*The Guardian* newspaper, 6 February 2003).

The Problem of Moral Luck

It seems, then, that sometimes people do dreadful things because of factors beyond their control. It is not that they were compelled to do them by some overwhelming force, but that background factors came together so that they made a particular choice which, if things had been different, they would not have made. To what extent can we hold them morally responsible for their choice? There were various factors that came together in the case of Venables and Thompson, not least that they were ten years old, but they were judged to be fully morally responsible for what they did and so were tried as adults and found guilty of murder. This seems to me to have been an obvious mistake because the background factors made such a significant contribution to their choosing violence that it is highly questionable how responsible they were for their actions. One reply to this defence, however, is that anything anybody chooses to do is, to some extent, dependent on factors beyond their control, such that if things had been different they would have chosen differently. If this argument excuses Venables and Thompson then it must excuse anybody. In other words, as an argument against holding these two boys morally responsible it is much too powerful, and undermines moral responsibility in general. The fact is that we *do* hold people responsible for their actions despite the fact that there are always uncontrolled background factors in play, and so I have failed to show that there was anything wrong in holding Venables and Thompson responsible for the killing of James Bulger. What we have encountered here is the problem of moral luck.

Chapter Seven

The Character of Evil

Moral Luck

The problem we examined in the previous chapter was one of moral judgement, and I argued that the way Venables and Thompson were judged was patently unfair. This is not only to dismiss the charge of 'evil' made against them, but also to question the extent to which they were morally responsible for what they did – any kind of moral judgement is therefore questionable in their particular case. This is because there were background factors that played a significant role in their actions, and those background factors and the role they played made it inappropriate to hold them morally responsible. However, it could be argued that examining these kinds of background contexts undermines moral judgement in general. While I want to close the space for the discourse of evil, it is not my intention to close the space for any level of moral judgement, and so in this chapter I need to explain how my approach can coherently both show the discourse of evil to be redundant and at the same time show that moral judgement – sometimes of the most severe kind – is possible. I will approach this particular problem through the concept of 'moral luck', because some theorists use this idea to show that moral judgement in general is impossible, and they do so precisely by focusing on the background conditions that influence people's actions. I need to show that there is a difference between the moral-luck argument and my own approach, and that my approach avoids this general moral scepticism.

Thomas Nagel defines moral luck like this: 'Where a significant aspect of what someone does depends on factors beyond his control, yet we continue to treat him in that respect as an object of moral judgement, it can be called moral luck' (Nagel 1993: 59).

Nagel has no doubt that moral luck occurs: 'Whether we succeed or fail in what we try to do nearly always depends to some extent on factors beyond our control' (Nagel 1993: 58). At the extreme, there are cases where moral judgement is clearly inappropriate – if I fall on you and injure you because an overwhelming and unpredictable gust of wind blew me against you, I am not morally responsible; this is just bad luck. But whatever we do rests on factors beyond our control, including those actions for which we are morally praised or blamed. 'And external influences in this broader range are not usually thought to excuse what is done from moral judgement, positive or negative' (Nagel 1993: 58). If I leap into a river to save a drowning child, I am a moral hero, but that I was there at the right time is a matter of luck, and so I am no more a moral hero than all the other people who *would* have saved the child if they had been there. However, I am the one who gets the moral praise here, not them, and therefore this is an example of moral luck. The crucial point for Nagel is that: 'We judge people for what they actually do or fail to do, not just for what they would have done if circumstances had been different' (Nagel 1993: 66). Similarly, if five of us all have murderous intent towards you, and I happen upon you walking down the road at night alone and so succeed in murdering you, I am morally condemned while they are not. The only difference between us was determined by factors beyond our control, and therefore that I am morally condemned and they are not is an example of moral luck. Nagel's point is that if we genuinely only hold people morally responsible for their motives and intentions, then all people with the same motives and intentions are equally praiseworthy or blameworthy. But in practice moral judgement is not like that – we praise or blame people for what they do, in which case we have to face the existence of moral luck, because what people actually do or don't do is importantly, though not completely, determined by factors beyond their control, such as being in the right or wrong place at the right or wrong time. There are different ways in which this can happen and Nagel identifies four (although he only gives a specific name to the first – the names for the other forms of moral luck have emerged through subsequent discussions by other writers): constitutive luck – 'the kind of person you are, where this is not just a question of what you deliberately do, but of your inclinations, capacities, and temperament'; circumstantial luck – 'the kind of problems and situations one faces'; causal luck – 'luck in how one is determined by antecedent circumstances'; and resultant luck – 'luck in the way one's actions and projects turn out' (Nagel 1993: 60).

According to Nagel, 'the problem posed by this phenomenon . . . is that the broad range of external influences here identified seems on close examination to undermine moral assessment as surely does the narrower range of familiar excusing conditions. If the condition of control is consistently applied, it threatens to erode most of the moral judgements we find it natural to make', and so 'it leaves few pre-reflective moral judgements intact. Ultimately, nothing or almost nothing about what a person does seems to be under their control' (Nagel 1993: 59). This seems absurd, but to get rid of the absurdity we have to 'pare down each act to its morally essential core, an inner act of pure will assessed by motive and intention' (Nagel 1993: 63). But even these 'stripped-down acts of will' are the product of antecedent circumstances beyond our control, and so: 'The area of genuine agency, and therefore of legitimate moral judgement, seems to shrink under this scrutiny to an extensionless point' (Nagel 1993: 66). In other words, there is no moral agency, only moral luck. This is a problem to do with the practice of moral judgement – as soon as we notice aspects of what people do which are not under their control, we withdraw moral judgement. But as soon as we do this we cannot stop – 'the ultimate consequence of such subtraction is that nothing remains' (Nagel 1993: 67). It is impossible to fix the point where conditioning factors end and moral responsibility begins, and so unless we want to deny the influence of conditioning factors altogether, moral responsibility disappears.

We can now see the challenge Nagel's conception of moral luck presents to my argument against the use of the concept of evil. I have argued that 'evil' as an idea is used to fill a space of incomprehension. Where we cannot understand how people could do dreadful things we describe them as evil and so have the illusion of an explanation. Instead, I have argued, we *can* understand why people do dreadful things if we are prepared to examine the detail of the background context against which they act. This is not to say that this background context determined their choice, but it is to say that this context contributes to making such choices possible – they would not be made without that context in place. This gives us the resources to understand what has happened, something we are deprived of by the idea of evil. However, Nagel's concern is that, as soon as we begin to focus on background conditions, we realise that anything anybody does is subject to factors beyond their control, such that even the most basic moral judgement becomes impossible – we lose any concept of moral agency. In other words, in closing the space for judgements that people are morally evil, I have closed the space for any kind of moral judgement at all, and this threatens my argument with absurdity.

A problem, though, with Nagel's argument is that he himself is sometimes not clear about its force. At times he comments that the problem of moral luck threatens to erode *most* of our moral judgements, that it leaves *few* such judgements intact, that *almost* nothing a person does seems to be under their control; but also that the consequence of his argument is that *nothing* remains. But there are reasons to suppose that the radically sceptical conclusion can be resisted. First, Nagel argues that it is impossible to fix the point where conditioning factors end and moral responsibility begins, but this argument could have two different conclusions – either that there is no such boundary, or that there *is* such a boundary but it is 'fuzzy'. There is nothing in Nagel's descriptions of moral luck to lead us to the conclusion that there is no boundary at all; the most plausible conclusion is that the boundary is less clear than we might hope. But a 'fuzzy' boundary is still a boundary, and although its 'fuzziness' means there will be hard cases – and perhaps cases which are genuinely impossible to judge – it allows that there are clear cases that fall either side of the boundary. If we look at resultant moral luck – the way things turn out – we can see that there is room for legitimate moral judgement. Nagel discusses resultant luck by using the example of a driver who knocks down and kills a child. To give the example more detail, let's suppose there are two drunken drivers, X and Y, and X drives home without incident, but Y hits a child who walks into the road – further suppose that if Y had not been drunk he or she could have reacted in time to avoid the child. Resultant luck is about how your actions work out, and in this case X was lucky to get away with doing something risky, but if X was lucky then Y must have been unlucky. The only difference between them is down to factors beyond their control. This means if we morally condemn Y more than X, then this is an example of moral luck. That Y did something dreadful that X did not do is not down to any of their decisions, intentions, motives and judgements; it is purely a matter of luck. One immediate response is, of course, to deny that we would pick out Y over X for moral condemnation, but our experience of moral judgement makes this response rather implausible.

Daniel Statman uses the example of someone being negligent in putting out a fire (Statman 1993: 13). In the case of X, the fire is put out by a shower of rain, but in the case of Y there is no shower of rain, and the fire spreads out of control and burns down a house, killing a child. Statman says: 'It is obvious that the outcome in both these cases is beyond one's control, in the sense that it was not within one's control to make it the case that a rainfall occurred or did not occur, or that a child was or was not in the house nearby. In this sense, the outcome was a matter of (good or bad) luck. Hence, because, *ex hypothesi*, the two agents were equally negligent, it may seem that both are guilty and responsible to the same degree. But despite these facts, we *do* judge these cases differently' (Statman 1993: 13). Again, as Nagel says, we judge people on what they do, not what they might have done under different circumstances, or what would have happened if things had been different, or rather if we do judge them on these latter aspects, we judge them less severely.

This final example of resultant luck is my own. X and Y both let off a loaded gun in a crowded room in order to frighten people. In the case of X no one is hit, but in the case of Y someone is hit and killed. Both are equally reckless, with the same intentions and motives, but X was lucky – and so Y was unlucky. If we pick out Y for special moral condemnation, this is a clear example of moral luck. But there is one thing to notice about resultant luck. In each case, there is something X and Y are equally morally to blame for: driving when drunk; lighting a fire and leaving it to burn; letting off a gun in a crowded room. Each of these is an appalling act, and we would condemn X and Y equally for them. There is another level of moral condemnation which is reserved for Y in each case, and it is this extra level of moral condemnation which is down to moral luck and therefore may be incoherent. But still, Statman agrees that there is a level of moral judgement that is immune from this incoherence, the negligent act itself (Statman 1993: 29), in which case resultant luck seems to lack the power to make all moral agency disappear. And so it may be that while resultant luck gives the clearest examples of something we can understand as moral luck, it lacks the destructive power Nagel attributes to moral luck in general.

The example of the loaded gun reveals another possible way out of the sceptical conclusion Nagel reaches. We might consider that X is outrageously lucky not to kill anybody, but we would certainly not consider that Y was outrageously unlucky that they did kill somebody. If someone deliberately set off a gun in a crowded room, it would seem ludicrous to describe them as unlucky if the bullets hit people, even if someone else did exactly the same and the bullets missed everybody. X, then, was very lucky, but this does not mean that Y was unlucky at all. This means that two people can perform the same risky action and one cause harm and the other not, and it makes sense to say that the latter was lucky while at the same time refusing to say that the former was unlucky. Judgements of luck, it seems, are not symmetrical, but Nagel assumes they are: he assumes that if we say X was lucky, we are compelled to say Y was unlucky, and the whole argument about the existence of moral luck may rest on this questionable assumption. If we apply this to the drivers, while we may think the driver who does not kill anybody was lucky to get away with it, we may not think the driver who kills was unlucky that he or she did not get away with it. In some cases judgements of luck *may* be symmetrical, and this, in some cases, may have something to do with the balance of probabilities – if there is a genuinely 50/50 chance of a card coming up and it does, the person who gambled that it would is lucky and the person who gambled that it would not is equally unlucky. But for now, we can surmise that judgements of *moral* luck are not centrally to do with probabilities, and are not necessarily symmetrical. A radical proposal would be that they are *never* symmetrical, in which case the moral-luck argument loses all of its teeth.

This may not be a decisive refutation of the moral-luck argument, but my concern here is merely to show that we can allow the significant role of background factors in contributing to what people do, and still have space for legitimate moral judgement. For the purposes of my arguments, the most interesting forms of luck are constitutive and circumstantial, and the examples of Venables and Thompson and others show that how one is constituted and the circumstances within which one has to act can be extremely significant in contributing to the choices people make. My position here, then, is a rejection of Nagel's conception of moral luck when it comes to constitution and circumstances, because in identifying constitutive and circumstantial luck as significant, I want to argue that they are not examples of *moral* luck – that is, allowing them a significant role *does* narrow the space for legitimate moral judgement. If we do believe that background factors to do with the constitution of Venables and Thompson and the circumstances in which they had to lead their lives played a significant role in the choice they made to kill James Bulger, then we *must* question the extent to which we believe they were morally responsible for that act. And there is a crucial difference between the moral-luck argument and my argument in the previous chapter. There we described a specific set of background conditions that can be shown to have specific outcomes when it comes to children, and so the argument cannot be generalised to cover all kinds of background conditions to any kind of action. The background factors we have looked at heighten the risk of particular criminal actions, including violence. There were other background factors in play as well, such as James Bulger happening to be in the wrong place at the wrong time, which, while they are uncontrolled background factors which come together to make his murder possible, are not the sort of conditions we have discussed here. The argument has not been a general appeal to the role of luck in shaping people's actions, but to the role of well-established patterns of conditions that have been shown to heighten the risk of specific outcomes for children. The argument from moral luck is not so well focused. However, others who criticise Nagel, especially on the question of constitutive moral luck, do so in a way which *extends* the scope of moral responsibility in unacceptable ways. Two critics who do this are Nicholas Rescher and John Kekes, and I will discuss their arguments next. Kekes is of special significance as he argues *for* the use of a secular conception of evil.

Bad Characters

Thomas Nagel describes constitutive moral luck as to do with 'the kind of person you are, where this is not just a question of what you deliberately do, but of your inclinations, capacities, and temperament' (Nagel 1993: 60). This is to do with whether you are greedy, vain, cowardly, envious, and so on (Nagel 1993: 64). This is 'largely a matter of constitutive bad fortune. Yet people are morally condemned for such qualities, and esteemed for others equally beyond control of the will: they are assessed for what they are *like*' (Nagel 1993: 65). Circumstantial moral luck is to do with 'the kind of problems and situations one faces' (Nagel 1993: 60), and here his example is of people living in Nazi Germany who went along with the fascist programme. People living under liberal-democratic regimes may well have acted just as badly if they had lived under the same regime, but as we judge people for what they do, not what they would have done if things had been different, then we condemn the citizens of Nazi Germany far more than we do those citizens of liberal democracies, when the only difference between them is down to luck.

Nicholas Rescher denies there is any such thing as moral luck, and in understanding his objection we have to keep clear what moral luck is supposed to be. This is not to deny there is such a thing as constitutive or circumstantial *luck*, but only to deny that we judge people morally despite knowing that what we are judging them for is due to luck. Rescher, then, has to insist that we do not judge these cases differently – in all the examples of lucky and unlucky motorists, citizens, and so on, we make the same moral judgement. In arguing this he extends the sphere of moral condemnation so that those who *would* have done wicked things under different circumstances are condemned alongside those who actually did do them. For Rescher the problem is not moral but epistemic. He asks what of the person who is 'venial by disposition and inclination, but has the good fortune to be able to stay on the good side of morality because the opportunity for malfeasance never comes his or her way?' (Rescher 1993: 154). He concludes: 'The difference between the would-be thief who lacks opportunity and his cousin who gets and seizes it is not one of moral conditions . . . their moral *record* may differ, but their moral *standing* does not' (Rescher 1993: 154). And therefore: 'the luck involved relates not to our moral condition but only to our image: it relates not to what we are but to how people (ourselves included) will regard us. The difference at issue is not moral but merely epistemic' (Rescher 1993: 154–5). This means that 'the moral significance of acts lies in their serving as evidence' (Rescher 1993: 157). And so we should extend our moral condemnation to include those who would do wicked things if they had the opportunity. We should distinguish between both groups when it comes to the law 'for very good reason' (Rescher 1993: 166), as we may 'want to differentiate such situations on *nonmoral* grounds; for example, to reward only *successful* rescues or to punish only *realized* transgressions as a matter of social policy *pour encourager les autres*' (Rescher 1993: 159).

Rescher specifically rejects the notion of constitutive moral luck: 'it makes no sense to say things like, "Wasn't it just a matter of luck for X to have been born an honest (trustworthy, etc.) person, and for Y to have been born mendacious (avaricious, etc.)?" For it is just exactly those dispositions, character traits, and inclinations that constitute these individuals as the people they are. One cannot meaningfully be said to be lucky in regard to who one is, but only with respect to what happens to one. Identity must precede luck. It makes no sense to envision a prior featureless precursor who then has the good (or bad) luck to be fitted out with one particular group of character traits rather than another' (Rescher 1993: 155). And this is to adhere to 'the fundamental moral presumption involving treating a person as a person' (Rescher 1993: 156). But there are two deep problems here. The first is Rescher's view of legal punishment, which takes on the form of utilitarian deterrence rather than Kantian retribution. Norvin Richards, who takes a similar line to Rescher, also makes clear that this utilitarian view of punishment has to emerge from this position (Richards 1993: 170). Notoriously, however, the deterrence theory of punishment does not adhere to the fundamental moral presumption involving treating a person as a person. Also, and more crucial for our discussion, it simply *does* make sense to ask the sort of questions Rescher dismisses. Who one is, to an important extent, is a matter of what happens to one. What makes no sense is to suppose that we come into the world with a fixed moral identity in place. Now, Rescher may not seriously believe that people can be 'born' an honest, trustworthy person, or a mendacious, avaricious person, despite what he says here, but certainly he has to hold that one's character is fixed at a very early stage and is then immune from being shaped by external factors to any significant extent. But it simply *does* make sense to envision a prior featureless precursor, who then has the good or bad luck to be fitted out with one particular group of character traits rather than another; it is the alternative view, which Rescher vaguely describes here, that is nonsensical.

But Rescher insists: 'People's moral attributes do not come to them by luck but emerge from them on nature as free individual agents' (Rescher 1993: 155). And 'even after all the needed complications and qualifications are made, the fact remains that these personality features are not merely things regarding which we happen to "have no choice" – they are by their very nature things to which the idea of choice does not apply' (Rescher 1993: 156). This is because 'although in some (morally irrelevant) sense one's inclinations, disposition, and character merely fail to be "matters within one's *control*", these factors are not things that lie outside oneself but, on the contrary, are a crucial part of what constitutes one's self as such' (Rescher 1993: 157). But this is simply to *declare* that the sense in which one's inclinations, dispositions and character are not under one's control is morally irrelevant – if there is an argument here that *demonstrates* that they *must* be morally irrelevant, I must confess that I fail to grasp it. And, as I have argued, this is to extend the scope of moral condemnation to a remarkable degree. Rescher's argument also applies to circumstantial luck, again on epistemic grounds, but as Daniel Statman observes: 'The difficulty in this approach is that too many people are held responsible and blameworthy for too many things, with the result that blame seems to lose much of its meaning and effectiveness' (Statman 1993: 20).

Moral Character and Human Evil

John Kekes outlines a secular theory of evil, which both recognises the extent to which people have certain moral characters which are formed by factors outside their control, but which at the same time holds that such people can be morally censured when those moral characters are such that they carry out evil actions. Indeed, certain people can justifiably be described as evil if their moral characters lead them to consistently carry out evil actions, and the point of describing them as evil is to hold them up to moral condemnation. They deserve to be morally condemned. This, on the face of it, is the worst of both worlds – the recognition that much wrongdoing results from factors for which the agent cannot be held responsible, and yet the determination to morally condemn the agent for this wrong doing. But for Kekes this only seems paradoxical from the point of view of a moral theory that focuses on choice and the capacity to choose. He offers a moral theory that focuses on moral character, such that the point of morality is to discourage certain kinds of moral character and encourage others. The point of the discourse of evil is precisely this – there are certain people who have an evil character, and by identifying them and condemning them as evil we discourage others from being like them, and hopefully discourage them from following their evil character to its fullest extent.

Evil actions are those that cause undeserved harm to others (Kekes 1990: 4), and Kekes argues that a great deal of undeserved harm is caused by people who have particular vices. 'They may be cowardly, lazy, intemperate, thoughtless, cruel, vain, or envious, and these vices are reflected in their actions' (Kekes 1990: 6).

For Kekes, the fact that people with these vices regularly cause evil in the form of undeserved harm to others means that we can justifiably describe the agents themselves as evil. 'The vices of some people are lasting and predictable sources of evil, and calling people dominated by their vices evil merely registers this fact' (Kekes 1990: 8). This is, of course, a derivative sense of evil; its primary sense is 'the undeserved harm human beings cause one another and themselves' (Kekes 1990: 48). The derivation takes three steps. The first is to describe the actions which produce undeserved harm as evil, and the second is to describe those human character traits – vices – which give rise to those actions as evil. The third and final step is to describe people dominated by their vices as evil: 'there are people in whose characters some traits acquire dominance, and the preponderance of their actions is attributable to these dominant traits. Such people become notable examples of certain ways of being and acting. If the dominant character traits are vices, then their agents are regular sources of evil. In another derivative sense, we can then identify them, and not merely their actions and character traits, as evil' (Kekes 1990: 48).

For Kekes, then, evil can be part of human character – it makes sense to describe certain people as evil. We have to keep in mind, though, that evil is only part of human character in a derivative sense. The primary sense is undeserved harm suffered by people. At this stage we should note that we are not *compelled* to take the steps Kekes describes, from the evil of undeserved harm to the evil of the people who cause it. For Kekes, we take those steps because there is a good moral reason for doing so, and I will look at that reason more closely below. A second issue to keep in mind is that Kekes is not suggesting a specific character trait called evil – an evil person is dominated by a number of vices, and it does not make sense, in Kekes' scheme, to identify a particular vice called evil. And third, Kekes' aim here is to justify moral description, not psychological explanation; the primary task is moral condemnation: 'from the point of view of understanding evil, the primary factor is that many people have vices of which evil actions are the predictable outcome; how they come to have their vices is secondary' (Kekes 1990: 7). 'Psychologising', therefore, is beside the point. However, we should note that 'because they are evil' is a coherent explanation of why a person caused undeserved harm within Kekes' scheme, and so in a sense he cannot avoid an element of psychological explanation. Much of his book is taken up with explaining how people can come to have particular character traits and how those traits can give rise to particular kinds of actions – evil ones. This looks to me like a psychological explanation. Kekes would not deny this, I suspect, but he would insist that this is a secondary element. The first and foremost point of his theory is not to allow us to explain why people perform evil actions, but to allow us to condemn them *as* evil, to make the discourse of evil a coherent and essential part of a secular account of humanity. The fact that it also offers a psychological explanation for evil is a side effect.

Although Kekes rejects the notion of moral luck (Kekes 1990: 14), his scheme follows from the discussion of it because he acknowledges that people do not choose their character traits. This is precisely the problem of constitutive luck, but Kekes holds that how people's characters come to be constituted raises few important moral questions. What he draws out of the problem is that the vast majority of evil actions are in fact unchosen, in the sense that they arise from character traits that are unchosen: 'much of the evil that jeopardizes human aspiration to live good lives is caused by characteristic but unchosen actions of human beings' (Kekes 1990: 6). These people 'do not *choose* to act in these ways'; instead, they 'spontaneously and naturally respond according to habitual patterns ingrained in their characters' (Kekes 1990: 6). But how, then, can we morally condemn the agents who carry out such actions? We can do this, says Kekes, if we reject what he calls the soft reaction to evil, which is based on an erroneous choice-morality, and instead take the hard reaction, which is based on character-morality. For Kekes, three kinds of human agents perform evil actions. The first are moral monsters: 'people who habitually choose to cause undeserved harm' (Kekes 1990: 84). The second are people who choose to perform evil actions but are not moral monsters – in fact they are not evil at all because their actions 'do not stem from the agents' characters; they are, rather, infrequent and uncharacteristic actions responding to strong provocation, stressful circumstances, or considerable temptation, or they are the symptoms of the agents' being disturbed, overpowered by some strong emotion, or unable to think clearly' (Kekes 1990: 84). These agents are acting out of character 'and this serves to weaken our condemnation of them' (Kekes 1990: 85). Such agents cannot be described as evil. Moral monsters *are* evil, because they regularly choose to cause others to suffer undeserved harms, but such people are rare because being a moral monster is very difficult. Legal sanctions and social pressures force most potential moral monsters into hypocrisy or self-deception. Hypocritical moral monsters know what they are doing but they conceal it from others, and this is very hard (Kekes 1990: 84–5). 'I suppose there are such people, but the talents, if that is the word, required for living in this way are so exceptional as to make it unlikely that many would possess them' (Kekes 1990: 85). The true moral monster, then, is a rare and highly talented individual. The self-deceptive moral monster manages to 'convince themselves of the truth of some account that makes their habitual evildoing appear in an acceptable moral light' (Kekes 1990: 85). But the result of this is that they becomes examples of the third kind of evil agency, those people who bring about *unchosen* evil.

Kekes' central claim is that 'unchosen evil may still be moral and thus an appropriate subject for moral concern and, possibly, for moral censure' (Kekes 1990: 66). Such agents are unable to do otherwise, and yet the evil they cause is not accidental, 'because their evil actions follow from their unchosen vices, they are symptomatic of enduring dispositions, and they occur when they act naturally and spontaneously, in accordance with vices they have developed but without choosing to develop them' (Kekes 1990: 66). On the one hand, we have to recognise that a large part of human character is produced through factors over which we have little or no control, and that this part has an enormous influence over what we are able to choose to do, making it debatable whether we are really choosing at all (Kekes 1990: 66). On the other hand, such unchosen character traits are appropriate subjects for moral condemnation (Kekes 1990: 67). But before we see how Kekes proposes to make these two statements fit together in one coherent moral scheme, we have to understand how he thinks actions can be unchosen.

For an action to be chosen certain very general conditions have to be in place. These are: (1) having the capacity to make a decision to bring about certain results; (2) having the belief that the action will achieve those results; (3) the absence of force preventing the action; (4) the capacities to aim at the results, perform the action, and, importantly, to choose some other action; (5) an understanding of the situation within which we act. Complications can occur with any of these conditions. So, for example, we may decide to bring about impossible results (condition 1), or the belief that a particular action will bring about a specific result is absurd (condition 2); force can take many subtle forms preventing us from undertaking the action (condition 3); the agent may feel that they have no option left, and that the proposed action is the *only* thing they can do (condition 4); or the agent may have a poor understanding of their situation (condition 5). 'In all these cases, the conditions of choice shade into lack of choice' (Kekes 1990: 69). Although there may be examples that are not clearly chosen or unchosen, Kekes believes that there are still clear cases of unchosen actions and these are the subject of his discussion: 'Actions are clearly unchosen if the agents did not decide to perform them, if they had no strong reason to believe that the actions would produce the results they did produce, if they were forced to perform the actions, if they were psychologically incapable of doing anything else, or if they lacked understanding of their situations' (Kekes 1990: 69).

The unchosen actions which are central to his project are those that produce undeserved harm and which occur systematically. Such actions arise because agents have certain character traits which are vices. Kekes goes on to discuss a number of such vices and the most interesting is his treatment of malevolence. He admits that malevolence is puzzling because while other vices generally aim to prioritise one's own wants and desires over others, malevolence has no positive purpose at all. 'It is a disposition to act contrary to what is good. Its emotional source is ill will, a desire for things not to go well' (Kekes 1990: 79), and it manifests itself as hate, resentment, envy, jealousy, rage, vindictiveness, cruelty and cynicism. The puzzle is that these are not pleasant feelings to have and acting on them does not improve the situation for the agent. 'So, if malevolent feelings are unpleasant, likely to be causally inefficacious, and detrimental to reasonable responses, then why would reasonable people allow themselves to be motivated by them?' (Kekes 1990: 79–80). However, says Kekes, this is only puzzling if we suppose that malevolent people choose their malevolence. 'To remove the puzzle, we need to understand how people can be malevolent and act malevolently without choice' (Kekes 1990: 80). Malevolence arises from a condition of oppression and consists of a response to that oppression of 'saying no to life – to their own, to the lives of people like them, and certainly to the lives of those who adversely judge them' (Kekes 1990: 80). This is 'a hate filled, resentful, enraged, no' (Kekes 1990: 80) which manifests itself in various actions: 'Casual vandalism, senseless crime, random violence, desecration of symbols, indifference to consequences due to contempt for self-interest, and delight in cruelty . . .' (Kekes 1990: 81). But this is not conscious choice – these

people 'have no choice left' (Kekes 1990: 81). They need an out-
let for their destructive feelings, and any object to hand will do,
including themselves. 'Such people do not choose malevolence.
They are overpowered by it; it is something that happens to them'
(Kekes 1990: 81). They are not moral monsters: 'they have not set
out to be evil and to do evil'; instead there is a lack of control here,
in that 'whether people are able to exercise control is often not a
matter within their control' (Kekes 1990: 83).

But given this account of how people are driven to harm and destroy through forces behind their control, how are we to respond
morally? It is here that the disagreement between the soft reaction
and the hard reaction to evil becomes most acute. For Kekes, the
soft reaction seeks 'to excuse the agents', while the hard reaction
seeks 'to censure them' (Kekes 1990: 86). Behind the soft reaction
lies choice-morality, the view that people are only morally responsible for what they choose, and so can only be morally responsible
for evil if they rationally and consciously choose it (Kekes 1990:
86–7). And so if Kekes is right that the vast majority of evil is
caused by unchosen actions, we cannot condemn the agents who
cause it. 'Their *actions* may be evil, but their actions do not reflect on them, because they have not chosen to perform them'
(Kekes 1990: 88). Three assumptions underlie this moral theory:
first, that 'the domain of morality coincides with the domain of
choice'; second, that all human agents have the capacity to choose
freely and therefore all possess the same moral worth; and third
that humans 'are basically good' (Kekes 1990: 88). This final principle is fundamental to choice-morality. 'Evil is not a constituent
of human nature but a corruption of it. Human beings cannot lose
their worth because their potential for good is basic, while their
potential for evil is merely a by-product of something going wrong'
(Kekes 1990: 88). All the features of choice-morality are plausible,
says Kekes, but are mistakenly generalised, and what this general-
isation obscures is that 'within human beings the evil-producing
essential conditions of life exist in a state of tension with the aspiration to live good lives. As a result, both chosen and unchosen
actions can systematically produce evil; lives dominated by such
patterns have less worth than lives that are beneficially directed;
and whether the primary potential of individual moral agents is
for good or for evil is an open question' (Kekes 1990: 88–9).

The recognition of all this leads us to character-morality, according to which 'the central question is what sort of person we
ought to *be*' (Kekes 1990: 91). Moral praise and blame are not

primarily about what we do but about what kind of person we are. Character-morality does take seriously the moral principle that ought implies can, but while that principle takes a central place in choice-morality and leads to the emphasis on acquittal, in character-morality it takes a less central place and its role is to extenuate. If an action is unchosen then it is to be morally condemned, but less seriously than if it was chosen. The dispute here is over how we should judge people. 'Should we judge them on the basis of what they have become through their choices or on the basis of their characters independently of how they came to possess them?' (Kekes 1990: 92). For Kekes and character-morality it is the latter.

As a way of questioning the coherence of Kekes' version of character-morality we can first question the coherence of his attack upon choice-morality. His fundamental distinction is between evil produced by chosen actions and evil produced by unchosen actions, and he argues that the latter are the most widespread form of evil. As choice-morality says we cannot censure unchosen actions at all, this leaves us with no moral defence against the most widespread cause of human suffering, and so choice-morality is a failure. But this is to suppose that choice-morality would accept Kekes' distinction between chosen and unchosen actions and where the boundary between them lies, while, as Kekes acknowledges at one point, it may well be that the choice-moralist would reply that 'the idea of unchosen evil is incoherent' (Kekes 1990: 132). From the point of view of choice-morality, as I understand it, there are clear cases where a person is overwhelmed by uncontrollable forces, often psychological ones, and here the ought-implies-can principle clearly does lead us to acquit. However, the field of human action is complex, and there are degrees of responsibility and therefore degrees of culpability. Here the principle plays exactly the extenuating role that Kekes claims it can only carry within character-morality. An 'unchosen' action in Kekes' sense is both chosen and unchosen, and the judgement of responsibility and therefore moral blame has to be balanced between these elements. At one stage Kekes talks of *purely* unchosen evil. 'They habitually act the way they do, because they have been indoctrinated by a pernicious morality, or because they make an understandable mistake in their moral commitments, or because their character defects make them incapable of acting otherwise, or because they are distracted, inattentive, or lethargic due to physiological or psychological causes they are powerless to alter' (Kekes

1990: 132). But from the point of view of choice-morality, a purely unchosen *action* would have to be something like a case of uncontrollable compulsion, and such a condition *would* acquit the agent and this seems perfectly reasonable. The majority of unchosen actions that Kekes describes would not count as pure in this sense. Indeed, much of Kekes' critique of choice-morality rests on this assumption that it would accept his category of unchosen actions. There are no good reasons why it should accept it, and many good reasons why it should not.

Another central principle of choice-morality which Kekes attacks is that all human agents have equal moral worth (Kekes 1990: 106). The capacity for choice confers equal and universal moral worth on all agents who possess it, and so agents of unchosen evil do not lose their worth. 'They may cause evil, but they have not chosen it, so their actions cannot reflect adversely on the source of their worth, which is their capacity to choose' (Kekes 1990: 106). Again, this assumes that we accept Kekes' distinction here. However, he then goes further to assert that choice-morality asserts that evil people 'have the same human worth and deserve the same treatment as benefactors of humanity', an 'absurd consequence' – how can Hitler and Einstein have 'equal human worth' (Kekes 1990: 121)? But my reading of choice-morality is very different – it asserts that all humans have a basic moral worth which is equal and universal and based on the capacity to choose, but it allows that people can make morally good or bad choices, and so it allows for different moral status, depending on what they choose. There is a moral baseline below which I cannot go in condemning and punishing immorality – any condemnation or punishment must take into account the fact that human agents are capable of free and rational choice, and must *respect* that moral status. But respecting it does not entail that we treat 'evil' people in exactly the same way as 'benefactors of humanity'; rather, we punish them *as* a chooser, not as an object. Significantly, this allows for the possibility of redemption. As Kant, the primary choice-moralist, observes, human agents, whatever they do, are 'still capable of improvement', and 'there remains hope of a return to the good...' (Kant 1960: 39; Kekes 1990: 107). And so again any punishment or condemnation must take into account the fact that the wrongdoer is capable of redemption. Kekes, on the other hand, argues that it seems 'reasonable and morally right that people with long patterns of evil conduct should not receive the same protection of their rights to freedom and welfare as people who have not shown themselves to be undeserving' (Kekes 1990: 122). He then lists how treatment should differ, but these are differences the choice-moralist would not dispute and which make perfect sense in the context of a choice-morality, except for one, where he asserts that 'school lunches should be more nutritious than prison lunches' (Kekes 1990: 122). It is in this perhaps throwaway remark that the harshness – and inhumanity – of Kekes' hard response becomes clear. The lives of people with evil characters have less worth than others: these *people* have less worth than others.

As I pointed out above, Kekes condemns the tendency to 'psychologise' about evil, and part of the virtue of character-morality is that it will reduce this tendency. He argues that if someone does something bad to us we have a tendency to try and understand their motives, because 'evil deeds and their agents cry out for an explanation' in a way that good deeds and their agents do not (Kekes 1990: 231). We see evil as an anomaly, and so 'we look at the motivation of evil-producing agents not merely to understand them but to remove the anomaly that threatens to undermine the assumption of our sensibility that the pattern of human conduct tends toward the good and that evil is a deviation from it' (Kekes 1990: 231). He complains about the 'epidemic of specious speculation about human motivation' (Kekes 1990: 231), the aim of which is to make evil less threatening: 'once we can tell an intelligible story, we feel better because we suppose ourselves to have understood what has gone wrong' (Kekes 1990: 232). Instead, we should reject the view that human agents are primarily good and that evil is always a corruption of that primary goodness. Instead, human nature is mixed, and 'contains a mixture of good and evil potentialities' (Kekes 1990: 142).

However, despite this mixed view and the argument that understanding evil is secondary to minimising it, Kekes has supplied an understanding of why people perform evil actions that is in fact very useful in seeking to minimise it, and in the end his account of why people perform evil actions rests on a negativity, a lack, rather than simply the positive presence of evil character traits. One of his examples is of Colonel Kurtz from Joseph Conrad's *The Heart of Darkness*. Kurtz has a destructive trait in his character, and we have to recognise that this 'barbaric and life-diminishing force of evil ... is an active force within us' (Kekes 1990: 25). If we recognise this and understand it, then we can restrain it. If Kurtz had a better understanding of his own character 'he would have known about its presence and motivating force' (Kekes 1990: 186). This would not have enabled him to remove the character trait, as it was part of him, but it would have enabled him to avoid placing himself in contexts where it became an overwhelming compulsion. This moral understanding is 'an action-guiding force that can, in some cases, minimize, neutralize, or override the expression of destructiveness' (Kekes 1990: 187). It makes it possible 'to erect obstacles, strengthen defenses, to remove the opportunities for and the temptations of destructiveness' (Kekes 1990: 187). Through this 'reflective self-modification' (Kekes 1990: 211) we can gain 'a greater clarity about our intentions, a growing impetus to develop capacities that enable us to choose, and a better understanding of our situation' (Kekes 1990: 207). And so while understanding evil, both in others and ourselves, is secondary to morally censuring those who produce it, we can see that understanding is a crucial aspect of Kekes' project. In the end Kekes' claim is that moral censure takes priority because it is far more effective in minimising evil. We can question the extent to which this is true. It seems more reasonable to see understanding and censure as partners in that project, and emphasising one over the other in the appropriate circumstances – even when one should clearly have priority, it would seem odd to exclude the other altogether.

There is one more puzzle in Kekes' account here. He argues that if we have a correct understanding of ourselves, we will seek to control and restrain our destructive aspects – we shall seek to minimise the evil we cause as well as that caused by others. But if human nature is a genuine mixture of good and evil traits, why would we choose to pursue the good over the evil however much we understand ourselves? This can only make sense if we suppose that rational human agents blessed with this kind of understanding will choose good over evil, which is to suppose that human agents are primarily good, that evil comes about through a corruption of that nature. Any sensible approach to moral character will surely acknowledge that human agents have a mixed nature and are capable of pursuing harm as well as benefiting others, but there is nothing incoherent in supposing that they will, in normal circumstances and with reasonable information, choose to minimise the harm they cause, as Kekes himself acknowledges. In the end, there is no great difference between choice-morality and Kekes' version of character-morality – the version of choice-morality he attacks is a very odd one. Equally nothing persuades me that there is much to be gained from condemning human agents as evil. There is something to be gained from acknowledging that human agents are capable of pursuing the suffering of others, but what we gain is not that certain human agents are evil and must be avoided and condemned, but that we, as human agents, are capable of doing the same under similar circumstances. And this is not a deeply pessimistic conclusion to reach. First, it makes such actions understandable – they do not come out of the blue, nor are they committed by some distinct group of humans who are in some sense less than human (as Kekes' evil characters seem to be). They are committed by people like us. Second, because we know that under similar situations we are capable of choosing to do such dreadful things to others, we also know that we are capable of choosing *not* to do them. And if those who actually have chosen them *are* people like us, then they were equally capable of not choosing them. They are, therefore, redeemable. By bringing 'evil' into the realm of the human, by humanising evil, we find that it can be opposed and defeated.

Part of the problem may be with a level of 'folk psychology' in the treatment of constitutive luck. Nagel defines it in terms of character traits such as greed, envy, cowardice, vanity, and so on, and this is how Rescher takes the discussion forward, talking of people being 'venial by disposition'. Kekes offers a more subtle picture which gives a sympathetic account of how people acquire these character traits but reaches an extremely unsympathetic conclusion. I observed in the conclusion to the previous chapter that arguments about moral luck take place at an extremely psychologically unsophisticated level, and that what emerges if we take a more serious view is that people are constituted into criminality, for example, by specific patterns of factors – we cannot simply say that someone is 'venial by disposition' and assume, at the extreme, that they were born that way, or that their criminality was somehow innate in their nature awaiting to emerge when the right conditions were in place. If the conditions are in place children are at risk of developing criminal behaviour, and the difference between those that do and those that do not has nothing to do with some criminal trait they were born with. What we are confronted with here is a crude, primitive model of psychological explanation which tries to explain why people steal, lie, commit violent acts in terms of their moral character without asking how they came to have this character. Kekes, oddly, does ask how they come to have this character and gives a reasonable answer to the question, only to dismiss this understanding. For him, constitutive luck carries little moral significance, when his argument cries out that it should have a central place.

Claudia Card shows us how we can take constitutive moral luck seriously, but in doing so changes its meaning. Her focus is on factors that have an impact on moral character: 'different combinations of circumstances in fact provide opportunities for, stimulate, nurture, or discourage the development of different virtues and vices, strengths and weaknesses of character' (Card 1996: ix); moral luck for her, then, is to do with the way in which background conditions contribute to the development of a person's moral character, such that we have to understand that character in the context of those conditions; moral luck therefore describes the extent to which one has been lucky or unlucky in the development of moral character. She argues that 'appreciating the impact of luck on our lives can add depth to our understanding of responsibility and increase our sense of morality's importance' (Card 1996: 21). The realisation of the extent to which factors beyond people's control shape their choices and character has a moral impact on the person who realises it, but a quite different one to that proposed by Kekes. 'It moves me toward humility and mercy, virtues that acknowledge the unfairness of life but also presuppose a morally structured context of interaction' (Card 1996: 22). Rather than make moral responsibility an irrelevance, it makes it central to our concerns. Williams, Nagel and others take a particular perspective of the problem, looking 'down and back, from relatively privileged standpoints and towards the past, focusing on such things as praise, blame, regret, punishment, and reward – the last two, historically, prerogatives of the powerful exercised for social control' (Card 1996: 23). She says we should look 'forward and up, towards the future and from the standpoints of those struggling to put their lives together' (Card 1996: 23). From this perspective it is more important to *take* responsibility rather than to attribute it. 'I am interested, from the agent's forward-looking perspective, in the implications for taking responsibility for oneself of a history of bad moral luck, such as comes with a history of child abuse or a heritage of oppression' (Card 1996: 24). This is to recognise a 'basic lack of justice in our ability to be moral' (Card 1996: 29), and to focus on the forward-looking struggle for integrity – 'wholeness, completeness, undividedness...' (Card 1996: 32). If we return to Jon Venables and Robert Thompson for the moment, our realisation that these were two damaged, broken children gives us a concern for their future, and the ways in which they can be assisted to become whole, to gain moral integrity. One important step is to allow that it is *possible* for them to gain moral integrity, to be redeemed, and it is precisely this possibility which is denied them by those who characterise them as evil little monsters. Even within Kekes' more subtle treatment, the possibilities of reform and redemption are marginalised.

Conclusion

Two objections to my critique of the discourse of evil still have to be faced. The first is that I am dismissing all human wrongdoing, or at least the kind of extreme wrongdoing that gets characterised as evil, as a form of sickness. Philip Hallie expresses this objection: 'The whole tendency of current historical thought – about slavery, about what happened in the third empire of Hitler, about psychological analysis, about philosophic work on good and evil – all of these things conspire to flatten out evil and make it a kind of sickness. That means, if somebody's done some destructive work – sick, sick, sick – the person is thought of as a patient in a hospital. How can you blame someone who is sick? How can you become angry at somebody who is sick?' (Hallie 1988: 62). 'Sick' here is a 'vague, vast metaphor' (Hallie 1988: 62). One obvious reply to this objection is that 'evil' is a vague, vast metaphor, and to ask to what extent claiming that these people are evil, evil, evil, is any improvement? The second reply is to point out that not all people who carry out extreme acts of violence are 'sick'; some undoubtedly are psychologically disturbed, but nothing I have said here implies that all the subjects we have discussed are mentally sick in anyway. What I *have* said is that some of these subjects are in situations which close off their options and make certain actions seem like the most obvious available to them, such as killing someone. And that in those cases we can properly ask whether the background situation was so overwhelming in contributing to what they did that it provides some degree of excuse, so that we cannot hold them fully morally responsible for what they did. This, I have argued and will continue to argue, is a coherent and meaningful approach. And so although I have labelled it the 'psychological' approach, I do not mean by this that all those who fall under it are psychologically disturbed, and that the choice is between Evil and Sickness. There are many other ways in which we can understand how background factors significantly contribute to wrongdoing to such an extent that moral condemnation of the wrongdoer becomes questionable.

The second objection is, I think, more serious. The question has been whether we should describe people as evil, and this is a moral as well as a psychological problem because it raises the question of moral responsibility. The objection to my account is that, in trying to understand the psychological, social, cultural factors that play a significant role in contributing to serious wrongdoing so that we can try to explain why people do dreadful things, we are finding excuses. There is a French saying, 'tout comprendre, c'est tout pardonner' – to understand all is to forgive all – which suggests that understanding and excusing are tightly connected. The more we understand, the less we can condemn. The corollary is, as we have seen, that in order to condemn, the less we need to understand. The examination of the case of Venables and Thompson does suggest that the project of understanding is closely tied to excusing. The whole point of looking at it in such detail was to argue that they should not have been held morally responsible to the extent that they were. If we apply this approach to adults then we end up with the kind of generalised moral scepticism that arose from Thomas Nagel's account of moral luck. In closing the space for the discourse of evil, I close the space for any kind of moral judgement.

But this is a mistake. The first point to make in reply is that we are looking at cases that people regard as examples of human evil. These are extreme cases and I do not intend to generalise what I say about them to every kind of moral wrongdoing. The discourse of evil itself picks out these extreme cases, and what seems to be the unifying theme is that they lie beyond human understanding. As Alison Young commented in the previous chapter, these are events that both demand and prohibit interpretation. It is within the space created by the failure to interpret that the discourse of evil takes root. With lesser kinds of wrongdoing interpretation does not fail – we can understand them and explain them perfectly well, and at the same time morally condemn them. The fact is that we are not baffled by these lesser forms of wrongdoing – if people lie or cheat we can perfectly well understand why they did it, and we do not feel that our capacity to morally censure them is lessened because of that understanding. Here I *do* want to generalise, but in the other direction – if we attend to the severe cases then we can, with sufficient effort, understand and explain them, and so make the discourse of evil redundant. The objection is that in attempting to understand them we condone them, but if this does not follow with lesser immorality, why should it follow for greater immorality? It could, of course, be replied that lesser immorality is as incomprehensible as the greater immorality is supposed to be, but this is surely unconvincing.

There is, of course, a play on the word 'understanding' here. In *Roget's Thesaurus* it appears in several places, one of which is 'pacification', alongside such words as 'conciliation' and 'reconciliation'. But it also appears under 'intelligibility' and 'comprehension' as opposed to 'unintelligibility' and 'incomprehension'. The objection to my account takes the first meaning, while I intend the second. My claim is that such actions, however terrible, are comprehensible. Comprehension may lead to reconciliation with the wrongdoer, but it may also lead to condemnation. In understanding how in some situations particular background factors can act as excuses for what a person has done we can also understand how, in other situations, they can not. There is a moral boundary here – a highly complex one, but it exists. It is the alternative to the boundary posed by the discourse of evil between humanity and inhumanity. The boundary I am posing here is much more complex, and is to do with understanding how background conditions contribute to an action, understanding a person's reasons for choosing a particular action over others given these conditions, and judging the extent to which there were more reasonable options available to that person which they should have considered and should have chosen. This is very much a choice-morality, and it focuses on the responsibility people have for making a particular choice. One aspect of this judgement is how easy or hard it was for a person to choose a particular option given their situation.

We can, therefore, understand the context in which a person acted, their reasons for acting, their mental condition, their past history, and so on – but this understanding not only provides grounds for excusing, it also provides the grounds for condemning. Without such a grounding our condemnation has no basis. We saw in Chapter 1 that, according to David Pocock, in 'primitive' societies there is a belief 'in creatures who are and are not human beings, at once within and beyond the limits of humanity' (Pocock 1985: 48), the paradoxically not human. Because motives of truly evil people are beyond understanding they cannot be judged: 'the evil act itself is beyond the comprehension of human justice' (Pocock 1985: 52). While Hannah Arendt thought she could give some account of the 'banal' evil of Adolf Eichmann, the 'radical' evil of the arch-Nazis were beyond the powers of normal moral judgement. 'All we know is that we can neither punish nor forgive such offenses and that they therefore transcend the realm of human affairs...' (Arendt 1958: 241).

Excusing and punishing therefore *both* rest on the foundation of understanding, and my claim is that this is possible even for the most severe cases that seem to prohibit it. Perhaps the nature of the prohibition is precisely the thought that understanding implies forgiveness and these acts cannot be forgiven. But this is a mistaken thought. Bearing witness to these horrific acts is difficult, but with understanding we can begin to speak about them. However unspeakable they may appear, they must be put into words. Friedrich Nietzsche makes the point in *Twilight of the Idols* when he says that: 'One has to learn to *see*, one has to learn to *think*, one has to learn to *speak* and *write*...' (Nietzsche 1968: 65). And 'Learning to *see* – habituating the eye to repose, to patience, to letting things come to it; learning to defer judgement, to investigate and comprehend the individual case in all its aspects... Learning to *see*, as I understand it, is almost what is called in unphilosophical language "strong will-power": the essence of it is precisely *not* to "will", the *ability* to defer decision' (Nietzsche 1968: 65). What the project of understanding demands is not excusing people for what they have done, but that we defer judgement and decision, and what is truly disturbing about the case of Venables and Thompson, and many others like them, is not primarily that they were judged and condemned (although the fact that they were judged and condemned as adults is truly disturbing), but the *rush* to judgement. The media and the public had already decided that these were evil little monsters, and one suspicion has to be that the trial was arranged to confirm that judgement. In that moment we became one of Pocock's 'primitive societies'. Nietzsche is surely profoundly right that the ability to defer judgement and decision in these cases takes an immense power of will.

And so the opposition between human understanding and moral condemnation is mistaken – moral condemnation is only possible on the basis of human understanding. If we reject the possibility of moral monsters then the challenge is that any such action can be understood and explained, and we can reject the charge that in seeking to understand and explain we are seeking to excuse. However, it can still be objected that in understanding and explaining these cases some degree of excuse is involved, in that we are excusing the perpetrators of being evil. But even this is a misunderstanding – we are not excusing them of being evil at all; we are rejecting evil as a category that can meaningfully be applied to human beings. We can still condemn such people to the fullest extent of our judgement, but the crucial and deeply ethical point is that we must condemn them as human beings, not as moral monsters. The deeply *unethical* aspect of the discourse of evil is that it closes any space for future redemption. In the previous chapter we saw Sean Sexton, the solicitor representing the Bulger family, condemn Venables and Thompson as evil and conclude that they should never be released because they were 'irredeemable'. The rejection of the discourse of evil does not rule out moral condemnation and legal punishment of the most extreme kind, but it does rule out the notion that such people are irredeemable. However, my claim that actions of the most extreme immorality can be both understood and morally condemned has to be tested against one of the most troubling examples in human history which stand against it, the Holocaust.

Chapter Eight

Facing the Holocaust

Introduction

Elie Wiesel was sent to Birkenau in April 1944, at the age of fifteen. He also spent time in Auschwitz, Monowitz and Buchenwald. His mother and younger sister were killed in Auschwitz, and his father was killed in Buchenwald shortly before it was liberated by the American army in April 1945. He has written a series of novels and other work in response to his experiences, and he presents two serious challenges to those who want to write about the Holocaust. The first is the problem for those of us who were not there. 'Ask any survivor and he will tell you, and his children will tell you. He or she who did not live through the event will never know it' (Wiesel 1990: 7). Indeed, can anyone comprehend it? Eve Garrard and Geoffrey Scarre comment in the introduction to their book, *Moral Philosophy and the Holocaust* (Garrard and Scarre 2003), that for some 'the fundamental non-rationality of the Holocaust made comprehending it impossible. To understand human actions is to map them within the space of reasons, yet the happenings at Auschwitz are for ever beyond that space' (Garrard and Scarre 2003: ix). We can ask further whether we *ought* to seek to understand the Holocaust. 'Wouldn't a contemplative, pain-filled silence be much more proper? Interpreting the moral dimensions of the Holocaust may seem to be something that we could not do if we would, and should not attempt if we could' (Garrard and Scarre 2003: ix–x). The Holocaust is the primary event which, in Alison Young's terms, 'both calls for and prohibits interpretation' (Young 1996: 112). And here we face once more the suspicion that 'attempts to comprehend Nazi deeds are tantamount to attempts to excuse them', that 'explanations are exculpations' (Garrard and Scarre 2003: x). Garrard and Scarre say this is 'very disputable' (Garrard and Scarre 2003: x), and their book contains a series of essays that seek understanding of the Holocaust. The writers whose ideas I explore in this chapter face up to this accusation and also reject it. Christopher Browning, whose book *Ordinary Men: Reserve Police Battalion 101 and the Final Solution in Poland* (Browning 2001) raises the disturbing problem that the people who carried out the killings could have chosen not to do so without penalty, observes: 'The policemen in the battalion who carried out the massacres and deportations, like the much smaller number who refused or evaded, were human beings. I must recognize that in the same situation, I could have been a killer or an evader – both were human – if I want to understand and explain the behaviour of both as best I can. This recognition does indeed mean an attempt to empathize. What I do not accept, however, are the old clichés that to explain is to excuse, to understand is to forgive. Explaining is not excusing; understanding is not forgiving' (Browning 2001: xviii). To refuse to demonise is not to forgive, and indeed, says Browning, the possibility of history rests on understanding. To demonise those who perpetrated the Holocaust is to refuse to face the lessons of history. Robert J. Lifton is perhaps less confident in his book, *The Nazi Doctors: Medical Killing and the Psychology of Genocide* (Lifton 1986), and quotes one Holocaust survivor who told him: 'The professor would like to understand what is not understandable. We ourselves who were there, and who have always asked ourselves the question and will ask it until the end of our lives, we will never understand it, because it cannot be understood' (Lifton 1986: 13). Lifton nevertheless believes we must try to understand – in doing so, though, we must just allow that 'certain events elude our full understanding, and we do best to acknowledge that a partial grasp, a direction of understanding, is the best that can be expected of any approach' (Lifton 1986: 13). The disturbing truth that must be understood is, he says, 'the ordinariness of most Nazi doctors I had interviewed' (Lifton 1986: 4). The fact is that 'they were by no means the demonic figures – sadistic, fanatic, lusting to kill – people have often thought them to be' (Lifton 1986: 4–5); and we have to face 'the disturbing psychological truth that participation in mass murder need not require emotions as extreme or demonic as would seem appropriate for such a malignant project' (Lifton 1986: 5). The lesson of history is that 'ordinary people can commit demonic acts' (Lifton 1986: 5).

The second of Wiesel's challenges is that the primary subject of many texts, including this chapter, are the victimisers not the victims. Wiesel comments: 'If the victims are my problem the killers are not. The killers are someone else's problem, not mine' (Wiesel 1990: 17). However, those of us who were not there do have the task of understanding what happened, even if we can never know it, and Wiesel does believe that the victimisers have to be understood, if not by him, then by someone else. 'Somebody will have to explain why so many killers were intellectuals, academicians, college professors, lawyers, engineers, physicians, theologians' (Wiesel 1990: 17). And there is a third challenge to be faced – that of all human atrocities the Holocaust comes closest to the mythology of evil, closest to a vision of hell. If diabolical evil existed anywhere in human history, surely it existed here. Here, surely, everything is in black and white.

The Grey Zone

But even in the Holocaust, there are what Primo Levi described as 'grey zones', where judgement becomes complex and difficult, and he warns against the rush to condemn. Levi's concern is primarily with those prisoners, both Jews and non-Jews, who collaborated in some way with their oppressors, and the difficulty, perhaps impossibility, in condemning them for doing so. Levi, who died in Turin in 1987 – either in a tragic accidental fall or a suicide – was a member of the Italian anti-Fascist resistance, captured and deported to Auschwitz in 1944, and liberated by the Russian army in January 1945. In his last book, *The Drowned and the Saved*, he says of Auschwitz: 'The inside of the Lager was an intricate and stratified microcosm; the "grey zone" ... that of the prisoners who in some measure, perhaps with good intentions, collaborated with the authority, was not negligible, indeed it constituted a phenomenon of fundamental importance for the historian, the psychologist and the sociologist' (Levi 1989: 9). The fact was that 'the first threats, the first insults, the first blows did not come from the SS but from other prisoners, from "colleagues", from those mysterious personages who nevertheless wore the same striped tunic that they, the new arrivals, had just put on' (Levi 1989: 9). Levi warns against the 'Manichean tendency' to oversimplify history into the 'we' and the 'they' (Levi 1989: 22). The history of the Holocaust shares 'the tendency, indeed the need, to separate good from evil' (Levi 1989: 23). But 'the network of human relationships in the Lagers was not simple: it could not be reduced to the two blocs of victims and persecutors' (Levi 1989: 23). The new arrivals to the Lager expected to find 'a terrible but decipherable world, in conformity to that simple model which we atavistically carry within us – "we" inside and the enemy outside, separated by a sharply defined geographical frontier' (Levi 1989: 23). Instead: 'The world into which one was precipitated was terrible, yes, but also indecipherable: it did not conform to any model, the enemy was all around but also inside, the "we" lost its limits, the contenders were not two, one could not discern a single frontier but rather many confused, perhaps innumerable frontiers, which stretched between each of us' (Levi 1989: 23).

Levi asks how we should judge those prisoners – both Jewish and non-Jewish – who in some degree cooperated with the murderous system that was oppressing them. First, there were the low-level functionaries, whom Levi absolves of responsibility: 'sweepers, kettle washers, night-watchmen, bed smoothers ... checkers of lice and scabies, messengers, interpreters, assistants' assistants' (Levi 1989: 29). These were people who, 'for an extra half-litre of soup, were willing to carry out these and other "tertiary" functions: innocuous, sometimes useful, often invented out of nothing' (Levi 1989: 29). But judgement becomes more difficult when it comes to those in commanding positions, such as the *Kapos* (who were mainly – but not all – non-Jewish) who ran labour squads, the barrack chiefs, clerks and people who worked in the administrative offices. Some of these, especially the latter, were members of secret defence organisations, but the great majority were not, and their power to impose violence was unlimited, and so 'it was not unusual for a prisoner to be beaten to death by a *Kapo*' (Levi 1989: 31). Still, in judging them we face a problem. 'Even if one did not want to take into account the infernal environment into which they had been abruptly flung, it is illogical to demand of them, and it is rhetorical and false to maintain that they all and always followed, the behaviour expected of saints and stoic philosophers. In reality, in the enormous majority of cases, their behaviour was rigidly preordained. In the space of a few weeks or months the deprivation to which they were subjected led them to a condition of pure survival, a daily struggle against hunger, cold, fatigue and blows in which the room for choices (especially moral choices) was reduced to zero; among these, very few survived the test and this thanks to the coming together of many improbable events: in short, they were saved by luck' (Levi 1989: 33–4).

Most disturbing of all the figures among the victims were the *Sonderkommando*, an extreme case of collaboration which brought with it no privileges but rather certain death. The *Sonderkommando* ran the crematoria. 'It was their task to maintain order among the new arrivals...who must be sent into the gas chambers; to extract the corpses from the chambers, pull gold teeth from jaws, cut the women's hair, sort and classify clothes, shoes, and the contents of luggage; transport the bodies to the crematoria and oversee the operation of the ovens; extract and eliminate the ashes' (Levi 1989: 34). There were between 700 to 1,000 active at a time in Auschwitz, and each squad worked for a few months and was then replaced by a new one, but none of the old squad lived as the SS ensured there were no witnesses to this aspect of the programme: 'as its initiation the next squad burnt the corpses of its predecessors' (Levi 1989: 34). These squads were largely made up of Jews, very few of whom have survived. Apart from the last squad, which rebelled in October 1944 and blew up one of the crematoria and was exterminated in its struggle to revolt, how does one understand this level of cooperation? 'One is tempted to turn away with a grimace and close one's mind: this is a temptation one must resist. In fact, the existence of the squads had a meaning...' (Levi 1989: 37). Levi finds that meaning in the report of a football match between members of the SS and members of the *Sonderkommando* during a workbreak, with other members watching and cheering encouragement and taking bets on the result. 'Behind this armistice one hears Satanic laughter: it is consummated, we have succeeded, you are no longer the other race, the anti-race, the prime enemy of the millennial Reich: you are no longer the people who reject idols. We have embraced you, corrupted you, dragged you to the bottom with us. You are like us, you proud people, dirtied with your own blood, as we are. You too, like us and like Cain, have killed the brother. Come, we can play together' (Levi 1989: 38).

As for judgement, Levi concludes: 'I believe that no one is authorised to judge them, not those who lived through the experience of the Lager and even less those who did not live through it. I would invite anyone who dares pass judgement to carry out upon himself, with sincerity, a conceptual experiment: let him imagine, if he can, that he has lived for months or years in a ghetto, tormented by chronic hunger, fatigue, promiscuity and humiliation; that he has seen die around him, one by one, his beloved; that he is cut off from the world, unable to receive or transmit news; that, finally, he is loaded on to a train, eighty or a hundred persons to a boxcar; that he travels towards the unknown, blindly, for sleepless days and nights; and that he is at last flung inside the walls of an indecipherable inferno' (Levi 1989: 42). More generally, ' . . . an infernal order such as National Socialism was, exercises a frightful power of corruption, against which it is difficult to guard oneself. It degrades its victims and makes them similar to itself, because it needs both great and small complicities. To resist it a truly solid moral armature is needed' (Levi 1989: 49). We can wonder what we would have done in their situation, but never really know: 'nobody can know for how long and under what trials his soul can resist before yielding or breaking. Every human being possesses a reserve of strength whose extent is unknown to him: it can be large, small, or non-existent, and only extreme adversity makes it possible to evaluate it' (Levi 1989: 42–3). There can, therefore, be no rush to judgement in these cases: 'it is imprudent to hasten to issue a moral judgement. It must be clear that the greatest responsibility lies with the system, the very structure of the totalitarian state' (Levi 1989: 28). This is not to say that judgement is impossible here, but it is to say that it must be carefully considered, and should be one of compassion not condemnation.

Levi's question of judgement extends to the victimisers themselves. It is more difficult to include them within the grey zone, but still there is a 'paradoxical analogy between victim and oppressor' (Levi 1989: 12). Levi says that 'both are in the same trap, but it is the oppressor, and he alone, who has prepared it and activated it, and if he suffers for this, it is right he should suffer' (Levi 1989: 12). Certainly, says Levi: 'The oppressor remains what he is, and so does the victim. They are not interchangeable . . . but both, faced with the indecency of the act which has been irrevocably committed, need refuge and protection, and instinctively search for them. Not all, but most; and often for their entire lives' (Levi 1989: 13). And in the end, when we examine the victimiser, we reach the same conclusion: 'More often and more insistently as that time recedes, we are asked by the young who our "torturers" were, of what cloth were they made. The term torturers alludes to our ex-guardians, the SS, and is in my opinion inappropriate: it brings to mind twisted individuals, ill-born sadists, afflicted by an original flaw. Instead, they were made of our same cloth, they were average human beings, averagely intelligent, averagely wicked: save for exceptions, they were not monsters, they had our faces . . .' (Levi 1989: 169). We have to resist the temptation, therefore, to think that the perpetrators are twisted monsters we can detect in advance, or are born with some sign of evil already upon them. It is not that these monsters have our faces – it is that they are not monsters at all. How, then, are we to protect ourselves from them?

Ordinary Men

The problem of what motivates 'ordinary' people to commit 'demonic' acts has been extensively debated, and at the heart of that debate is the dispute between Daniel Goldhagen and Christopher Browning. Goldhagen's book, *Hitler's Willing Executioners: Ordinary Germans and the Holocaust* (Goldhagen 1997), was in part a reply to Browning's thesis that many of those who carried out the killings did not do so because they hated Jews and wanted to see them exterminated, but for a cluster of more 'banal' reasons. They were, says Browning, 'willing' but not 'genocidal executioners' (Browning 2001: 216). Goldhagen, however, rejects any attempt to explain away the genocidal motivation of ordinary Germans. It is not plausible 'that the perpetrators contributed to genocide because they were coerced, because they were unthinking, obedient executors of state orders, because of social psychological pressure, because of the prospects of personal advancement, or because they did not comprehend or feel responsible for what they were doing, owing to the putative fragmentation of the tasks' (Goldhagen 1997: 379). There could be no fear of retribution because there is no evidence of any German ever being executed or imprisoned for refusing to participate in the killing of Jews, and there is plenty of evidence that they knew this (Goldhagen 1997: 381). Germans cannot be characterised as routinely obeying orders as there are many examples where they did not, especially when it came to disobeying orders *not* to kill Jews (Goldhagen 1997: 381–3). The notion that peer pressure played a significant role may be true in a small number of cases, but Goldhagen points out that if we suppose it played the most significant role in pushing Germans into killing Jews it becomes incoherent – if the majority of Germans really did not want to kill Jews, that would have been the relevant peer pressure, not the other way around (Goldhagen 1997: 383–4). Career advancement was not an option for most of the perpetrators who were actually doing the killing (Goldhagen 1997: 384). And the argument that the Holocaust was a fragmented programme such that individuals did not know what was happening around them, and so could not understand the role they were playing, is 'fanciful' for both the face-to-face killers and the bureaucrats. 'Most of them understood perfectly well, and there is no reason to believe that those who did not would have acted otherwise had they more knowledge' (Goldhagen 1997: 385).

The argument seems to be, says Goldhagen, that the Germans had inner moral scruples opposed to the genocide which had to be overcome in order to get them to participate. If that is true we have to explain why the Germans would act against those inner scruples, and there is no such explanation available. This puzzle is solved, says Goldhagen, when we realise that there were no such inner scruples. 'Explanations proceeding in this manner cannot account for Germans taking initiative, doing more than they had to, or volunteering for killing duty when no such volunteering was necessary – all of which occurred routinely' (Goldhagen 1997: 385). Nor can it account for the extreme cruelty that was involved in the killing of the Jews, which was not present in the killing of other groups, such as the mentally ill or physically handicapped (Goldhagen 1997: 385–9). 'None of the conventional explanations can explain why the Germans did not take advantage of their ready opportunities either to avoid killing or to ameliorate Jewish suffering. None can explain why, by and large, the Germans did the opposite, producing unnecessary Jewish suffering and carrying out their lethal tasks with zeal and, for many, apparent eagerness' (Goldhagen 1997: 389). For Goldhagen there is only one explanation that can account for all of this – that the Germans, ordinary Germans, hated Jews to such an extent that they were happy to see them exterminated. 'The one explanation adequate to these tasks holds that a demonological antisemitism, of the virulent racial variety, was the common structure of the perpetrators' cognition and of German society in general. The German perpetrators, in this view, were assenting mass executioners, men and women who, true to their own eliminationist beliefs, faithful to their cultural antisemitic credo, considered the slaughter to be just' (Goldhagen 1997: 392–3). It was this deeply held eliminationist anti-Semitism which moved them to kill.

This version of anti-Semitism held that there was a Jewish conspiracy aimed at the destruction of Germany, a 'demonological view of Jews' which was 'common to German society' (Goldhagen 1997: 394). This conviction was so intensely held that they would 'accept the genocide as an appropriate "solution", if not the only "final solution to the Jewish Problem"' (Goldhagen 1997: 394). The conception of the Jew was of a 'terrestrial demon' (Goldhagen 1997: 398) and this explains the difference between the killing of the Jews and other programmes. Those who killed the mentally ill and severely handicapped were not eager or cruel, but 'the Germans' killing of the Jews was often wrathful, preceded and attended by cruelty, degradation, mockery, and Mephistophelean laughter' (Goldhagen 1997: 398). The Jews were demons and: 'Demons must be destroyed, after all' (Goldhagen 1997: 401). From this perspective the annihilation of the Jews '*made sense*' (Goldhagen 1997: 403). Goldhagen draws his most disturbing conclusion from the same evidence on which Browning based his own work, the records of Reserve Police Battalion 101. Because these were ordinary Germans, 'the conclusions drawn about the overall character of the members' actions can, indeed must be, generalized to *the German people in general*. What these *ordinary* Germans did also could have been expected of other *ordinary* Germans' (Goldhagen 1997: 402). In other words, any German would have done the same, not under duress, but because he or she wanted to.

For Goldhagen, while there were other causal factors in play which explain how the Holocaust happened, this 'virulent brand of German racial antisemitism' is sufficient by itself to explain the motivation of the killers: 'racial eliminationist antisemitism was a sufficient cause, a sufficiently potent motivator, to lead Germans to kill Jews willingly' (Goldhagen 1997: 417). But while Browning agrees with Goldhagen on the ordinariness of the Germans involved and on the high degree of voluntarism, he differs sharply on the motivation (Browning 2001: 192). Goldhagen is arguing that the Nazi regime was enabling the German people to do what they wanted to do, but Browning replies that the Nazi regime itself was significant in shaping German attitudes and behaviour (Browning 2001: 193). This is made plausible by what happened in Germany after 1945, when anti-Semitism became a much less significant element in German culture. And so 'if Germany's political culture in general and anti-Semitism in particular could be transformed after 1945 by changes in education, public conversation, law, and institutional reinforcements, as Goldhagen suggests, then it seems to me equally plausible that they could have been equally transformed in the three or four decades preceding 1945 and especially during the twelve years of Nazi rule' (Browning 2001: 193). Goldhagen identifies one all-encompassing kind of 'eliminationist' anti-Semitism, while in fact, says Browning, there were different types in play. Certainly Germany took a relatively distinct path which led to anti-Semitism playing an important role in political and cultural life. In the nineteenth century, says Browning, the German conservatives associated anti-Semitism with 'everything they felt threatened by' (Browning 2001: 195), and so it became 'an integral part of the conservative political platform', and became 'more politicized and institutionalized than in the western democracies of France, Britain, and the United States' (Browning 2001: 196). However, this anti-Semitic conservatism remained a minority view in the late nineteenth century, and even for these conservatives the Jews were not the major issue. Browning concludes that the Jewish 'problem' was of little interest to most Germans at the turn of the century (Browning 2001: 196–7). The series of disasters that beset Germany between 1912 and 1929 transformed politics in that country as the right grew in power and the influence of the radical right grew within it, with the National Socialist movement growing in importance until it came to power in 1933. But still, even this has to be kept in perspective. Their best electoral performance was 37 per cent, less than the socialist/communist vote in that election (Browning 2001: 197), and Browning observes that we do not know how many people voted for the National Socialist party for anti-Semitic reasons (Browning 2001: 198). He concludes that: 'Beginning in 1933 all the factors that Goldhagen credits with dismantling German anti-Semitism after 1945 . . . were operating in the opposite direction to intensify anti-Semitism among the Germans, and indeed in a far more concerted manner than in the post-war period' (Browning 2001: 198). It is more plausible that people were drawn to anti-Semitism because they were drawn to the Nazis, rather than the other way around.

After 1933 there were still different forms of anti-Semitism in German politics and culture. The German conservatives favoured Jewish de-emancipation and segregation, but 'it is unlikely that the conservatives on their own would have proceeded beyond the initial discriminatory measures of 1933–34' (Browning 2001: 199). As for the German people at large, the prevailing historical view is that anti-Semitism was not a priority. They did not oppose – indeed they approved of – the legal measures against Jews between 1933 and 1939, but there is evidence that they did not support violence against the Jews. On 9 November, 1938, ninety-one Jews were killed in a night of violence in Germany known as *Kristallnacht*, the night of broken glass. Tens of thousands of shops and homes were broken into, and 191 synagogues in Berlin were set on fire or otherwise destroyed. More than 30,000 Jews were arrested and sent to concentration camps, where thousands were murdered before the survivors were released (Gilbert 1987: 69–70). Browning argues that *Kristallnacht* had a negative impact on most of the German people and the Nazi leadership recognised that such overt violence had little support (Browning 2001: 199–200). Goldhagen recognises that *Kristallnacht* was unpopular, but reads criticisms of it as 'the limited criticism of an eliminationist path that the overwhelming majority of Germans considered to be fundamentally sound, but which, in the case, had taken a momentary wrong turn' (Goldhagen 1997: 102). For Browning, though, it is evidence that 'the anti-Semitic priorities and genocidal commitment of the regime were still not shared by ordinary Germans' (Browning 2001: 200). Certainly, it cannot be argued that the German population were 'indifferent' to the anti-Jewish programme being pursued, and historians have suggested other terms, such as 'passive complicity' and 'objective complicity' to describe their attitude. But, says Browning, 'I do not think that choice of language alters the basic point . . . namely that in terms of the priority of anti-Semitism and commitment to killing Jews a useful and important distinction can be made between the Nazi core and the population at large' (Browning 2001: 201).

How, then, did ordinary Germans become mass murderers of Jews? Browning points out that the Germans in eastern Europe were in the frontline of what was understood to be 'a "race war" of imperial conquest' (Browning 2001: 202) – an ideological crusade against Bolshevism which was a war of mass destruction, in which the rules that governed the war in the west did not hold. By the end of the Second World War, as well as six million Jews, more than ten million other non-combatants would be killed, including a quarter of a million Gypsies, tens of thousands of homosexuals, tens of thousands of those considered mentally defective, and several million Soviet prisoners of war (Gilbert 1987: 824). Martin Gilbert reports that prior to the invasion of the Soviet Union in June 1941, around 30,000 Jews had already perished: 10,000 in individual killings, street massacres and reprisals, and in the ghettos and labour camps, and 20,000 who had starved to death in the ghettos of Warsaw and Lodz. But there was no Jewish community in which more than 2 or 3 per cent of the population had been killed (Gilbert 1987: 155). This changed with the eastern invasion: 'From the first hours of Barbarossa . . . throughout what had once been eastern Poland, Latvia, Lithuania and Estonia, as well as in the Ukraine, White Russia and the western regions of the Russian Republic, a new policy was carried out, the systematic destruction of entire Jewish communities' (Gilbert 1987: 155). The Reserve Police Battalions were sent into the occupied territories to assist and relieve the SS *Einsatzkommandos*, who were bearing the brunt of the killing. Browning has studied the record of Reserve Police Battalion 101, a unit of just under 500 'ordinary' Germans who, in Poland, killed around 38,000 Jews between July 1942 and November 1943, and deported 45,200 to Treblinka between August 1942 and May 1943 (Browning 2001: 225–6).

As opposed to Goldhagen's account, Browning says he gives a 'multilayered' account of the activities of the battalion, which broke down into three groups. The first two were the eager killers and those who chose not to kill (the smallest group). The third and largest group did what they were asked to do: 'but they did not volunteer for or celebrate the killing. Increasingly numb and brutalized, they felt more pity for themselves because of the "unpleasant" work they had been assigned than they did for their dehumanized victims. For the most part, they did not think what they were doing was wrong or immoral, because the killing was sanctioned by legitimate authority. Indeed, for the most part they did not try to think, period' (Browning 2001: 215–16). Goldhagen, says Browning, sets up only two possibilities: either they agreed wholeheartedly with Hitler's vision of the Jews and were enthusiastically murdering them, or they believed they were doing something terribly morally wrong – and, argues Goldhagen, as the second option makes no sense at all, the first must be true. But Browning says neither of these options is true for the vast majority of the killers, and so offers a 'multicausal explanation of motivation' (Browning 2001: 216). These killings were 'crimes of obedience' (Browning 2001: 219), showing degrees of compliance from enthusiastic identity with the values of the campaign to nominal compliance when under supervision and noncompliance when unsupervised. 'I believe that the perpetrators not only had the capacity to choose but exercised that choice in various ways that covered the spectrum from enthusiastic participation, through dutiful, nominal, or regretful compliance, to differing degrees of evasion' (Browning 2001: 221). And the fundamental challenge, concludes Browning, 'is not to explain why ordinary Germans, as members of a people utterly different from us and shaped by a culture that permitted them to think and act in no other way than to want to be genocidal executioners, eagerly killed Jews when the opportunity offered. The fundamental problem is to explain why ordinary men – shaped by a culture that had its particularities but was nonetheless within the mainstream of western, Christian, and Enlightenment traditions – under specific circumstances willingly carried out the most extreme genocide in human history' (Browning 2001: 222).

Browning identifies the factors behind this transformation as 'wartime brutalization, racism, segmentation and routinization of the task, special selection of the perpetrators, obedience to orders, deference to authority, ideological indoctrination, and conformity' (Browning 2001: 159). These are all 'applicable in varying degrees, but none without qualification' (Browning 2001: 159), and some do not seem to apply at all to Police Battalion 101. For example, the men had not been brutalised by wartime action, as none had served on the frontline – they became brutalised as an *effect* of what they did (Browning 2001: 161). However, the war situation was still an important context for motivation: 'War is the most conducive environment in which governments can adopt "atrocity by policy" and encounter few difficulties in implementing it' (Browning 2001: 162). This is especially so in a 'race' war, because 'when deeply embedded racial stereotypes are added to the brutalization inherent in sending armed men to kill one another on a massive scale, the fragile tissue of war conventions and rules of combat is even more frequently and viciously broken on all sides' (Browning 2001: 159–60). And so 'race' wars, such as that between Germany and the Soviet Union, the USA and Japan in the Pacific, and the Vietnam war, are contexts within which atrocities become all too easy to commit. Another factor is that of 'distancing': 'Distancing, not frenzy and brutalization, is one of the keys to the behavior of Reserve Police Battalion 101. War and negative stereotyping were two mutually reinforcing factors in this distancing' (Browning 2001: 162). The effect of distancing is most pronounced when it comes to bureaucratic 'desk murderers', but is not irrelevant to Police Battalion 101, where a division of labour did help in some cases when 'specialists' were brought in to do the killing and when deportations took the Jews to be murdered in Treblinka (Browning 2001: 162–3).

Browning says there is no evidence that members of the battalion were a 'special' type of person, attracted to its activities, and he cites two famous psychological experiments to show that one does not have to be a 'special' type of person to become involved: Philip Zimbardo's Stanford prison experiment and Stanley Milgram's experiments on obedience to authority. What Zimbardo's experiment seemed to show – setting up a simulated prison and separating a random sample of people into 'prisoners' and 'guards' – was that it was the prison situation alone which produced the behaviour. Browning notes that Zimbardo's 'guards' split into three groups that strikingly resembled the members of Police Battalion 101: a third were enthusiastic about their roles, a large middle group kept to the rules but did not go out of their way to apply them, and a very small group 'opted out' in the sense that they subverted the rules when they thought they could. Milgram's experiment on authority simulated the application of electric shocks. Two-thirds of the randomly selected subject group applied shocks to the most extreme level – where the 'victim', after protests and cries of pain, fell silent – when instructed to do so by an authority figure. In the absence of such a figure, compliance fell to zero. Milgram and his team concluded that obedience to authority does not rest on duress – there is a tendency to obey authority. Milgram observed: 'Men are led to kill with little difficulty' (Browning 2001: 173). Milgram did not test for conformity to peer pressure, but thought this was a factor, and Browning speculates that in the case of Police Battalion 101 'conformity assumes a more central role than authority' (Browning 2001: 175). Between 80 and 95 per cent of its members killed despite expressing horror and disgust at their work. 'To break ranks and step out, to adopt overtly nonconformist behavior, was simply beyond most of the men. It was easier for them to shoot' (Browning 2001: 184). To step out would mean leaving the 'dirty work' to colleagues, carried the risk of ostracism, and could be interpreted as moral criticism; those who did refuse to kill characterised themselves as weak rather than ethical, and therefore presented no moral challenge to what was happening around them (Browning 2001: 184–5). It was easier to conform with the immediate community and the larger society, and this was made easier still by the war situation and by Nazi propaganda (Browning 2001: 186).

   While the 'ordinary' men of Police Battalion 101 may have lacked the education to critique the Nazi programme, the fact is that German intellectuals, for the great majority, also failed to mount any serious critique, and indeed joined in with the programme, some of them to the fullest extent. The intellectual framework in Europe during this period was dominated by 'scientific' racism, the view that there were distinct races arranged in a hierarchy of superiority and inferiority, with the 'Aryan' race at the summit. This view was so embedded in much of the European mind that Carl Jung could write in 1930 about the United States: 'The Negro by his mere presence is a source of temperamental and mimetic infection, which the European can't help noticing just as much as he sees the hopeless gap between the American and the African Negro. Racial infection is a most serious mental and moral problem where the primitive outnumbers the white man. America has this problem only in a relative degree, because the whites far outnumber the coloured. Apparently he can assimilate the primitive influence with little risk to himself. What would happen if there were a considerable increase in the coloured population is another matter' (Jung 1970: 509). Of the Jews he wrote in 1934: 'The Jew, who is something of a nomad, has never yet created a cultural form of his own and as far as we can see never will, since all his instincts and talents require a more or less civilized nation to act as host for their development' (Jung 1970: 165–6). And so: 'The "Aryan" unconscious has a higher potential than the Jewish . . .' (Jung 1970: 166). Although this is, of course, far from eliminationist anti-Semitism, and although Jung heavily criticised the Nazi regime, we can see that he shared the view that there was a Jewish 'problem'. Writing, again in 1934, against charges that he agreed with the Nazis, his defence was partially that he had identified the Jewish 'problem' before they did (Jung 1970: 543), and that the fact that the Nazi regime was reprehensible should not discourage 'scientific' discussion of that problem. 'The Jewish problem is a regular complex, a festering wound, and no responsible doctor could bring himself to apply methods of medical hush-hush in this matter' (Jung 1970: 539).

Others did go further. A notorious example is Martin Heidegger, who was elected as Rector of Freiburg University in April 1933, and soon afterwards joined the Nazi party. John Cornwell describes the scale of support for the Nazi leadership from intellectuals and academics in *Hitler's Scientists: Science, War, and the Devil's Pact* (Cornwell 2003), but those who went the furthest were those doctors who worked in the extermination camps, at the heart of the Holocaust, as described by Robert J. Lifton in *The Nazi Doctors: Medical Killing and the Psychology of Genocide* (Lifton 1986). He explains that the doctors were central to the functioning of Auschwitz in particular: 'doctors were given much of the responsibility for the murderous ecology of Auschwitz – the choosing of the victims, the carrying through of the physical and psychological mechanics of killing, and the balancing of killing and work functions in the camp. While doctors by no means ran Auschwitz, they did lend it a perverse medical aura' (Lifton 1986: 18). Prior to the extermination camps, doctors oversaw the policy of direct medical killing of those judged unworthy of life. This began with euthanasia, but progressed to the killing of 'impaired' children in hospitals, then the killing of 'impaired' adults – mostly from mental hospitals – in special centres using carbon-monoxide gas, and culminated in the killing of 'impaired' inmates of concentration and extermination camps (Lifton 1986: 21). The final escalation in their involvement came with their supervision of the killing of the Jews and others in the camps.

Lifton asks how this could take place? How could the physician become a killer? From his interviews with Nazi doctors who worked in the camps, Lifton concludes that the psychological process of 'doubling' was an essential aspect of their work. They were, he says, offered a 'Faustian bargain' – they would participate in the vilest work of the Nazi programme, and in exchange were 'offered various psychological and material benefits'. There was also a larger temptation: 'that of becoming the theorists and implementers of a cosmic scheme of radical cure by means of victimization and mass murder' (Lifton 1986: 418). In order to participate, though, they had to double themselves into an 'Auschwitz self', who could 'function psychologically in an environment so anti-thetical to his previous ethical standards', and a 'prior self', in order to see themselves as 'humane physician, husband, father' (Lifton 1986: 419). This was not the radical disassociation and sustained separateness one finds in cases of multiple personality disorders: it was a response to a specific situation, and was resolved once that situation was resolved, and was 'more focused and temporary and occurs as part of a larger institutional structure which encourages or even demands it' (Lifton 1986: 423). The Auschwitz self and prior self were autonomous but connected, with the former enabling the doctor to function within the environment of Auschwitz with a clear conscience. This doubling enabled them to avoid guilt 'not by the elimination of conscience but by what can be called the *transfer of conscience*' (Lifton 1986: 421). The demands of conscience were transferred to the Auschwitz self, so that it could be answered in terms of doing one's duty within that context. What was repudiated by the prior self was not reality as such – they knew what they were doing – but what it meant: they were 'altering the meaning of murder' (Lifton 1986: 425).

Lifton argues that Auschwitz as an institution depended on doubling. It was so structured that 'the average person entering it...will commit or become associated with atrocities' (Lifton 1986: 425). For an atrocity-producing institution to function, it has to be able to motivate individuals to engage in the atrocity. Auschwitz was a particularly powerful atrocity-producing institution, and demanded doubling so that its members could adapt to killing without regarding themselves as murderers (Lifton 1986: 425). Here it became 'a shared psychological process, the group norm' (Lifton 1986: 425). This enabled them to see their work as a larger healing project: on the large scale, the healing of the world, and on the smaller scale the healing of the camp itself by ensuring that it continued to function. And so 'sending typhus patients or potential carriers to the gas chamber did control that disease, and doing the same to the large numbers of weak and sick prisoners did indeed improve the hygienic situation in Auschwitz. If one entered into the healing-killing paradox with a comprehensive Auschwitz self, it could seem to make sense, to "work"' (Lifton 1986: 433). In this context, then, what they were doing made sense, and in the wider context there was a war in which they believed. Auschwitz was, therefore, 'the moral equivalent of war' (Lifton 1986: 431).

The Holocaust was, from this perspective, 'an absolute form of killing in the name of healing' (Lifton 1986: 467), and this was the wider project that motivated the doctors. Lifton comments: 'Genocidal projects require the active participation of educated professionals – physicians, scientists, engineers, military leaders, lawyers, clergy, university professors and other teachers – who combine to create not only the technology of genocide but much of its ideological rationale, moral climate, and organizational process' (Lifton 1986: 489–90). Intellectuals, he says, are susceptible to 'extreme environments', and the doctors 'reflect the more general tendency to claim virtue for maintaining under duress the function of a profession, especially a healing profession, even when that duress includes participating in genocide' (Lifton 1986: 490). When the project is portrayed as one of healing, the professionals 'can move to the farthest shore of evil' (Lifton 1986: 490). This requires 'the kind of immersion in ideology with its promise of a unified worldview and of knowledge put to passionate purpose, an immersion toward which the educated are especially inclined' (Lifton 1986: 490). He concludes: 'Intellectuals can all too readily welcome relief from the burden of thought, as described by Karl Stern in depicting "a peculiar brand of irrationalism" that took hold of German colleagues at the psychiatric institute where he worked – a "mysticism which opposed itself to Reason" – but, we may add, came to do so always in the name of science' (Lifton 1986: 490). And so: 'The dynamism of genocide offers considerable temptation to the professional to become the "spiritual engine" of change, revolution, renewal,' and one participates in these things 'with the conviction that they are "in accord with the natural history and biology of man", and that one is acting as healer and savior' (Lifton 1986: 491). This is not to deny that there was some resistance from the academic community, including some doctors and psychiatrists (see Lifton 1986: Chapters 3 and 5), but the fact remains that intellectuals and academics are easily seduced by the powerful when they are told that their discipline – science, medicine, philosophy, history – lies at the centre of the renewed political life of the 'nation'.

Extraordinary Monsters

The context for this understanding of the Holocaust was, of course, an extreme form of anti-Semitism. Historians identify different strands of anti-Semitism that play a centrally important role in shaping German politics and culture under the Nazi rule. Gavin Langmuir identifies a new kind of Jewish stereotype which he calls 'chimerical' (Langmuir 1990b: 306), which emerges as early as the thirteenth century in northern Europe. A chimera is a 'fabulous monster' (Langmuir 1990b: 334), and during this period a strand of anti-Semitism emerges which portrays Jews as 'imaginary monsters' (Langmuir 1990b: 306). This is distinct from a xenophobic anti-Semitism, in which dislike or hatred is based on certain characteristics the group actually has – the way it dresses, certain religious or cultural practices, and so on. In contrast, chimerical stereotypes contain no truth about the group. Langmuir identifies two fantasies about Jews that emerged by the end of the thirteenth century. The first was that of ritual murder, which became firmly rooted in northern European prejudices against the Jews, and the second was to do with the dogma of transubstantiation issued by the Catholic Church in 1215, that the consecrated bread and wine in the eucharist contained Christ's body and blood. A cult of the body of Christ grew, and Jews were accused of torturing Christ by assaulting the bread and wine – as

a consequence thousands of Jews were massacred as Christ torturers (Langmuir 1990b: 308). Such chimerical accusations are especially vindictive as they are directed against every member of the
group, and since they are unobservable they cannot be disputed –
they are part of its hidden, secret life. Certainly, the picture of the
Jew at the heart of the anti-Semitism held by Hitler and other core
members of the Nazi movement was chimerical in this sense.

Such was the nature of this chimerical anti-Semitism that it took
an apocalyptic form, according to Saul Friedländer in his study
of German treatment of the Jews from 1933 to 1939 (Friedländer
1997: 87). Fear of racial degeneration combined with religious belief in redemption to bring about what he describes as 'redemptive
anti-Semitism' – the struggle against the Jews was a 'struggle to
the death' (Friedländer 1997: 87). The source of this version of
anti-Semitism in Germany lay in the late nineteenth century with
the Bayreuth circle, 'that meeting point of German Christianity,
neoromanticism, the mystical cult of sacred Aryan blood, and
ultraconservative nationalism' (Friedländer 1997: 87). Richard
Wagner, while undoubtedly anti-Semitic, was not the key figure
as the 'intellectual foundations' were laid by others in the circle mostly after his death (Friedländer 1997: 89). Circle member
and English historian Houston Stewart Chamberlain's book *The
Foundations of the Nineteenth Century* was published in 1899,
and described the opposition between 'Germandom' and 'Jewry'
as the central theme of world history, and the need for a German–
Christian religion purged of all Jewish elements in order for regen-
eration. By 1915 the book had sold 100,000 copies in Germany.

Other events came together to reinforce this view of world history, with the Russian Revolution and the defeat of Germany in
the Great War. The leaders of the Russian Revolution were identified as Jewish, and the revolution itself was proof of the Jewish
world conspiracy to destroy Christianity. Another English historian, Nesta H. Webster, outlined the case for this world view in
her book *World Revolution: The Plot against Civilization*, published in 1921, as did many others (Friedländer 1997: 90–1). And
so in Germany there was the 'most explosive ideological mixture',
which was 'a fusion of constant fear of the Red menace with nationalist resentment born of defeat' (Friedländer 1997: 91). The
Red uprisings in Berlin and Bavaria and other parts of Germany
were all evidence of the Jewish conspiracy. Friedländer describes
the main atrocity committed by the Reds in April 1919 in Munich,
when they took ten hostages and shot them after hearing that Red

prisoners had been murdered by counter-revolutionary volunteer units elsewhere in Germany. 'These executions, an isolated atrocity, became the quintessential illustration of Jewish Bolshevik terror in Germany' (Friedländer 1997: 92), despite the fact that none of the leaders of the Reds in this instance was Jewish and one of their victims was.

There were undoubtedly many Jews in the radical movements in Germany during this period. These were secular Jews 'who had abandoned the framework of religious tradition for the ideas and ideals of rationalism and, more often than not, for socialism (or Zionism)' (Friedländer 1997: 93). But the great majority of Jews in central and western Europe were politically liberal, and most German Jews supported the liberal centre German Democratic Party. The radical revolutionaries, however, were held to represent the Jewish people in general. An important text in this growing mood of anti-Semitism was the *Protocols of the Elders of Zion*. This was fabricated in the mid-1890s by the head of the Czarist secret police in Paris, the Okhrana, in order to fight the spread of liberalism in Russia (Friedländer 1997: 94). The source was a political pamphlet published in 1864 attacking the emperor Napoleon III by using the imagery of a diabolical plot in hell, entitled 'Dialogues in Hell: Conversations Between Machiavelli and Montesquieu' (Bronner 2003: 83). It made no mention of the Jews and was intended as political satire, but a German anti-Semite, Herman Goedsche, writing under the name of Sir John Retcliffe, adapted it as part of a series of novels, *Biarritz*, which appeared in 1868 (Bronner 2003: 81). One chapter describes a secret rabbinical conference which meets regularly to review Jewish plans for world domination. It was translated into Russian in 1872, and the chapter describing the meeting appeared in Russia in 1891. It was during the Dreyfus case of 1893–95 that agents of the Okhrana in Paris produced the text which is known as the *Protocols of the Elders of Zion*, which itself was printed in Russia in 1897. However, they were not publicly published until 1905, when Russia's defeat in the Russo-Japanese War and the revolutionary instability of 1905 led the reactionary 'Union of the Russian Nation' to incite violence against the Jews, whom they blamed for the revolutionary movement. They used the *Protocols* as part of a propaganda campaign which accompanied the pogroms of 1905, inspired by the Okhrana. In the civil war following the Russian Revolution of 1917 the reactionary White armies made use of the *Protocols* to incite widespread massacres of Jews. They appeared in Britain and the

United States in the 1920s, and in 1927 Henry Ford was ordered by an American judge to destroy a large printing he had personally financed. Although they were exposed as a forgery very early in their history, they continued to be influential in anti-Semitic movements and are still believed by some today. The *Los Angeles Times* of 28 November 1993 reports the leader of the Russian radical nationalist group Pamyat, Dmitiri Vasiliev, declaring that 'the entire history of Russia after 1917 is solid proof that they are genuine'. This followed a ruling by a Russian court that they were an anti-Semitic forgery, the first official verdict on them in Russia.

The *Protocols* appeared in Germany in 1919, and their appearance 'exacerbated to the most extreme degree the paranoia prevalent in those years of crisis and disaster. If the Jewish threat was supranational, the struggle against it had to become global too, and without compromise. Thus, in an atmosphere suffused with concrete threats and imaginary forebodings, redemptive anti-Semitism seemed, more than ever before, to offer answers to the riddles of time. And for the anti-Jewish believers, the ultimate struggle for salvation demanded the unconditional fanaticism of one who could show the way and lead them into action' (Friedländer 1997: 95). That figure was Adolf Hitler, who shared the apocalyptic picture of the Jewish 'threat' – that Jewish domination meant the total destruction of the world, not only Germany (Friedländer 1997: 98). The Jews therefore represented a devilishly evil threat to humanity as such. Here was a mythological world history of Good versus Evil, the outcome of which would be 'perdition or redemption' (Friedländer 1997: 100). The imaginary Jewish enemy was both a superhuman force of destruction through their diabolical cleverness and conspiracy, and also a subhuman force of destruction through bringing with them infection, disintegration and disease (Friedländer 1997: 100). Friedländer comments: 'Images of superhuman power and subhuman pestilence are contrary representations, but Hitler attributed both to one and the same being, as if an endlessly changing and endlessly mimetic force had launched a constantly shifting offensive against humanity' (Friedländer 1997: 100). This was a view Hitler shared with anti-Semitism in general, with the 'past representations of the Jew as endlessly changing and endlessly the same, a living dead, either a ghostly wanderer or a ghostly ghetto inhabitant' (Friedländer 1997: 100). And so the Jewish 'threat' becomes 'formless and unrepresentable; as it leads to the most frightening phantasm of all: a threat that looms everywhere, that, although it penetrates everything, is an invisible carrier of death' (Friedländer 1997: 100–1). And so for Adolf Hitler, 'the struggle against the Jews was the immutable basis and obsessional core of his understanding of history, politics, and political action' (Friedländer 1997: 102).

But the question then arises, how should we understand Hitler himself? The temptation to find some mental abnormality is, of course, very strong, and the thought is that if we can find it, then it *must be* the explanation for what he did. In April 2005, there was great interest in a report written in 1943 for the Office of Strategic Services, a forerunner of the CIA, by a prominent personality expert at Harvard, Dr Henry A. Murray, which sought to explain Hitler's motivation in these terms (*The Independent*, 1 April 2005, 12). The report, recently discovered at Cornell University Law Library, speculates that Hitler was unable to come to terms with his sexuality. Jonathan Brown reports in *The Independent* newspaper: 'According to Dr Murray, the future dictator being caught engaged in a sexual encounter with a young girl aged 12 left him with syphilophobia – a morbid fear of contamination of the blood through contact with a woman. He was also deeply scarred from seeing his three-times married, highly promiscuous and illegitimate father having sex with his mother. Confusing sexuality, which he considered "exceedingly filthy" with the act of excretion, Hitler was both impotent and a "fully fledged masochist". But his inability to consummate the sex act left him with "exorbitant cravings for superiority". To further complicate matters, the Führer may also have been a closet homosexual. According to Dr Murray he found himself in awe of strong sexual characters. His recurrent nightmares were reminiscent of "homosexual panic", argues Dr Murray. While on one hand he had an "Oedipal complex" he was also beaten by his sadistic father, a man he both idealised and loathed.'

There is a simple philosophical objection to this kind of account. Just because we find a mental abnormality, it doesn't follow that it was the cause of the abnormal actions of the agent; it is tempting to suppose that the two abnormalities are connected but there is no reason why they should be. And of course the more dramatically abnormal the actions, the more dramatic the mental abnormality has to be, such that Hitler becomes insane and we can explain away the Holocaust as the programme of a mad man. Saul Friedländer questions the value of such an approach: 'any such interpretation usually appears to be highly speculative and often reductive. Moreover, similar anti-Jewish images, similar threats, a similar readiness for violence were shared from the outset by hundreds of thousands of Germans belonging to the extreme right and later to the radical wing of the Nazi party. If "pathology" there was, it was shared. Rather than an individual structure, we must face the social pathology of sects' (Friedländer 1997: 99).

The other temptation, beyond pathologising Hitler, is of course to demonise him, and this is reflected in the titles of a number of recent books about him and those around him – *The Devil's Disciples: The Life and Times of Hitler's Inner Circle*; *Hitler's Scientists: Science, War and the Devil's Pact*; *The Devil's Doctor: Felix Kesten and the Secret Plot to Turn Himmler against Hitler*; *To Kill the Devil: The Attempts on the Life of Adolf Hitler*. All these are deeply serious books and in fact make no attempt to equate Hitler with the Devil, but such is the 'naturalness' of this diabolical image that the titles, in attracting our imagination, play on it powerfully. In 2005 German film director Oliver Hirschbiegel released *Der Untergang* (*Downfall*), a film about the last days of Adolf Hitler and his staff in the bunker in Berlin. The film was controversial because of its 'portrait of the Führer as a very human dictator whose insane rages jostle with acts of charity and tenderness' (BBC news). German tabloid newspaper *Bild* asked: 'Should a monster be portrayed as a human being?' The problem is, of course, the other way around, whether a human being should be portrayed as a monster, and Hirschbiegel replied: 'We all know he was not a crocodile or an elephant, but a human being. The worse thing that can happen to an evil man like that is if he becomes a myth, which is what has happened for decades. He's among us now, and if we accept he was a human being, we have to accept that some of that evil is in all of us.' The film was well received by British film critics. Anthony Quinn, writing in *The Independent* newspaper, says: 'the picture does show Hitler as incontrovertibly human, which is why it is disturbing as well as magnificent. Much as we recoil at the notion, the quintessential hate-figure of the 20th century was a man, not a monster, and if we are to put his crimes in the dock, then all that we mean by "humanity" must be hauled up there too' (*Independent Arts and Books Review*, 1 April 2005, 6). Dave Calhoun, writing in *Time Out* (30 March–6 April 2005, 74), says: 'The shock of the new – of seeing Hitler as a human being – allows us to view a specific period of history with fresh eyes. To accuse Hirschbiegel of doing a disservice to the past is unfair. Instead, he should be praised for contributing

an intelligent, daring film to our understanding of Nazi Germany.'
Unfortunately, the *Time Out* headline writer could not resist
the temptation to entitle Calhoun's piece: 'Sympathy for the
Devil?'

No one has tried to 'humanise' Josef Mengele, the doctor who
worked in Auschwitz and who carries a particularly horrifying
place in the Holocaust. Robert J. Lifton gives the deeply shocking
details of Mengele's career in Auschwitz, but argues against holding an 'image of Mengele as an evil deity' (Lifton 1986: 379), and
against the 'cult of demonic personality' in general (Lifton 1986:
338). He describes the play *The Deputy* written by Rolf Hochhuth,
who has a Mengele-like character called 'the doctor' who, says
Hochhuth, 'has the stature of Absolute Evil, far more unequivo-
cally so than Hitler.' This figure resembles an 'uncanny visitant
from another world' (Hochhuth quoted in Lifton 1986: 338). Lifton
warns against attempts, like Hochhuth's, 'to simplify Nazism by
constructing a figure of such pure evil as to no longer belong to
the category of human being' (Lifton 1986: 380). For many of the
survivors of the Holocaust that Lifton interviewed, Mengele represented Auschwitz itself, to such an extent that only his capture
and trial could bring meaning back to their lives. One survivor
said of such a trial: 'I would be very interested to hear the details
and to see him pass [through] this metamorphosis of turning back
into a person instead of God Almighty' (Lifton 1986: 381). Lifton
comments: 'Mengele's imagined trial ... involved both the legend
and the man: justice for Mengele came to represent a restoration
of a just cosmos – a means of overcoming a vast "wound in the
order of being", in Martin Buber's phrase, that Auschwitz has represented. It also came to signify the desacrilization of a terrible
deity: the god must be rendered not only human but vulnerable
to truth and retribution' (Lifton 1986: 381). But the key to understanding Mengele is to understand the context, says Lifton. One
of the prisoner doctors, forced to work alongside Mengele, said:
'There's not only one Mengele. They are all part of Mengele – all
the doctors' (Lifton 1986: 381).

Mengele was never apprehended and was reported to have died
in South America in 1979 of a heart attack. 'Yet that resolution
was psychologically unsatisfactory, especially for Auschwitz survivors. The need was to capture him and put him on trial, to hear
his confession, to put *him* at *their* mercy. Failing that, many survivors refused to believe the remains in the Brazilian grave were
Mengele's' (Lifton 1986: 382). They have not been 'provided with a

psychological experience of that "metamorphosis" from evil deity to evil human being' (Lifton 1986: 382). Lifton concludes: 'Mengele's many-sidedness in Auschwitz was both part of his legend and a source of his desacrilization. In the camp he could be a visionary ideologue, an efficiently murderous functionary, a "scientist" and even a "professor", an innovator in several areas, a diligent careerist . . . and, above all, a physician who became a murderer. He reveals himself as a man and not a demon, a man whose multifaceted harmony with Auschwitz can give us insight into – and make us pause before – the human capacity to convert healing into killing' (Lifton 1986: 383). We must therefore resist the temptation to regard such figures as mysterious and inexplicable visitors from another world.

Banal Evil?

One wonders whether the trial of Mengele would have provided any kind of closure and peace for the survivors of Auschwitz. Although Mengele was never found, another notorious figure in the Holocaust was. Adolf Eichmann, head of the Department for Jewish Affairs in the Gestapo from 1941 to 1945, was chief of operations in the deportation of three million Jews to the extermination camps. After the war he fled to Argentina, but was kidnapped by Israeli Mossad agents in 1960, and stood trial in Jerusalem in 1961. He was sentenced to death and executed in 1962. Hannah Arendt famously witnessed his trial and wrote a report, in which she made one of the most influential and at the same time confusing comments about the evil of the Holocaust (I discuss Arendt's thoughts about evil extensively elsewhere (Cole 1998: 103–12), and I draw heavily on that material here, though to reach different conclusions). She says of his closing comments, when he attempted to justify his actions: 'It was as though in those last minutes he was summing up the lesson that this long course in human wickedness had taught us – the lesson of the fearsome, word-and-thought-defying *banality of evil*' (Arendt 1976: 252). However, Paul Clarke observes: 'It was never entirely clear from Arendt's account of the trial of Eichmann exactly what the phrase "the banality of evil" meant' (Clarke 1988: 194). In a postscript to the *Report* she says: 'when I speak of the banality of evil, I do so only on the strictly factual level, pointing to a phenomenon that stared one in the face at the trial' – this was that, beyond personal advancement, Eichmann 'had no motives at all' (Arendt 1976: 287). Arendt concludes: 'That such remoteness from reality and such thoughtlessness can wreak more havoc than all the evil instincts taken together which, perhaps, are inherent in man – that was, in fact, the lesson one could learn in Jerusalem. But it was a lesson, neither an explanation of the phenomenon nor a theory about it' (Arendt 1976: 288). In a later work she comments on: 'a manifold shallowness in the doer that made it impossible to trace the uncontestable evil of his deeds to any deeper level of roots or motives. The deeds were monstrous, but the doer – at least the very effective one now on trial – was quite ordinary, commonplace, and neither demonic nor monstrous' (Arendt 1978: 4). Arendt writes as though she expected to see a demon or a monster on trial, and was taken aback that Eichmann was neither; he was a very ordinary human being, neither 'perverted nor sadistic', but 'terribly and terrifyingly normal' (Arendt 1976: 276). It was this normality that was most terrifying of all.

The accounts of the Nuremberg trials contain much the same observations about the defendants, and the defendants said much the same as Eichmann about what they had done. Peter Padfield writes: 'When William Shirer, anticipating the moment he had been awaiting "all these black, despairing years" entered the courtroom the prisoners were in their places. He found his first sight of them in their changed condition indescribable. Shorn of their former glittering symbols of power, "how little and mean and mediocre" they looked. At the left of the lower row, Göring was scarcely recognizable in a faded *Luftwaffe* uniform shorn of insignia; he had lost weight and reminded Shirer of "a genial radio operator on a ship". Above him at the left of the second row Dönitz sat wearing a civilian suit and looking "for all the world like a grocer's clerk. Hard to imagine him as the successor of Hitler"; next to him Raeder looked "a bewildered old man" ' (Padfield 1984: 441). Werner Maser comments of the same scene: 'All were downcast and cut sorry figures, with their lined faces, some without ties, and the officers in faded uniforms without badges of rank or decorations' (Maser 1979: 74). And so what is most terrifying and indescribable about these people is not that they are monsters, but that they are human. Of course it could be argued that the true monster was not present at the trials, but then how would Hitler have appeared? As a demonic monster or as a mediocre human? And so one aspect of the banality of evil is that those who perform it are staggeringly, disturbingly normal.

If this is all Arendt meant by the 'banality' of evil it is a valuable counter-point to its mythology, but she expanded her comment into a wider thesis about 'thoughtlessness'. For her, Eichmann was a new type of criminal who 'commits his crimes under circumstances that make it well-nigh impossible for him to know or feel that he is doing wrong' (Arendt 1976: 276). This context was bureaucracy, which enabled Eichmann to make decisions about the fate of millions and yet be at a distance from that fate. Paul Clarke describes 'pure' bureaucracy: 'a form of organisation which, as far as the goals of the organisation are concerned, requires the suspension of reflective judgement by its members. The ideal type bureaucrat does not reflect on the larger issues surrounding his work and his role' (Clarke 1988: 207). Christopher Browning thinks this kind of distancing through bureaucratic structures was significant in contributing to the Holocaust: 'modern bureaucratic life fosters a functional and physical distancing in the same way that war and negative stereotyping promote a psychological distancing between perpetrator and victim' (Browning 2001: 162). And so many of the perpetrators were 'so-called desk murderers whose role in the mass extermination was greatly facilitated by the bureaucratic nature of their participation' (Browning 2001: 162). He concludes: 'Segmental, routinized, and depersonalized, the job of the bureaucrat or specialist . . . could be performed without confronting the reality of mass murder' (Browning 2001: 162). In fact this description does not fit Adolf Eichmann, who Browning admits is 'not in fact the best example of the "banal bureaucrat" ', although he does believe the concept is still valid for others: 'the extent to which ordinary bureaucrats, performing functions vital to the mass murder program in exactly the same routine way they performed the rest of their professional duties, made the Holocaust possible. The evil was not banal; the perpetrators most certainly were' (Browning 2001: 250). Eichmann is not the best example because he was involved at the highest level of planning the Holocaust, attending the Wannsee Conference on 20 January 1942, as Richard Heydrich's right-hand representative. We have no reason to suppose whatsoever that Eichmann did 'not reflect on the larger issues surrounding his work and his role'. This raises two challenges: first, are we in a position to know that there *any* 'banal' bureaucrats in the sense that Clarke and Browning describe? And second, as Arendt attended Eichmann's trial she was fully aware of his involvement in the Holocaust, and so when she comments on the 'banality' of evil, she cannot have meant that Eichmann was this kind of minor cog in a great and evil machinery. So what did she mean?

In her later comments, Arendt describes Eichmann as 'thoughtless' (Arendt 1978: 4), and says: 'The manifestation of the wind of thought is not knowledge; it is the ability to tell right from wrong, beautiful from ugly' (Arendt 1978: 193). Elsewhere she says that one of the 'outstanding characteristics of our time' is thoughtlessness, 'the heedless recklessness or hopeless confusion or complacent repetition of "truths" which have become trivial and empty'. And she says: 'What I propose, therefore, is very simple: it is nothing more than to think what we are doing' (Arendt 1958: 5). But again we have to ask what Arendt meant by 'thoughtlessness'? As Clarke points out, Eichmann had an inner mental life. 'Arendt was undoubtedly correct in regarding Eichmann's *appearance* as banal, but if that banality of appearance reflected anything of Eichmann's inner condition, then he could hardly have been held culpable for his actions for we would take it that he was incapable of reason, thought, will and judgement.' Rather, Eichmann was thoughtless because he *chose* not to think about certain crucial aspects of what he was doing. 'The faculties of thinking, willing and judging may be freely abnegated or the opportunities available to cultivate and develop them freely, passed by' (Clarke 1988: 202). Eichmann was someone who willed not to will, and was therefore an example of what Clarke describes as 'heteronomous evil', as opposed to autonomous evil. Autonomously evil agents choose to pursue evil; heteronomously evil agents choose to place themselves in a situation where some other agency is directing them towards a particular goal, and that particular goal is evil. Heteronomous evil has three conditions: first, the agent's behaviour must have evil consequences; second, the agent must have adopted a maxim of heteronomy – he or she must have chosen not to choose; and third, 'he must have deferred in act, will and judgement to some evil person, tradition or practice' (Clarke 1988: 204).

This kind of agent need not have an actively evil disposition or have independently adopted any explicitly evil maxim or principle of action. Adopting heteronomy is 'a decision to avoid further choosing'. This need not be '*consciously* formulated; it can be expressed, indeed is best expressed, in the activity and manner of a person's life' (Clarke 1988: 204). Clarke believes that Eichmann is 'an almost paradigmatic case' (Clarke 1988: 205), but, crucially, he is still fully morally culpable. 'The ground of his moral, and not merely his legal culpability, is established if it is shown that he was a free and willing tool of his masters, rather than an involuntary automaton; and this is readily established' (Clarke 1988: 205). Therefore: 'Although Eichmann did do great evil, he achieved this not so much through the adoption of a fundamental maxim to do evil, as through a fundamental maxim not to make a personal choice, or stand, in situations where this was required if he was to retain his autonomy' (Clarke 1988: 205). This is the most politically significant form of evil, because 'heteronomous agents present a permanent possibility of political evil' (Clarke 1988: 205–6), and heteronomous evil 'takes place only in certain structured situations' (Clarke 1988: 206). The structure is, once more, the bureaucracy, which 'permitted many of those who were active in executing the policies of genocide, to stand at a significant "moral distance" from the offences in which they participated. They could argue, perhaps even believe, that any evil lay either in the intentions of their superiors or in the direct violence of their subordinates, but that their own activities were morally insignificant' (Clarke 1988: 206). But again the problem is how to make sense of Adolf Eichmann in this scheme. In what sense did Eichmann believe his activities were morally insignificant, and that the intentions of his superiors were evil, or that the activities of his subordinates were evil? He believed none of these things. The most that can be claimed is that he may have believed the actual activity of killing was a *necessary* evil – dirty work that was beneath him but that had to be carried out by someone. But to the extent that Eichmann believed in the Holocaust as necessary to save Germany and the Aryan race in general from the Jewish conspiracy to destroy them, he was not heteronomous in Clarke's sense.

But Arendt believed Eichmann to be thoughtless, and that this thoughtlessness was a key factor in the Holocaust and other human evils. What is crucial to understand, then, is not what Arendt meant by 'banality', but what she meant by 'thoughtlessness'. Eichmann is important to the development of her own thinking because he showed that monstrous deeds can be committed 'without being motivated by monstrous evil intentions' (Bernstein 2002: 218). For Richard Bernstein, Arendt's portrayal of Eichmann 'is much more damning than simply characterizing him as some sort of demonic monster' (Bernstein 2002: 220). She shows his ordinariness, his banality: 'her portrait of Eichmann revealed him to be *human-all-too-human*. According to her account, neither blind anti-Semitism, sadistic hatred, nor even deep ideological convictions motivated him. He was motivated by the most mundane, and petty considerations of advancing his career, pleasing his superiors, demonstrating that he could do his job well and efficiently. *In this sense*, his motives were at once banal and all too human' (Bernstein 2002: 220).

In a deep sense, Eichmann did fail to think beyond this context and question what was happening around him. For Arendt, thinking liberates judgement because it enables people to judge the particular without resorting to old general or universal rules. Thinking is a capacity all possess, but thoughtlessness is 'an ever-present possibility for everybody' (Arendt 1978: 191). Crucial to thinking is the imagination, because even where there is a crisis in understanding, where old categories of thought collapse, people can still judge and understand what is happening. Imagination 'allows us to view things in their proper perspective and to judge them without the benefit of a pre-given rule or universal' (D'Entreves 1994: 106). Arendt says: 'Imagination alone enables us to see things in their proper perspective, to put that which is too close at a certain distance so that we can see and understand it without bias and prejudice, to bridge abysses of remoteness until we can see and understand everything that is too far away from us as though it were our own affair' (Arendt 1953: 392). And: 'Without this kind of imagination, which actually is understanding, we would never be able to take our bearings in the world. It is the only inner compass we have' (Arendt 1953: 392). The imagination is therefore important both to those trying to understand the Holocaust from the outside, and for those embedded within it. Through the use of imagination we can come to terms with a reality that may initially defy human comprehension. And Eichmann himself failed to use his imagination, says Maurice D'Entreves in his commentary on Arendt: 'Eichmann's guilt resided in his banal thoughtlessness, in his failure to engage in responsible judgement when confronted with Hitler's orders to exterminate the Jews. Those few individuals who refused to carry out the orders of their superiors were thus left entirely to their own resources' (D'Entreves 1994: 108). They had to be able to tell right from wrong, even though all that was left to guide them was their own judgement (Arendt 1976: 294–5). Arendt concludes: 'Those few who were still able to tell right from wrong went really only by their own judgments, and they did so freely; there were no rules to be abided by, under which the particular cases with which they were confronted could be subsumed. They had to decide each instance as it arose, because no rules existed for the unprecedented' (Arendt 1976: 295). And so in the end people cannot rely on the application of rules and principles to decide what is the right or wrong thing to do – to the extent that we do depend on such rules we elect for heteronomy. Our power of judgement can be overwhelmed by desire, propaganda, illusion, by force of circumstances. For Arendt, the power of judgement is a particularly political capacity, and its possession and practice is therefore a political issue. What happened in Germany is an extreme example of what happens when, for whatever reason, people's capacity to make autonomous judgements is overwhelmed by circumstances or set aside for the sake of some vision of the greater good. That a few were able to retain their capacity to judge is of little comfort here, and the overall lesson is that the autonomy of human agents does not only rest on their own power of rational decision-making, their own self-understanding; it also rests on the nature of the community, the presence of a particular form of social context.

Radical Evil?

But for Arendt there is still something more that has to be said about the Holocaust, because although Eichmann and others like him were banal, the evil of the Holocaust was radical. Richard Bernstein draws on her correspondence with Karl Jaspers to try to flesh out what she might have meant by this. At first Arendt saw the arch-Nazis as being beyond human justice, but Jaspers warned against this, saying that such a view places a streak of 'satanic greatness' upon them. This, he says, is 'as inappropriate for the Nazis as all the talk about the "demonic" element in Hitler and so forth' (Bernstein 2002: 214–15). Arendt replies that she too rejects suggestions of mythical or satanic 'greatness' for the Nazi leaders. 'We have to combat all impulses to mythologize the horrible, and to the extent that I can't avoid such formulations, I haven't understood what actually went on' (Bernstein 2002: 215). The main difficulty in arriving at an understanding is precisely how to understand how 'perfectly normal men' could come to participate in what happened (Bernstein 2002: 216). In replying to critics of her report on Eichmann's trial, and to the idea that his evil was 'banal', she became reluctant to speak of 'radical' evil at all. Bernstein comments on her correspondence here: 'When she now says that evil is extreme but not radical, that it lacks depth, she is calling attention to the fact that evil is on the *surface*. Insofar as "radical" suggests digging to roots that are hidden, she no longer thinks that evil is radical in *this sense*. It is "thought-defying" because thought seeks something that has depth' (Bernstein 2002: 218).

But Bernstein believes that Arendt did retain some notion of a radical evil, and again finds glimpses of it in her correspondence with Jaspers. There she speaks of radical evil having something to do with 'making human beings as human beings superfluous' (Bernstein 2002: 208), and that this in turn has something to do with the 'elimination of human unpredictability and spontaneity' (Bernstein 2002: 208). For Immanuel Kant, who had an enormous influence on Arendt's thought, spontaneity is 'the essential characteristic of our human rationality and freedom' (Bernstein 2002: 208). But Arendt takes the step of 'thinking that even this apparently *transcendental* condition of a human life *can* be eliminated *empirically*, by totalitarian means. This . . . stands at the heart of her understanding of radical evil' (Bernstein 2002: 208). She focuses on the absence of rights, which means that one is expelled from the human community as such. 'It is because of the threat of superfluousness that Arendt insists that the most fundamental right is "the right to have rights", the right to belong to a community that protects one's rights – a community in which one can exercise those rights' (Bernstein 2002: 209). But 'the deepest and most shocking sense of superfluousness – one that reveals what she means by radical evil – is epitomized in the concentration and death camps' (Bernstein 2002: 209–10). In this context, 'her phrase "making human beings as human beings superfluous" has a much more horrifying and specific meaning. It means literally the attempt to transform human beings in such a way that they are no longer *human*' (Bernstein 2002: 211). In *The Origins of Totalitarianism* (Arendt 1951) Arendt says: 'The camps are meant not only to exterminate people and degrade human beings, but also to serve the ghastly experiment of eliminating, under scientifically controlled conditions, spontaneity itself as an expression of human behavior and transforming the human personality into a mere thing, into something that even animals are not' (Arendt 1951: 438; Bernstein 2002: 211).

Conclusion

In April 2005 I visited New York City as a tourist, and spent part of my trip at the Ellis Island Museum of Immigration. The island became an immigration station in 1892 to handle the influx of immigrants from Europe into the United States, and only fell out of use in 1954. It was renovated and opened as a museum in 1990. It is an impressive and moving experience, and one aspect that stayed with me was the practice of marking those the immigration officials felt were unfit to be admitted to membership of the American nation with a chalk cross on their clothing. According to one display, a young girl was the only member of her family to be marked this way and feared being separated, until an older person told her to remove her coat and reverse it, so concealing the mark. She entered America with the rest of her family. According to the museum, only 2 per cent of potential immigrants were turned away, but this conceals a larger story that connects with the Holocaust. In an earlier book about immigration I wrote: 'Whether we make them with paint, wire, walls or only on maps, borders remain imagined constructs, and what is banal about them is their arbitrariness' (Cole 2000: x). What the Holocaust shows us is that in our desire to make real the boundary we imagine between ourselves and others – with, in Primo Levi's words, the 'we' inside and the enemy outside, 'separated by a sharply defined geographical frontier' – we mark not only the border, but also those we feel do not belong inside it, with yellow stars or chalk marks. As we eject asylum seekers and refugees from our borders we can comfort ourselves with the thought that – if proper procedures are followed – there must be somewhere safe for them to go. But if we rush to judgement, compelled by irrational panic, we may find that we are not simply ejecting people from our territory, but that we are expelling them from humanity itself.

That was certainly the case for many of the Jewish refugees who sought refuge in the United States from the oppression they faced in Europe before the Second World War. What the Ellis Island '2 per cent' figure fails to represent are all those who never made it even that far. In his superb and important book *The Mismeasure of Man*, the late Stephen Jay Gould notes the passing of the US Immigration Restriction Act of 1924, heavily influenced by the same eugenicist theories of racial inferiority that inspired the Nazi leadership and its supporters. 'The eugenicists battled and won one of the greatest victories of scientific racism in American history' (Gould 1997: 262). The Act set quotas designed to restrict immigration from southern and eastern Europe, in favour of the 'superior' northern and western Europeans. These quotas slowed immigration to the United States from southern and eastern Europe 'to a trickle' (Gould 1997: 263). Gould observes the connection with the Holocaust: 'Throughout the 1930s, Jewish refugees, anticipating the holocaust, sought to emigrate, but were not admitted. The legal quotas and continuing eugenical propaganda, barred them even in years when inflated quotas for western and northern European nations were not filled' (Gould 1997: 263). Between 1924 and 1939, perhaps up to six million southern, central and eastern Europeans were barred from entering the United States by the quotas.

Robert S. Wistrich also notes the connections. He says: 'The Holocaust was a *pan-European* event' (Wistrich 2002: 5), and observes that it could not have happened if there had not been a consensus about the Jewish 'problem', especially strong in eastern Europe, but 'there was also a growing anti-Semitism in western Europe and America, tied to the hardships caused by the Great Depression, increased xenophobia, fear of immigration and the influence of fascist ideas' (Wistrich 2002: 6). Three criticisms can be aimed at the United States in particular. First, it adopted a 'highly restrictive immigration policy', and did so 'in response to racist and xenophobic pressures in American society, which it was unwilling to seriously confront' (Wistrich 2002: 191). Second, it obstructed German offers of negotiation to remove Jews from Europe. And third, although the network of transport and camps that made up the Holocaust were known of and could be reached by the Allied air forces, there was never any attempt to disrupt its operations by bombing campaigns. The latter two charges stem from the first, the political influence of anti-Semitism in America, which, although it 'never crystallised into a coherent, organised political movement or seriously infiltrated into the mainstream political parties, it was nonetheless pervasive enough in the 1930s and 1940s to affect American responses to the Holocaust' (Wistrich 2002: 192–3). Wistrich gives the example of Breckinridge Long Jr, Assistant Secretary of State in the administration, who was 'a paranoid anti-Semite who thought Hitler's *Mein Kampf* "eloquent in opposition to Jewry and to Jews as exponents of Communism and Chaos" ' (Wistrich 2002: 193). Because of people like Long, attempts to relieve and rescue Jews were sabotaged to such an extent that an internal investigation published a report in January 1944 entitled 'Report to the Secretary on the Acquiescence of this Government in the murder of the Jews' (Wistrich 2002: 194).

Of those turned away, the passengers of the SS *St Louis*, a liner with 937 passengers, almost all of them Jews fleeing from Germany in May 1939, has a special place in the history of the Holocaust.

They aimed to enter the United States, but planned to stay in Cuba until their entry was arranged. However, the situation in Cuba was hostile and when the ship arrived in Havana only twenty-eight people were allowed to disembark, six of whom were not Jewish, the rest having valid entry documents. The *St Louis* was ordered out of Cuban waters, and although it sailed so close to Florida they could see the lights of Miami, the United States' administration refused to grant entry. On 6 June 1939, the ship sailed back to Europe. However, after negotiations Great Britain, France, Belgium and the Netherlands agreed to share the refugees, and the *St Louis* finally docked at Antwerp on 17 June 1939. In less than three months the Second World War began, and it is not known how many of the former passengers of the *St Louis* were trapped in German-occupied Europe and met their end in the extermination camps (the story of the *St Louis* can be found on the Holocaust Encyclopedia website, www.ushmm.org).

The British government was equally obstructive to assisting the European Jews, perhaps because of its political interests in the Middle East. In order not to provoke the situation there, 'a supposedly sympathetic Britain was busy sealing off the escape routes for Jewish refugees, especially those bound for the Jewish National Home in Palestine. An intense British diplomatic effort was undertaken to pressure European governments during the war to *actively prevent* "illegal" Jewish immigration' (Wistrich 2002: 207). The British navy used its ships in the eastern Mediterranean to intercept ships carrying immigrants. 'So draconian was Britain's policy that by 1945 even the miserly permitted quota of 75,000 Jewish immigrants to Palestine throughout the war years had not yet been achieved' (Wistrich 2002: 207). It is another ship, the *Struma*, which illustrates what this policy meant for Jewish refugees. The *Struma* was commissioned to carry around 790 Jewish refugees from Romania to Palestine in December 1941. The ship was in an awful condition and when the engine gave out it was towed to Istanbul, where it remained until February 1942, as the British government consistently refused to allow the refugees into Palestine. Eventually the Turkish authorities towed the *Struma* into the Black Sea, where it was abandoned, its engine still not working. A huge explosion destroyed the ship on 24 February and only one man survived.

There are connections here which, if we ignore them, will return to haunt us. I write this after a general election in Britain in which both main political parties have used immigrants and asylum seekers as political tools, making their humanity, once more, superfluous. The Labour Party promised a reduction in asylum numbers by introducing 'tougher' rules on settlement and increasing deportations; an electronic register of all border crossings; and a skills-based points system for permanent immigrants. The Conservative Party promised 24-hour surveillance of British ports as it claimed to 'take proper control of our borders'; to opt out of the 1951 Geneva Convention on refugees; to fix an annual limit on immigration including the number of asylum seekers accepted; and to take asylum seekers 'outside Britain' to process their claims, without defining what 'outside' Britain means in this context (Conservative Party manifesto: 21). All this displays Arendt's 'thoughtlessness', the subsuming of thought under general rules and abstract principles, the inability to think about the particular case, or to use one's imagination. I make no apologies for reproducing her words in full for the second time: 'Imagination alone enables us to see things in their proper perspective, to put that which is too close at a certain distance so that we can see and understand it without bias and prejudice, to bridge abysses of remoteness until we can see and understand everything that is too far away from us as though it were our own affair'. And: 'Without this kind of imagination, which actually is understanding, we would never be able to take our bearings in the world. It is the only inner compass we have.' I said in the introduction to this chapter that to demonise others is to fail to learn the lessons of history. I close the chapter with the same thought.

Chapter Nine

Twenty-First-Century Mythologies

The Return to Satan

I began this book by speaking of the Devil, and that is how I close it. I looked at the figure of Satan in detail in Chapter 2, concluding that he had an ideological role in Jewish and Christian thought, as communities who felt themselves both under external attack and endangered by an enemy that hid within used the idea of the Devil to attack and destroy that internal threat. Rather than metaphysical, here Satan's presence is political, but I also identified another presence for him, a literary one, and it is this particular role I want to examine now. Neil Forsyth has written two important books here, one, *The Old Enemy: Satan and the Combat Myth* (Forsyth 1987), which looks at the historical role of Satan in the Judaeo-Christian tradition, and the other, *The Satanic Epic* (Forsyth 2003), which examines his presence in Milton's *Paradise Lost*. Forsyth is clear that 'Satan is first, and in some sense always remains, a character in a narrative' (Forsyth 1987: 4). We do not need to try to understand his character or his motivation – rather, we need to understand the plot in which he has a role to play. In that sense it is always a mistake to worry about the motivation of evil agents in fictional narratives, to wonder what makes Iago tick for example; he has no motivation, only a narrative purpose. Of course, as we read these texts for their psychological meaning we search for the motive, but perhaps this is to mis-read them. For Forsyth: 'The essential role of Satan is opposition' (Forsyth 1987: 4), and this of course goes back to the original Hebrew meaning of the word as 'adversary'. 'He took his function for his title ... so Satan's name is both paradoxical and tragic. It defines a being who can only be contingent: as the adversary, he must always be a function of another, not an independent entity. As Augustine and

Milton show, it is precisely when Satan imagines himself independent that he is most deluded. His character is, in this sense of
the word, a *fiction*' (Forsyth 1987: 4). Satan, therefore, has a narrative purpose, and he gets his meaning from his role in a Christian
mythological world history. 'The role of Satan in that narrative
is to be the Opponent, the Adversary, the one who motivates the
plot, who drives the story into motion. The idea that Christ, or
God, is good and Satan evil, though very widespread, is not universal and is in any case secondary; it is an interpretation of the
primary texts and traditions which are narrative and may reverse
(or simply ignore) good and evil markers. Characters ... are produced by the plot and function as the plot requires: evil comes
later' (Forsyth 2003: 26). For example in *Paradise Lost*, Satan begins as the opponent of God and chooses evil later as a strategy,
'just to be different'; this is not a difference in essence, but of
'structure and direction' (Forsyth 2003: 27). We therefore misunderstand Satan if we characterise him as *embodied evil* – evil by
nature; he *chooses* evil. In this sense, Satan is by no means a monster. He is, essentially, the opposition to the hero of a particular
myth.

Although contemporary fiction is more complex than myth and
has layers concerned with psychological character and motivation, it may be that the 'evil enemy' in modern literature and film
still has this mythological element, such that they play a specific
and prescribed role which makes *their* psychological character
and motivation irrelevant or at least marginal, or even, as Adam
Morton commented in Chapter 3, as 'diabolically alien' (Morton
2004: 98). Perhaps it is because we are trying to place an essentially mythological figure into a modern narrative that the character of evil agents become 'archetypal horrors' (Morton 2004: 102).
One place where we can see the importance of the evil character
more clearly is in fairy tales, which follow the mythological narrative structure more closely. In her study of evil in fairy tales, Verena Kast says: 'let us call evil that which opposes and obstructs the
fairy tale hero and his will, or which disrupts his pre-existing situation' (Kast 1992: 18). And: 'By understanding evil as that which
obstructs, various levels and qualities of evil emerge' (Kast 1992:
19). One important point that does emerge is that 'evil is not simply evil' (Kast 1992: 16), as the character that obstructs can be both
good and evil at the same time. Animals which are vicious and
dangerous can turn out to be helpful when tamed, and princesses
can be beautiful but destructive when their suitors are killed if

they fail a seemingly impossible task. But another mythological sense of evil is not merely obstruction, but rebellion. Vitautas Kavolis looks at two classic myths of rebellion, of Prometheus and Satan. In both we have 'the general theme of rebellion by an individual against the supreme authority in the established normative order and against the rules by which this order operates' (Kavolis 1984: 18). The Promethean model comes out of Greek culture. In Greek mythology, Prometheus rebels against Zeus to bring fire to humanity, and so is the patron of civilisation. Here: 'Rebellion is . . . a "noble crime", and in the life history of the rebel . . . the substantive personal virtue of the individual overcomes the formal criminality of the rebellious act' (Kavolis 1984: 18). The Satanic model dominates Judaeo-Christian thought, and here Satan rebels through resentment, or in Nietzsche's terms, *ressentiment* – a grudge-filled hatred. This resentment has various causes in the traditional writings, pride among them (Kavolis 1984: 18–19). Here, the rebel is not concerned with the welfare of others; he does not rebel against an unjust order for the sake of humanity as does Prometheus, but rebels against an order which deprives him of power and status. He rebels not against the order of things, but against his place in that order, and he seeks to invert it rather than create a new one. In Christian thought, therefore, there is a strong connection between rebellion and resentment and destruction – rebellion against the established order is evil. Kavolis concludes: 'We have . . . two interpretative models of rebellion, both potentially applicable to the behaviour of actual rebels in any civilisation. The first model suggests that rebellion, motivated by humane sympathy for the sufferings of others and expressed through particular acts of practical assistance, results in an enduringly valuable change in the structure of the moral universe. The other model contends that rebellion, motivated by personal resentment and expressed in global attempts to create an alternative style of life and impose it on others, is destructive in its consequences' (Kavolis 1984: 20).

It should not be a surprise that the latter is how the contemporary problem of 'Islamic terrorism' is presented – as people motivated by *ressentiment* against the west and engaged in a global campaign to impose their own way of life upon others, a project which is apocalyptic in its destructive potential. Kavolis says: 'The dominant Judeo-Christian tendency, shaped or reinforced by Iranian influences and surviving in a variety of secular ideologies of western European derivation, has been to adopt a *mobilising* or *reifying* attitude towards moral issues' (Kavolis 1984: 21). This means that we seek to promote good and oppose evil 'by rigidly separating them, as objects of total worship and of absolute condemnation... The good is... identified with lawful order, the evil with disorder that automatically arises from refusal to submit to lawful order' (Kavolis 1984: 21–2). Rebellion is judged as 'arising outside the normative order and as constituting a threat not only to the current political manifestation of that order, but to the principle of order itself' (Kavolis 1984: 24). Kavolis agrees with the account we developed in Chapter 2, that the Satanic myth emerged during a period when the Jewish community felt itself to be in extreme danger. 'Satan emerged as a religious interpretation of the perceived readiness of members of a community in which high value has been traditionally placed on group solidarity to abandon the moral ties of mutual obligation' (Kavolis 1984: 26). And, as we saw in Chapter 4: 'A similar situation developed in Christian Europe at the peak of the power of the devil and fear of witchcraft, toward the end of the Middle Ages' (Kavolis 1984: 26). Evil, then, is that which opposes us, that which rebels against the authoritative order of things, and by describing others as evil we condemn them as negative, resentful destructive rebels – we assign them a narrative role in a mythological world history.

Mythologies

As Kavolis observes the witch trials in Europe and North America in the sixteenth and seventeenth centuries are a powerful example of the destructive power of the myth of the evil enemy. In Chapter 4 I suggested that the vampire epidemics of eastern Europe in the eighteenth century give us another example of the fear and panic that can grip a community that feels that it is under siege, and I argued that what is fundamentally disturbing about the vampire and the witch is their ability to pass among us undetected, to appear to be part of humanity but to be secretly scheming its destruction. The person sitting next to you now as you read this could be a witch or a vampire. This is by far the most frightening aspect of them. The evil enemy renders borders insecure and meaningless. In the case of witches the border becomes meaningless because they are already *inside* the community; in the case of vampires they have the demonic power to cross borders without detection, however secure we make them. There are

important parallels here with contemporary fears over mass migration and global terrorism, and these are further examples of
the irrational fear of imaginary monsters. One objection to such a
claim is, of course, that while witches and vampires are obviously
the product of the imagination, migrants and terrorists are not –
they *do* exist while the witch and the vampire did not, and so any
attempt to draw lessons about our current 'panics' from the witch
craze and the vampire epidemic must be flawed.

But there are two reasons to think we can illuminate the present
with the past here. First, so far as European intellectuals and peas-
ants were concerned up until the eighteenth century, witches did
exist. Even those who protested most vigorously against the trials
did not question the existence of witches; they merely suggested
that the confused peasant women being executed were innocent,
and the real witches were evading capture. And as far as the people
of eastern Europe were concerned there was no question that vampires existed. What follows from this is that terrorists and global
migrants do exist, but in the same way that vampires and witches
existed in the epistemological/political frameworks of perception
of the time. It can be objected that the evidence that terrorists and
migrants have an existence beyond our frameworks of belief is
overwhelming, but again the evidence that witches and vampires
existed was also considered to be overwhelming. However, the
most important and significant point is that there was undeniably
some real process underlying the witch craze and the vampire
epidemics which, to some degree, caused people to believe in the
reality of these events. People were undeniably practising magical rituals with the intention of causing harm to their neighbours.
What lay behind the vampire epidemics is more complex, but
again *something* was happening. So certainly there are real processes in the world today that underlie our perceptions of a *crisis*
of migration and the war on terror, but those processes may be
very different to the way they are represented by the political authorities and in the media – the 'official' picture of the migrant
and the terrorist may be exactly parallel with the demonological picture of the witch, an entirely fantastical picture designed
through, in Hugh Trevor-Roper's words, 'political exploitations
of a social fear' (Trevor-Roper 1978: 54). These figures may have
been demonised to such an extent that they are no longer reliable
representations of the processes that are actually taking place in
the world around us. And so the terrorist and the migrant as represented by the political authorities may well be imaginary.

There is a second, crucial aspect to this argument – that they are not only imaginary, but that they are monsters. What we have here is a mythology of the evil enemy, such that that enemy possesses the demonic, supernatural powers needed to destroy our communities. This, surely, is a step too far – nobody seriously believes that migrants and terrorists have supernatural powers. But this is *exactly* what happens through the discourse of evil: the migrant and the terrorist, while they are not represented as agents of Satan, *are* represented as possessing demonic and supernatural powers. With respect to mass migration, I argued in Chapter 4 that the example of the movement of Jews from eastern Europe to the west was entangled with the supernatural figure of the vampire, and the Jews were attributed with the ability to ghost across borders and threaten national identities. And I argued that contemporary migrants are still granted the same demonic powers and are still represented as a vampiric threat to the 'national' community. The same pattern can be seen in the representation of contemporary global terrorism. In Chapter 4 we saw how Christendom understood itself to be under ferocious attack from Satan in the sixteenth and seventeenth centuries, and how this led to the suspension of legal procedures, mass arrests, the use of torture, and indiscriminate use of the death penalty. There are dramatic parallels here with the contemporary war on terror: the normal rules of justice have been suspended or simply ignored as new rules have been written to enable thousands to be detained and imprisoned, some without the prospect of trial; and the use of torture has been widespread. Here, there is the imaginary element – the extent to which the threat of global terrorism has been imagined and exaggerated; and there is the monstrous element – the extent to which the 'evil enemy' is represented as possessing demonic powers they intend to use to destroy us.

Changing the Rules

In the United Kingdom new terrorism laws were passed in late 2001 in response to the September 11th attack on New York, and the government also opted out of an element of the European Convention on Human Rights (news.bbc.co.uk/go/pr/fr/-/1/hi/uk/3666235.stm). This allowed the Home Secretary to order detention of foreign terrorist suspects without trial, in the absence of sufficient evidence to bring a criminal case to the courts. Fourteen people were arrested as soon as the law was passed, two of whom took the option of leaving the United Kingdom. The others were held in a high-security prison, and appealed to the Special Immigration Appeals Commission (Siac). This commission, described by the BBC as 'one of the most controversial – and certainly the most secret court within English law', hears appeals of foreign nationals facing detention, deportation or exclusion from the UK on grounds of national security, presided over by senior judges and with the same powers as the High Court. Its hearings are not fully revealed to the appellants because they include testimony from members of the secret security services. Siac was established in 1996 after the British government lost a case at the European Court of Human Rights, which criticised the old system on the grounds that appellants or their lawyers could not hear all the evidence against them. Siac is supposed to solve this problem with a system of security-vetted lawyers, separate from the appellant's lawyers. These lawyers are subjected to intensive security checks before they are accepted as 'special advocates' for the appellants, and they are able to see all the secret evidence, but they cannot reveal any of it to the appellant or the appellant's lawyers. The special advocate can challenge whether certain evidence should be made open, and, if Siac agrees, then the government must disclose it or may withdraw it. During the hearing the appellant and his or her team can sit in court to hear open evidence, but must then withdraw. The special advocate can then challenge the closed evidence, but obviously without instruction from the appellant. The commission, once it makes a decision, makes an open judgement for public consumption, but also a closed judgement which once more cannot be revealed. The commission was designed to prevent appeal over decisions, except to the House of Lords on a point of law, although a lower court, the Court of Appeal, did back the commission's decision to release one of the detainees, ruling against the government. Amnesty International has criticised the system on the grounds that the burden of proof for the commission's judgements is 'shockingly low', and that it may be in breach of international law as it relies on evidence that may have been extracted through the use of torture of suspects in other countries. Historically, evidence gained through torture has been dismissed by courts as unreliable, except, of course, during the witch-trial period.

In December 2004 the law lords, the highest court in Britain, ruled that detention of foreign terrorist suspects without trial broke human rights law (news.bbc.co.uk/go/fr/-/1/hi/uk/ 4100481.stm). One of the senior law lords, Lord Bingham, said the rules were incompatible with the European Convention on Human Rights as they allowed detentions 'in a way that discriminates on the ground of nationality or immigration status' by justifying detention without trial for foreign subjects but not British nationals. The last eight detainees – three of the them being held in the high-security mental hospital Broadmoor because of concerns about their mental condition – were released on bail in March 2005. New legislation enabled the government to impose electronic tagging and control orders, which include a night-time curfew from 7 p.m. to 7 a.m., a ban on using mobile phones and the internet, obtaining permission from the Home Office if suspects wish to meet someone outside their home, living at an address notified to the police, who can search the property without warning, and having no visitors unless the Home Office has been informed in advance except for people under sixteen (news.bbc.co.uk/go/fr/-/1/hi/uk/4338849.stm). In June 2005, the Council of Europe's human rights commissioner, Alvaro Gil-Robles, criticised these arrangements on the ground that they violated the fundamental human right of the presumption of innocence (*The Independent*, 9 June 2005). He also criticised the British government's view that it had the right to use evidence obtained by the use of torture in another country, a view upheld by the Court of Appeal in 2004. His report also criticised the criminalising of children through government policies on anti-social behaviour, and the detention of asylum seekers for long periods of time.

After terrorist attacks in London in July 2005, however, the British government is now considering more expansive legislation. The proposals include new offences of encouraging and glorifying terrorism, disseminating terrorist publications, and preparing terrorist acts and training. Police want to be allowed to detain terrorist suspects without charge for up to three months instead of the current fourteen days, and the rules on allowing security service phone tap evidence are likely to be changed. The government also wants to increase the powers of the Home Secretary to order deportations or exclusions of foreigners judged to be extremists, including those who express support of terrorist acts anywhere in the world through the internet, in bookshops, written word or preaching. The power to ban extremist groups will be extended from those directly involved in terrorism to include those who 'glorify, exalt or celebrate' terrorist acts (*The Guardian*, 16 September 2005).

There were similar developments in the United States, with the passing of what is known as the USA Patriot Act in October 2001, or, to give it the full title, The Uniting and Strengthening America by Providing Appropriate Tools Required to Intercept and Obstruct Terrorism Act. The Act allowed for the indefinite imprisonment without trial of non-US citizens that the Attorney General believed to be a threat to national security (en.wikipedia.org/wiki/usA_Patriot_Act). The government is not obliged, under the Act, to provide detainees with counsel, or to make any announcement or statement concerning the arrest. It also allowed the security services to employ a wide range of methods to gather information, raising fears that it violated the Constitution and was an attack on civil liberties. By late November 2001, more than 1,200 people in the United States had been detained and were being held at secret locations under the Act (en.wikipedia.org/wiki/September_11%2C_2001_Terrorist_Attack/ Detentions). These were mostly male Arabic or Muslim non-citizens. As with the British example, there were concerns about the lack of legal review, lack of evidence and the lack of publicity for these detainees. A report by Amnesty International expressed concerns about the situation of the detainees (available from its United States website, www.amnestyusa.org). Of the around 1,200 people initially arrested, 327 were still in custody by February 2002. An unknown number have been released on bail or deported from the United States. Amnesty observed 'a disturbing level of secrecy surrounding the detentions, which has made it difficult to monitor the situation', but concluded that 'a significant number of detainees' were 'deprived of certain basic rights guaranteed under international law'. The Immigration and Naturalization Service (INS), which carried out the arrests, was given sweeping powers after the September 11th attack, including the power to detain people without charge for up to 48 hours or, in an emergency or other extraordinary circumstances, for a further undefined period. The INS also has the power to override decisions by immigration judges to grant bail in certain cases. Beyond the concern that people were being detained without trial and without access to legal counsel, Amnesty was also concerned 'that some people may be returned to countries where they are at risk of human rights abuses'. It also received reports of detainees being 'routinely shackled with belly chains and leg shackles, with no regard as to whether they have a record of violent behaviour or flight risk. Some have been held in prolonged solitary confinement. Other complaints include lack of exercise, poor medical care and failure to adhere to religious dietary requirements. Despite being held on non-criminal charges, INS detainees have not always been separated from criminal detainees, contrary to international standards.'

The United States has also been accused of disregarding international law when it comes to detention and imprisonment of terrorist suspects at its base in Guantanamo Bay in Cuba. More than 700 people from 44 different countries have been held there, many of them for more than two years (Human Rights Watch, *The Road to Abu Ghraib*: 5). The US government has argued that Guantanamo Bay itself is a place where no court has jurisdiction, American or international, and that the detainees are 'enemy combatants', and so neither civilians nor prisoners of war, which again places them beyond both US and international law, specifically the Geneva Convention. It has also argued that the detentions are not based on military orders, but on presidential common-law war powers. Adam Brookes reported the legal procedures of Guantanamo Bay for the BBC in April 2005 (news.bbc.co.uk/go/fr/-/1/hi/world/americas/4422825.stm). Detainees go through three procedures. The first is a Combat Status Review Tribunal to decide if the detainee is an 'enemy combatant'; an Administrative Review Board decides if the detainee should be released because he poses no threat to the United States or whether he should be held for another year; and a military commission tries those considered to have committed serious crimes. It is not known how many of the Guantanamo detainees have actually appeared before any of these bodies.

On 28 June 2004, the US Supreme Court ruled that the Guantanamo detainees could challenge their detention in federal courts. A six-three majority stated that they had a right of *habeus corpus*, a right that extended outside the territorial boundaries of the nation. However, while the decision does give the Guantanamo detainees the right to challenge their detention, the ruling does not challenge the legal right of the government to hold both its own citizens and foreign nationals without charges or trial under the anti-terrorism legislation – those affected can challenge their detention on a case-by-case basis, but there is absolutely no guarantee that they would win those cases. Although two of the Supreme Court justices wanted to declare the detentions improper, that was not the overall position arrived at by the Court. Another problem is that it only covers those held in the United States and at Guantanamo Bay, and one disturbing feature identified by Human Rights Watch has been the practice of 'disappearances' (*The Road to Abu Ghraib*: 12). The most sensitive detainees are held at undisclosed locations, and are therefore beyond any scope for monitoring. Human Rights Watch has identified thirteen people 'apprehended in places like Pakistan, Indonesia, Thailand, Morocco, and the United Arab Emirates, who have "disappeared" in U.S. custody' (*The Road to Abu Ghraib*: 12). At the time of writing this in May 2005, many have been released into the custody of their own countries and once there have been released without charge. However, about 500 detainees remain in Guantanamo Bay.

Torture

Another issue that carries a deep resonance with the witch-trial period is that of torture. Once more this raises the issue of the suspension of international law. According to American news service CNN, a United States government classified report argued that the detention of al-Qa'ida and Taliban suspects was not covered by the Geneva Convention regarding the use of torture (edition.cnn.com/LAW/, posted 9 June 2004). According to the *Wall Street Journal* on 7 June 2004, it was an incomplete document prepared for the US government reviewing the laws of war under the Geneva Conventions regarding the use of torture. The report noted the US ratification of the Convention against Torture and Other Cruel, Inhumane, or Degrading Treatment or Punishment, but said it 'did so with a variety of reservations and understandings'. One of these reservations was that 'the United States has maintained consistently that the covenant does not apply outside the United States or its special maritime and territorial jurisdiction, and that it does not apply to operations of the military during an international armed conflict'. It concluded 'that customary international law cannot bind the executive branch under the Constitution because it is not federal law', and that 'any presidential decision in the current conflict concerning the detention and trial of Al Qaeda or Taliban military prisoners would constitute a "controlling" executive act that would immediately and completely override any customary international law.' This meant that 'in order to respect the president's inherent constitutional authority to manage a military campaign [the prohibition against torture] must be construed as inapplicable to interrogations undertaken pursuant to his [authority as] commander-in-chief'. The report lists cases where anti-torture laws could be set aside, and a set of 'torture techniques' that were justifiable. As for the detainees at Guantanamo Bay, 'The U.S. criminal laws do not apply to acts committed there by virtue of [Guantanamo's] status as within the special maritime and territorial jurisdiction', and the detainees 'do not have constitutional rights under the Fifth Amendment of due process'. Although the report was not published, it seems fair to say that it was a reflection of the thinking of the US government with regard to international law, Guantanamo Bay and the use of torture. Another factor has been the transfer of detainees from American custody to countries in the Middle East that are known to practise torture, such as Syria, Uzbekistan, Pakistan, Egypt, Jordan, Saudi Arabia and Morocco (*The Road to Abu Ghraib*: 10).

There is now overwhelming evidence that prisoners in United States custody in Iraq faced the possibility of torture. There were three levels of abuse of detainees at Abu Ghraib prison and elsewhere: first, a level the US government sanctioned throughout; second, a level it sanctioned between December 2002 and dropped in April 2003; and third, a level it claims it did not sanction at all, but was carried out by personnel. The first level of official interrogation techniques, according to *The Independent* newspaper on 24 June 2004, includes providing a reward or removing a privilege beyond those required by the Geneva Convention; significantly increasing the fear level in a detainee; adjusting the sleeping time of a detainee; boosting or attacking the ego of a detainee; invoking the feeling of futility in a detainee. The second level included forced shaving of the beard or head; hooding during transport and interrogation; interrogations for up to twenty hours; use of mild, noninjurious contact; stress positions for a maximum of four hours; removal of clothing; and use of dogs to frighten the detainee. Part of the US government's reply to the charges of torture has been that the practices employed at Guantanamo Bay, Abu Ghraib and other locations fall short of it, except for some lapses which had no official sanction, and the internal documents which outlined the above practices that it released on 23 June 2004 were supposed to establish that case. But legal and medical experts have argued that even the officially approved practices violate the Geneva Convention in that some may amount to torture and are specifically banned by international courts and torture conventions, and others would violate those aspects of the Convention which prohibit inhumane and degrading treatment. Robert Verkaik, reporting in *The Independent* newspaper on 24 June 2004, quotes Sherman Carroll, director of public affairs at the Medical Foundation for the Care of Victims of Torture: 'The documents from the White House authorised specific interrogation techniques by U.S. forces abroad that amount to torture.'

However, it was the third level of abuse that received the greatest media attention in May 2004, and in Chapter 1 I looked at the suggestion that it was the background set in place by the political leadership that led to the horrific acts that took place at Abu Ghraib prison. Human Rights Watch concluded the same in a report called *The Road to Abu Ghraib* published on 10 June 2004. According to that report: 'This pattern of abuse did not result from the acts of individual soldiers who broke the rules. It resulted from decisions made by the Bush administration to bend, ignore, or cast rules aside. Administration policies created the climate for Abu Ghraib' (*The Road to Abu Ghraib*: 1). The worst abuses at Abu Ghraib occurred after a decision by the US government to 'step up the hunt' for intelligence, and Major General Geoffrey D. Miller, who oversaw interrogation methods at Guantanamo Bay, was sent there in August 2003 to review methods in Iraq. In addition, between three and five interrogation teams were sent from Guantanamo Bay in October 2003 'for use in the interrogation effort' (*The Road to Abu Ghraib*: 33).

What resulted included the following. According to the International Committee of the Red Cross Report of February 2004, 'methods of physical and psychological coercion were used by the military intelligence in a systematic way to gain confessions and extract information' (*The Road to Abu Ghraib*: 25). Those methods included hooding to disorient and prevent detainees from breathing freely; being forced to remain for prolonged periods in painful stress positions; being attached repeatedly over several days for several hours each time to the bars of cell doors naked or in positions causing physical pain; being held naked in dark cells for several days and paraded naked, sometimes hooded or with women's underwear over their heads; sleep, food and water deprivation; prolonged exposure while hooded to the sun during the hottest time of day. Another investigation was carried out for the US authorities by Major General Antonio Taguba, who concluded that 'numerous instances of sadistic, blatant, and wanton criminal abuses' were inflicted on several detainees. These in-cluded punching, slapping and kicking detainees; jumping on their naked feet; videotaping and photographing naked male and female detainees; forcibly arranging detainees in various sexually explicit positions for photographing; forcing groups of naked de-tainees to masturbate themselves while being photographed and videotaped; arranging naked detainees in a pile and then jumping on them; placing a dog chain or strap around a naked detainee's neck and having a female soldier pose with him with a picture; a male military police guard having sex with a female detainee (not described as rape in the Taguba report); beating detainees with a broom handle and a chair; threatening male detainees with rape; sodomising a detainee with a chemical light and perhaps a broom stick; forcing male detainees to wear women's under-wear (*The Road to Abu Ghraib*: 25–7). In addition, around thirty people have died in detention in Iraq. Some of these cases are be-ing investigated as possible homicides (*The Road to Abu Ghraib*: 27). Human Rights Watch concludes: 'What is clear is that U.S. military personnel at Abu Ghraib felt empowered to abuse the detainees. The brazenness with which the soldiers at the center of the scandal conducted themselves, snapping photographs and flashing the "thumbs-up" sign as they abused prisoners, suggests they felt they had nothing to hide from their superiors. The abuse was so widely known and accepted that a picture of naked de-tainees forced in a human pyramid was reportedly used as a screen saver on a computer in the interrogation room' (*The Road to Abu Ghraib*: 34).

This is a story with no end in sight. On 4 August 2004, *The Independent* newspaper published details of a report published by the Centre for Constitutional Rights based in New York, which revealed that the prisoners at Guantanamo Bay 'were subjected to Abu Ghraib-style torture and sexual humiliation in which they were stripped naked, forced to sodomise one another and taunted by naked female American soldiers'. According to the newspaper, 'the report details a brutal yet carefully choreographed regime at the U.S. prison camp in which abuse was meted out in a manner judged to have the "maximum impact". Those prisoners with the most conservative Muslim backgrounds were the most likely to be subjected to sexual humiliation and abuse, while those from westernised backgrounds were more likely to suffer solitary con-finement and physical mistreatment'. And in May 2005, a US army report was leaked detailing abuses of Afghan detainees at

Bagram air base. The report detailed abuses including the torture and killing of two Afghans. Details of the report were published by the *New York Times*, and include the claim that one prisoner was chained to a ceiling by his wrists for four days and beaten on his legs more than a hundred times during a 24-hour period (news.bbc.co.uk/1/hi/world/south_asia/4570631.stm). In February 2005, four British soldiers were prosecuted for similar offences after 'trophy' photographs were found of abuses committed at an aid depot near Basra in Iraq. However, there was no prosecution 'for some of the most shocking of the 22 images – Iraqi men stripped naked, being forced to simulate oral and anal sex, their humiliation completed by being made to smile and give a thumbs-up for the camera' (*The Independent*, 24 February 2005). Other cases are still being investigated – more than 160 charges of abuse have been investigated by British military prosecutors, and a number of British soldiers have been charged with murder.

The Imaginary Iraq

In April, 2005, the Iraq Survey Group (ISG), the US team investigating whether Iraq had weapons of mass destruction, published its final report: its 1,700-member team had found no evidence that Iraq possessed biological, chemical or nuclear weapons (*Financial Times*, 27 April 2005). The head of the ISG, Charles Duelfer, said: 'As matters now stand, the WMD investigation has gone as far as feasible. After more than 18 months, the WMD investigation and debriefing of WMD-related detainees has been exhausted.' There was no evidence, said the report, that Iraq had moved its weapons of mass destruction to Syria before being attacked by the United States and Great Britain in 2003, as claimed by some members of the US administration. 'Based on the evidence available at present, ISG judged that it was unlikely that an official transfer of WMD material from Iraq to Syria ever took place,' said Mr Duelfer. The *Financial Times* also reported the concerns of Democrat Senator Carl Levin, a member of the Senate armed services committee, that members of the US administration continued to raise an alleged meeting of one of the September 11th attackers of the World Trade Center in New York, with an Iraq intelligence officer in Prague, despite a CIA report disputing that this meeting had ever taken place. There has been no evidence of any connection between Iraq and the September 11th attack. This is the state of the world in 2005: Iraq had no connection with the September 11th attack and possessed no weapons of mass destruction. Someone visiting the planet for the first time would not find these reports remarkable; in fact, if that person had a journalistic background, he or she might wonder why they were being published at all: surely, that something had *never* happened, that a certain situation had *not* existed, is not news? However, what makes the reports news, indeed makes them remarkable, is the extent to which the world has changed in three years. As those of us who have been here that long know, three years ago there was no doubt that Iraq possessed weapons of mass destruction, and there was a firm possibility of a link between its regime and al-Qa'ida and global terrorism in general. So strong was the evidence that the United States and Great Britain felt they had the authority to attack Iraq and overthrow its government in order to save the world from these twin threats. Indeed, by March 2003, almost half of American citizens believed Saddam Hussein was personally involved in the September 11 attacks, and around 60 per cent believed him to be an immediate threat to the United States (Chomsky 2004: 18). Saddam Hussein was the 'demonic enemy', but it turns out he was an imaginary monster.

The full extent of the fabrication of the imaginary Iraq has yet to be written, and has to be pieced together from news reports and government statements. The Central Intelligence Agency (CIA) and the British intelligence services have been blamed for seemingly persuading their governments that Iraq posed a serious threat through its possession of weapons of mass destruction. In 2002 the evidence was clear enough for the White House to release a report claiming that Saddam Hussein was, among other things, 'continuing to seek and develop chemical, biological, and nuclear weapons, and prohibited long-range missiles' (White House press release, 12 September 2002, www.whitehouse.gov/news/releases/2002/09/20020912.html). According to that report, an Iraqi defector claimed to have visited 'twenty secret facilities for chemical, biological and nuclear weapons'. Also there was evidence to 'strongly suggest that Iraq maintains stockpiles of chemical agents, probably VX, sarin, cyclosarin and mustard'. Not only that, but Saddam Hussein 'continues his work to develop a nuclear weapon'; he could 'build a nuclear bomb within months if he were able to obtain fissile material'. The British government was equally convinced. Prime Minister Tony Blair told the House of Commons on 10 April 2002, 'Saddam Hussein's regime is despicable, he is developing weapons of mass destruction, and we cannot leave him doing so unchecked'; and 'He is a threat to his own people and to the region and, if allowed to develop these weapons, a threat to us also' (news.bbc.co.uk/go/pr/fr/-/1/hi/uk_politics/3054991.stm). The government published a dossier of intelligence evidence to back its case against Iraq on 24 September 2002 (see news.bbc.co.uk.nol/shared/spl/hi/middle_east/02/uk_dossier_on_iraq/html/full_dossier.stm). In its foreword, Tony Blair states: 'despite his denials, Saddam Hussein is continuing to develop WMD, and with them the ability to inflict real damage upon the region, and the stability of the world'; and 'What I believe the assessed intelligence has established beyond doubt is that Saddam has continued to produce chemical and biological weapons, that he continues in his efforts to develop nuclear weapons, and that he has been able to extend the range of his ballistic missile programme.' He says the intelligence also discloses 'that his military planning allows for some of the WMD to be ready within 45 minutes of an order to use them. I am quite clear that Saddam will go to extreme lengths, indeed has already done so, to hide these weapons and avoid giving them up.' In its executive summary, the report says Iraq has:

- continued to produce chemical and biological agents;
- military plans for the use of chemical and biological weapons, including against its own Shia population. Some of these weapons are deployable within 45 minutes of an order to use them;
- command and control arrangement in place to use chemical and biological weapons . . . ;
- tried to covertly acquire technology and materials which could be used in the production of nuclear weapons.

The British intelligence services and the CIA produced reports of Iraq's capabilities regarding weapons of mass destruction which their governments used to justify the attack upon Iraq to their public. However, as we have seen, no evidence has since been found to show that Iraq possessed these capabilities, and both in Britain and the United States enquiries have criticised the intelligence services for their misleading information, while clearing governments of pressuring them into producing such reports. In Britain the Butler Report was published on 14 July 2004. On the intelligence dossier of September 2002, the report concluded: '. . . in translating material from Joint Intelligence Committee (JIC) assessments into the dossier, warnings were lost about the limited intelligence base on which some aspects of these assessments were being made' (All extracts of the Butler Report are taken from an edited version published in *The Independent* on 15 July 2004). And 'the language in the dossier may have left with readers the impression that there was fuller and firmer intelligence behind the judgements than was the case: our view, having reviewed all the material, is that judgements in the dossier went to (but not beyond) the outer limits of the intelligence available'. The statement by the Prime Minister to the House of Commons on the day the dossier was published that it was 'extensive, detailed and authoritative' may, says the Butler Report, 'have reinforced that impression'. The report concludes that 'it was a serious weakness that the JIC's warnings on the limitations of the intelligence underlying its judgements were not made sufficiently clear in the dossier'; and that 'making public that the JIC had authorship of the dossier was a mistaken judgement'.

The claim in the dossier that Iraq possessed weapons of mass destruction that were 'deployable within 45 minutes of an order to use them' made a particular impact in the British media, with the *Sun* newspaper using the headline 'Brits 45 minutes from doom', and the *Star* claiming 'Mad Saddam ready to strike: 45 minutes from a chemical war'. In fact this claim referred to battlefield weapons although this was not made clear in the Executive Summary, nor in the Prime Minister's introduction. However, British ministers took no steps to put this unfounded fear to rest. Indeed, Tony Blair told the House of Commons on 4 February 2004, that he did not know that the 45 minute claim only referred to battlefield weapons. On this the Butler Report said: 'Much public attention has been given to the Prime Minister's statement that he was not aware until after the war that this report should have been interpreted as referring to battlefield weapons. If this report was regarded as having operational significance, and if in particular it had been regarded as covering ballistic missiles (as was reported in some newspapers), this indeed would have been surprising. If, however, it referred to forward-deployed battlefield munitions, the time period given would not have been surprising or worth drawing to the Prime Minister's attention. But it was unclear both in the JIC assessment of 9 September and in the Government's dossier which of the two it was. The JIC should not have included the "45-minute" report in its assessment and in the Government's dossier without stating what it was believed to refer to. The fact that the reference in the classed assessment was repeated in the dossier later led to suspicions that it had been included because of its eye-catching nature.'

In the United States, the Senate Select Committee on Intelligence published its 'Report on the U.S. Intelligence Community's Prewar Intelligence Assessments on Iraq' on 9 July 2004. Its primary conclusion was: 'Most of the major key judgements in the Intelligence Community's October 2002 National Intelligence Estimate (NIE), *Iraq's Continuing Programs for Weapons of Mass Destruction*, either overstated, or were not supported by, the underlying intelligence reporting. A series of failures, particularly in analytic trade craft, led to the mischaracterization of the intelligence' (Senate Report on the US Intelligence Community's Prewar Intelligence Assessments on Iraq: 1). In particular, the NIE's major judgements concerning Iraq's nuclear programme and chemical and biological weapons capacities were 'either overstated, or were not supported by, the underlying intelligence reporting provided to the Committee' (Senate Report: 1). However: 'The Committee found no evidence that the IC's [Intelligence Community's] mischaracterization or exaggeration of the intelligence on Iraq's weapons of mass destruction (WMD) capabilities was the result of political pressure' (Senate Report: 2). Democratic members of the committee disagreed with this last finding, and argued that 'questioning from the White House was almost exclusively in one direction. Analyst assessments that were generally sceptical were much more likely to be sent back with queries scrawled in the margins than assessments that found that there were indeed weapons of mass destruction in Iraq, and links between Baghdad and al-Qaida' (*The Guardian*, 10 July 2004).

Three paragraphs of the Senate Report summarise the failings of the Intelligence Community:

> At the time the IC drafted and coordinated the NIE on Iraq's weapons of mass destruction (WMD) programs in September 2002, most of what intelligence analysts actually 'knew' about Iraq's weapons programs pre-dated the 1991 Gulf War, leaving them with very little direct knowledge about the current state of these programs. Analysts knew that Iraq had active nuclear, chemical, biological, and delivery programs before 1991, and had previously lied to, and was still not forthcoming with, UN weapons inspectors about those programs. The analysts also knew

that the United Nations was not satisfied with Iraq's efforts to account for its destruction of all its pre-Gulf War weapons, precursors, and equipment. Additionally analysts knew that Iraq was trying to import dual-use materials and equipment and had rebuilt or was continuing to use facilities that had been associated with Iraq's pre-Gulf War weapons programs, and knew that WMD were likely within Iraq's technological capabilities.

The IC did not know whether Iraq had retained its pre-Gulf War weapons, whether Iraq was intending to use those dual-use materials and facilities for weapons or for legitimate purposes, or even if Iraq's attempts to obtain many of the dual-use goods it had been trying to procure were successful. The IC thought that Iraq had retained its pre-Gulf War weapons and that Iraq was using dual-use materials and facilities to manufacture weapons. While this was a reasonable assessment, considering Iraq's past behavior, statements in the 2002 NIE that Iraq 'has chemical and biological weapons', 'Iraq has maintained its chemical weapons effort,' and 'is reconstituting its nuclear weapons program,' did not accurately portray the uncertainty of the information. The NIE failed in that it portrayed what intelligence analysts thought and assessed as what they knew and failed to explain the large gaps in the information on which the assessments were based.

In the cases in the NIE where the IC did express uncertainty about its assessments concerning Iraq's WMD capabilities, those explanations suggested, in some cases, that Iraq's capabilities were even greater than the NIE judged. For example, the key judgements of the NIE said 'we judge that we are seeing only a portion of Iraq's WMD efforts, owing to Baghdad's vigorous denial and deception efforts. Revelations after the Gulf War starkly demonstrate the extensive efforts undertaken by Iraq to deny information . . . ' While this did explain that key information on Iraq's programs was lacking, it suggested that Iraq's weapons programs were probably bigger and more advanced than the IC had judged and did not explain that . . . analysts did not have enough information to determine whether Iraq was hiding activity or whether Iraq's weapons program may have been dormant. (Senate Report: 3–4)

This confirms Dani Cavallaro's distinction between horror and terror in Gothic fiction which we encountered in Chapter 5: that horror is a matter of spectacle, while terror is a matter of invisibility (Cavallaro 2002: vii) – terror is 'deemed intangible and resistant to definition' (Cavallaro 2002: 2), and 'disturbs because of its indeterminateness', such that 'it cannot be connected with an identifiable physical object and the factors that determine it accordingly elude classification and naming' (Cavallaro 2002: 2). Its causes are always 'uncertain and obscure' (Cavallaro 2002: 3), such that 'if horror makes people shiver, terror undermines the foundations of their worlds' (Cavallaro 2002: 2–3). It is what we cannot see that scares us most. Unfortunately, our inability to see what terrifies us allows the possibility that there is nothing there at all.

The Monster of Terrorism

In Chapter 4 we saw that the witch trials represented the belief that Christendom was under a ferocious assault by the forces of Satan, an apocalyptic assault that signalled the end of the world. Witches were part of a vast and highly organised conspiracy, working in league with each other, with demons, and with the Devil to overthrow Christian civilisation. Where one witch was found there had to be others, as they never worked alone. This perception of a global conspiracy is certainly an important part of how global terrorism is represented by political authorities. In his State of the Union address in 2002, George W. Bush said: 'Thousands of dangerous killers, schooled in the methods of murder, often supported by outlaw regimes, are now spread throughout the world like ticking time bombs, set to go off without warning.' A few sentences later, this threat had grown tenfold: 'tens of thousands of trained terrorists are still at large. These enemies view the entire world as a battlefield and we must pursue them wherever they are.' He went on to identify a 'terrorist underworld' which operated in remote jungles and deserts and also in the centres of large cities. There are clear parallels here between the witch craze and the contemporary perception of global terrorism, to the extent that it is represented as a global conspiracy bent on the destruction of western civilisation, consisting of enemies bent on bringing about an apocalypse. On 11 December 2001, Bush described terrorism as a 'great threat to civilisation' (remarks at The

Citadel, Charleston, South Carolina, www.usinfo.state.gov), and on 8 November 2001, said: 'We wage a war to save civilisation itself' (Address to the nation, World Congress Centre, Atlanta, Georgia, www.usinfo.state.gov). The second way in which global terrorism takes on the form of a demonic enemy is that the discourse draws on the conception of monstrous evil I described in Chapter 1. According to that conception, diabolical evil is a human capacity, but those humans who possess it take the form of monsters. In that monstrous form they pursue our destruction for its own sake. What is important here is that there is no history behind this, no set of grievances motivating this monster, and so no possibility of negotiation and compromise. That they are evil is a complete explanation for whatever they do and we need search no further. The only defence against such a monster is its complete destruction. In his remarks on 11 December 2001, Bush described terrorists as 'defined by hate', with a 'mad intent', and the vice-president Dick Cheney said in August 2002 that the war against terror would not end in a treaty or negotiations with terrorists, but only 'in their complete and utter destruction' (www.defendamerica.mil/archive/2002-08/20020807.html).

Robert Jay Lifton notes the apocalyptic nature of the conflict in an article, 'American Apocalypse', published in *The Nation* on 22 December 2003. He comments: 'The apocalyptic imagination has spawned a new kind of violence at the beginning of the 21st century. We can, in fact, speak of a worldwide epidemic of violence aimed at massive destruction in the service of various visions of purification and renewal.' Lifton regards both Islamic forces and American forces as motivated by this apocalyptic vision. 'Both sides are energized by versions of intense idealism; both see themselves as embarked on a mission of combating evil in order to redeem and renew the world; and both are ready to release untold levels of violence to achieve that purpose.' The war on Iraq itself 'was a manifestation of that American visionary projection'. The American government, he argues, has a 'cosmic ambition' to control history. But the war on terror has not made the American people feel more secure. 'Despite the constant invocation by the Bush Administration of the theme of "security", the war on terrorism has created the very opposite – a sense of fear and insecurity among Americans, which is then mobilized in support of further aggressive plans in the extension of the larger "war".' And so: 'The projected "victory" becomes a form of aggressive longing, of sustained illusion, of an unending "Fourth

World War" and a mythic cleansing – of terrorists, of evil, of our own fear.'

Not only is the struggle apocalyptic, but the evil enemy possesses demonic powers. This is seen most starkly in a study of the conflict in Sri Lanka between the majority Sinhalese and the minority Tamil communities, as Tamil separatists used violence against the Sinhalese-dominated state in order to gain some degree of political autonomy. E. Nissan and R. L. Stirrat examined in particular the reprisals against the Tamil community after the 'Eelam Tigers', the Tamil resistance, attacked a military patrol in Jaffna in 1983 (Nissan and Stirrat 1987). These reprisals were especially brutal, and included several massacres of Tamils held in custody by the political authorities, who did little to prevent them. Nissan and Stirrat comment: 'The brutality of the killings seems to have been linked, at least in part, with fearful representations of the "terrorist" which were very widely shared among Sinhalese at the time' (Nissan and Stirrat 1987: 20). The distinction between 'Tamil' and 'terrorist' became blurred – 'almost any Tamil might be a terrorist, might be a threat to Sinhala life' (Nissan and Stirrat 1987: 20). And, critically, 'At times of crisis, strong parallels are evident between representations of the terrorist and representations of the demonic among the Sinhalese' (Nissan and Stirrat 1987: 20). This is not to say that Tamils and terrorists were seen as demons in some crude and primitive way, but 'they were endowed with characteristics similar to those which are attributed to demons', and 'they were dealt with in a manner which might be compared with exorcism' (Nissan and Stirrat 1987: 20). The violence 'came to be a matter of "purifying" Sinhala space, of dealing with what was represented as an almost demonic threat to Sinhala intregrity' (Nissan and Stirrat 1987: 20). As with other struggles against an 'enemy within', limits which would hold in conflicts *between* states were ignored. 'Tamil victims were not just knifed, they were slashed or cut into pieces; people were not just shot but were beaten to death, or doused in petrol and set on fire. Reports of torture at other times, too, have been frequent' (Nissan and Stirrat 1987: 20).

The Tamils were accused of demon-like attacks on people, of committing atrocities which had 'demonic characteristics', such as drinking the blood of their victims or even cannibalism (a constant theme in the representation of demonic enemies). Most interestingly for this argument, 'Like demons, they could move around at will, often unseen, and were believed to have extraordinary strength and power' (Nissan and Stirrat 1987: 21). The best example of the fear created by this possession of demonic power came a few days after the worst of the 1983 reprisal attacks upon the Tamils. A shooting incident in Colombo, the capital of Sri Lanka, was interpreted as a terrorist attack and provoked mass panic as huge numbers fled the city, including members of the police and army. Nissan and Stirrat comment: 'Given that the Tigers then numbered at the most a few hundred, and that there had been no guerilla shootings within 200 miles of Colombo, such a panic was not based on any reasonable assessment of the situation. It was based rather on the belief in the almost supernatural powers of the Tamil activists: on their ability to enter Colombo unseen, and on their ability to mount a successful urban attack with guns. The shooting incident . . . seems, instead, to have involved two army patrols firing on each other. There was no attack by Tigers in Colombo, but many people expected there to be. Tigers had even been "seen" hanging beneath trains bringing them the 250 miles from Jaffna – even though the trains weren't running' (Nissan and Stirrat 1987: 21).

In important respects, then, the Tamils were 'represented as something akin to the demonic' (Nissan and Stirrat 1987: 21), and this had horrific consequences in the nature and viciousness of the reprisal attacks on the Tamil community. While the violence in Sri Lanka continued after 1983, its nature changed, taking a less intense form, and an important factor was a changed perception of the 'enemy'. 'The violence of 1983 was directed against generalized Tamilness; against a constructed Tamil "other": dangerous, demon-like and threatening' (Nissan and Stirrat 1987: 24). But what became apparent was that this kind of violence was not going to destroy the Tamil presence in Sri Lanka or subdue the separatist activists; in fact it made things worse by seeming to intensify Tamil resistance. 'And from this period the Tamil separatists were transformed from semi-human demon-like beings in the press to being named people who the government had to negotiate with' (Nissan and Stirrat 1987: 24).

To portray an evil enemy, then, is to close off all possibility of understanding and communication and negotiation, to make all history disappear. But in the case of global terrorism surely this is the only rational response? Here we have an enemy with no demands, who does not wish to communicate or negotiate, and who is clearly intent on destruction with no comprehensible aim beyond that destruction. Surely here we have people who can justly be represented as evil monsters? What appeared deeply monstrous about the events of 11 September 2001 was their unexpectedness and their arbitrariness. It has been pointed out since that to see them as unexpected and arbitrary is to misunderstand them and what they signify. The governments of the developed nations should certainly have expected some kind of attack upon their own territories at some stage, and there is evidence that these attacks were anticipated at some level but not adequately. And to see them as arbitrary is to fail to understand how the Pentagon and the World Trade Center can be taken to represent military and economic oppression. However, there is a level of arbitrariness which should not be lost, because it constitutes a central element of those acts which needs to be understood. The terrible bombings in Bali in October 2003, which killed 202 people, carried out by a group called Jemaah Islamiyah, and Madrid in March 2004, which killed 191 people, carried out by the Moroccan Islamic Combatant Group, and in London in July 2005, in which at least 52 people died, enable us to see the sheer monstrous arbitrariness of the victims. There was no attempt by the perpetrators to distinguish their victims in any of these attacks, in terms of their nationality, their class, their ethnicity, their religion or their politics. It could be argued that they could have anticipated that representatives of a certain class, nationality and religion would be present on the hijacked planes and in the destroyed buildings. But even allowing for this level of foresight, there was still something shockingly random about those who died. Surely this arbitrariness fits the model of monstrous evil?

But there is no need to deny the arbitrariness in order to gain the kind of understanding that moves us beyond accounting for these events in terms of evil, or trying to grope for symbolic meanings in the destruction of the World Trade Center or the attack on the Pentagon. The arbitrariness itself is loaded with meaning. The symbolism of monsters in fact works against the model of monstrous evil here, because literary monsters most often have a history of grievance. We can see this best in the symbolism of Mary Shelley's monster, Victor Frankenstein's awful creation. Chris Baldick observes that those the monster destroys in seeking revenge against Frankenstein are horrifically innocent victims (Baldick 1987). He says, for example, 'he is ... driven by a conscious sense of equity rather than mere frustration of vengeful rage; which is not to say his actions are just. On the contrary, the victims of his attacks are all *innocent*, which is exactly his grim but satirical point' (Baldick 1987: 52). The framing of the servant girl Justine for murder will shock the fair-minded reader. However: 'It is criminal madness, but there is certainly a method in it, since what the monster is doing is providing an illustration of the arbitrary injustice of the human society which condemns him on sight' (Baldick 1987: 52). There is a list of victims who are punished by the monster for crimes they did not commit, as he stages 'parodies of the injustice he suffers...' (Baldick 1987: 53). The only parallel I want to read between the actions of the monster and the attacks on New York, Bali, Madrid and London concerns this arbitrariness of victims, because it seems to me that the arbitrariness of the victims of those attacks can be understood when compared with the extreme arbitrariness and randomness of the victims of the developed world's domination and exploitation of the rest of the globe. The identity of the people who are oppressed, displaced, or killed through that domination and exploitation are of no interest to the governments of the developed nations, and are never commemorated, if their existence is known at all, just as the identity of the victims of the September 11th attacks were of no interest whatsoever to those who executed them. The extreme injustice of one is mirrored in the extreme injustice of the other. To see these attacks as coming from a monstrously evil enemy with no history, whose only aim is our suffering and destruction, is to deeply misunderstand them, and if the example of the armed reprisals against the Tamil community in Sri Lanka is a sound one, it will not work. It will only make the enemy stronger, or, worse, create one where it never existed before. The truth of the crisis of global terrorism is that the developed world is plagued by monsters of its own making, and these monsters have a history which we would do well to understand.

Conclusion

To close this chapter, and the book, I want to draw attention to three arguments that have run through it. The first is that we ought to dispose of the concept of evil. The argument is not that we *can* do without it, but that there are good moral and political reasons why we *should* do without it. In trying to eliminate the discourse of evil we may well be confronted by situations, actions and people that we feel compelled to condemn as evil, and we may have extreme difficulty in expressing our beliefs about them in any other way. Was not the Holocaust an evil? Was not Hitler an evil person? But in the end we have to ask ourselves what it *means* to say these things. Does the concept of evil explain anything here? My main target has been those approaches that identify some kind of evil agency, such that the evil *nature* of this agency explains what they do. It may be protested here that such a notion of evil agency is so obviously nonsensical that it is a waste of time to attack it. But the fact is that this idea of evil – closest to the monstrous conception I described in Chapter 1 – pervades popular culture, the media, and much political and legal culture too. It's all very well to 'play' with such mythological characters in fiction, but this fiction has a devastating effect when it invades and dominates conceptions of reality. And I do not accept the validity of the discourse of evil when it comes to mere *description* of people's character or motives or actions, or the consequences of their actions, as proposed by John Kekes and others. Nor do I accept that the idea of evil, while it does not explain anything, is nevertheless an indispensable part of the moral description of the world, helping us to *understand* that world, as suggested by Raimond Gaita. On the contrary, the idea of evil does not help us to understand these things at all; rather, it takes on the role of the *satan* of the Hebrew Bible: it *obstructs* our understanding, blocks our way, brings us to a halt. 'Evil' is a black-hole concept which gives the illusion of explanation, when what it actually represents is the failure to understand. Not only that, but it brings with it a package of historical commitments which those who argue for its current use may well reject but will find it hard to resist – the complete condemnation of those described as evil and their rejection as not *really* human, the impossibility of communication and negotiation, reform and redemption. The discourse of evil is so dangerous that we *must* try to do without it. In the face of events like the Holocaust, we have to remember that one major factor in bringing it about was a particular discourse of evil, the anti-Semitism that drove Hitler and his followers, the belief that the Jews represented a cosmic evil enemy bent on the destruction of the German people and civilisation in general. And so my rejection of the discourse of evil is complete: we should treat it as it urges us to treat its victims – no negotiation, no reform or redemption.

The second argument has been that the idea of evil is not a philosophical concept at all, nor even a religious one. It is a mythological concept that has a specific role to play in certain narratives.

Satan is a meaningful character only in the context of the Christian mythological world history, and he makes no sense outside of it; indeed, a Christianity that abandons that mythological world history has as much trouble making sense of the idea of evil as any secular philosophy. Evil itself is an idea that only makes sense in a narrative context, in a story we tell about people and about the world. When we describe someone as evil, we are not saying anything about their character or their motivations – we are instead making them a figure in a story in which they play a specific and prescribed role. And in making them such a figure we do away with any need to understand their history, their motives, their psychology. Narrative characters have no such features, or rather they simply have the history, motives and psychology ascribed to them by the narrative plot, those required to drive the story forward. If we were to look beyond the narrative of evil, we may discover people very different to those we have imagined.

What the mythical nature of the concept of evil shows is the power of the monstrous conception I described in Chapter 1. According to that view, there are people with a distinct nature, inhuman/humans, who pursue human suffering for its own sake – they have a demonic aspect. This is often accompanied by a two-world model, that evil agents enter our world from another, so that all we have to explain is their journey, not their nature. In taking this view we draw a boundary between us and them, so that we are not infected with this kind of evil. Although this conception obviously has its place in the worlds of mythology and fiction, we have seen it erupt again and again as a representation of actual human agency – serial killers, paedophiles, children who kill, migrants, Jews, those engaged in global terrorism, dissident women, and those who participated in the Holocaust and other atrocities. Once these take on the dimension of the demonic, then there can be no negotiation, no understanding, and no possibility of redemption. In Chapter 1 I used the American television series *Buffy the Vampire Slayer* as an illustration of the monstrous conception of evil along with the two-world view. Some of the demons Buffy and her friends battle against live in our world, but the most dangerous and potentially apocalyptic enter from a demon dimension through the hellmouth over which the Californian town of Sunnydale is situated. In the early episodes of the series, the demons that are found in Sunnydale are exterminated brutally and quickly, and there is something faintly disturbing about the way in which Buffy and her comrades perform this task with relish and very little evidence of what we might call thinking. Their intellectual guide is the Englishman, Rupert Giles, who uses ancient texts to identify the evil demons, their powers, and how to destroy them – a combination, if you like, of Houston Stewart Chamberlain and the *Protocols of Zion*. However, as the series progresses a more complex view is taken, and the vampires and demons can no longer be condemned as malignant enemies in any simplistic sense. They have their own underworld in the back streets of Sunnydale, where they lead their lives out of sight of humans for the most part, running businesses and performing services – in other words, a typical community of illegal immigrants. Angel, the vampire with a soul, is an ally in the struggle against evil, and Spike, a vampire without a soul, eventually joins that struggle and performs heroic acts of self-sacrifice in attempting to protect Buffy's younger sister Dawn from a ferocious enemy that seeks her destruction; and in the series finale he has acquired a soul and is the figure who saves the world from the ultimate apocalypse.

However, the most shocking moments in the series are not demonic at all. The first is the killing by the slayer Faith of a human being who works for the demonic mayor of Sunnydale, and who is actually trying to assist the Buffy gang in their struggle against this latest apocalypse. She kills him by mistake, believing herself to be under attack by supernatural enemies; it is a moment of misjudgement in a battlefield, when a tragic mistake is made which has enormous consequences for all the characters in the series. The second occurs when Warren, a human attempting to be a super-villain, shoots and kills a member of the Buffy gang, Tara. He is in a state of irrational rage, having had his masculinity humiliated. In Chapter 6 we saw Katharine Kelly and Mark Stotten identify 'how we socialize boys to be male' as leading to an increased risk of violent behaviour, especially where 'young men ... report feelings of being "disrespected", shamed, and humiliated by others and their circumstances' (Kelly and Totten 2002: 10). Warren takes a gun and, in his rage and humiliation, lets off a stream of bullets at Buffy, hitting her and wounding her – but a stray bullet kills Tara. This plunges the narrative into darkness, with the shock of the suddenness of death caused by irrational anger. Neither Faith nor Warren are demonic, and neither are their victims. Faith is eventually redeemed, but Warren never gets the chance, killed in an act of terrible revenge by Tara's partner, Willow, an act for which Willow herself must seek redemption. And so within all the demonic and supernatural dangers, the most shocking moments are human, all too human. This is Freud's uncanny in reverse. In Chapter 5 Freud observed that writers of fiction can produce a sense of the uncanny by presenting what seems to be a profoundly ordinary world and then throwing in a sudden instance of the supernatural. Here the supernatural world is disrupted and disturbed by the ordinary – what is most shocking is what ordinary people do. In the end, *Buffy* forces us to look away from the comforts of the monstrous conception of evil, with its clear boundaries and sharp distinctions. We are left to choose between the pessimism of the pure conception – that all humans have the capacity for inflicting suffering for its own sake; or the optimism of the psychological conception – that under specific and extreme circumstances people will do dreadful things, but we can understand these contexts, and there is always the possibility of redemption.

The third argument I want to draw from the many that take place in this book is about fear. What the examples of global terrorism, the Iraq 'war', and world migration have shown is that we are most scared of what we cannot see, and this terror undermines the foundations of our world. The first challenge is, of course, to actually study these phenomena in their detail – to understand their *history* – to look beyond the imaginary monsters fabricated by our political leaders and the media. But there is a second challenge which is far more difficult, and that is to stop being scared. If we are scared of the dark because we believe there is some horrible thing that hides in it, we can illuminate the darkness and show there is nothing there to be scared of at all – if there *is* something there, it is far less dangerous and threatening than we imagined. But the problem is that once the light goes out again the fear returns: there may be a gap between what we know and what we fear. Earlier I used the example of someone who, after watching the film *Jaws,* refused to swim in the seas off British beaches despite knowing full well that there were no great white sharks hidden below the waves. I doubt they are unusual – how many of us, after seeing a horror film about vampires, for example, would walk back from the cinema at night through a graveyard; or not get 'spooked' by noises that wake us later that night when the house is filled with darkness? We know there are no vampires, but we fear that there might be; we know there is no one in the attic as the house creaks, but we are petrified. This gap between what we know and what we fear is the *real* black hole, where the discourse of evil, the *myth* of evil, takes root and grows.

It may be that we can only make sense of the world through mythologies, that we will never free ourselves of them because in the end the rational world view is too stark, a world without meaning or significance, or at least one in which *we* have no meaning or significance. All kinds of myths give us a framework, a narrative, which makes our experiences coherent. Philosophy, psychology, science, history, politics, intellectual disciplines of all kinds at their best reveal these frameworks to be myths, but still do not tell us how to cope without them. We should remember that while Friedrich Nietzsche critiques the myth of the slave morality, he also considers it invaluable in that it made human suffering meaningful, and so gave humanity meaning. And in general for Nietzsche, myth is 'an absolutely central element of culture – indeed, the only escape from the malaise from which he believed "modern man" was suffering' (Megill 1985: 65). It is not that we can do without myths, but new myths are required. But my concern here is only with the myth of evil, one of the most powerful and enduring, and the most dangerous. In the face of it the question of whether we can make *some* philosophical sense of it seems marginal, which is why I have not focused exclusively on that question. My main purpose has been to attack it on moral and political grounds – even if it can be shown to be philosophically coherent, it still remains pernicious.

But I keep returning to the same place in the argument, that even though we know there is nothing evil there as the object of our fear, the fear remains. It may be that there is no philosophical or even rational response to this problem. I was recently introduced to the 'Emotional Freedom Technique' which aims to help people to control phobias by a system of physical tapping on 'meridian' points on the body. Of course in our rational moments we ask for evidence that such a method is successful, and then if it is, we further ask for an explanation of how it works. But if we are in the grip of a phobia none of this may matter any more. At the level of individual phobias we need to find ways of preventing our fears from controlling our lives, and at the political level we need to find ways of preventing politicians from controlling our lives through exploiting them. In *The Republic* Plato criticises the Sophists as educators, but in a way that has similarities to his critique of democratic political leaders: 'It is as if a man were acquiring the knowledge of the humours and desires of a great strong beast which he had in his keeping, how it is to be approached and touched, and when and by what things it is made most savage or gentle, yes, and the several sounds it is wont to utter on the occasion of each, and again what sounds uttered by another make it tame or fierce, and after mastering this knowledge by living with the creature and by lapse of time should call it wisdom . . . ' (Plato 1935: 39; 493a–c). Oppressive governments maintain their power by making their people terrified of them, but democratic governments increasingly maintain their power by making their people terrified of something else. Neither method has much to recommend it, although the 'democratic' method may be more efficient because all the governing group need do is invent objects of fear instead of having to invest in actual mechanisms of control. Even so, in the longer term the search for new evil enemies may drag democratic states towards these kinds of expensive and intrusive measures, such as the British government's proposals to introduce an identity-card system. One possibility is that this approach will create a highly paranoid society, very willing to support the political leadership as it takes these steps (the evidence is that the majority of the British public support the identity-card plan), but also capable of making more extreme demands and punishing those governing groups which refuse to take them seriously. In the general election of 2005 in the United Kingdom, the ruling Labour government found itself struggling to keep pace with the public anxiety over immigration, which had been fed by the opposition Conservative Party, but had earlier been inflamed by the Labour Party itself. There are similar fears about immigration throughout Europe which opposition parties exploit and those in power have to respond to. In this sense Plato is right that a democratic people are a dangerous and unruly beast, but the added insight is that it is the democratic leaders themselves who have created this paranoid monster.

So even if it is true that we depend on countless little mythologies to get us through the day or to drive us forward creatively, there are larger and more dangerous myths that we have to question and oppose at every stage. The myth of evil is one of these, perhaps the strongest and the darkest. As I observed at the end of Chapter 5, we the people are the monsters, and it is our fear of evil that makes us so.

Bibliography

Anderson, Benedict (1991), *Imagined Communities* (Verso, London and New York).

Arendt, Hannah (1951), *The Origins of Totalitarianism* (Harcourt Brace and Co., New York).

Arendt, Hannah (1953), 'Understanding and Politics' *Partisan Review*, no. 4, pp. 377–409.

Arendt, Hannah (1958), *The Human Condition* (Chicago University Press, Chicago).

Arendt, Hannah (1976), *Eichmann in Jerusalem: A Report on the Banality of Evil* (Penguin Books, New York).

Arendt, Hannah (1978), *The Life of the Mind 1: Thinking* (Secker and Warburg, London).

Auerbach, Nina (1995), *Our Vampires, Ourselves* (Chicago University Press, Chicago).

Baldick, Chris (1987), *In Frankenstein's Shadow: Myth, Monstrosity, and Nineteenth-century Writing* (Clarendon Press, Oxford).

Barker, Meg (2001), 'Women, Children and the Construction of Evil', www.wickedness.net/Barker.pdf.

Baumeister, Roy F. (1997), *Evil: Inside Human Cruelty and Violence* (W. H. Freeman and Company, New York).

Benedette, Jean (1971), *Gilles de Rais: The Authentic Bluebeard* (Peter Davies, London).

Bernstein, Richard J. (2002), *Radical Evil: A Philosophical Interrogation* (Polity Press, Cambridge).

Boyce, Mary (1984), 'Persian Religion in the Achemenid Age', in W. D. Davies and Louis Finkelstein (eds), *The Cambridge History of Judaism*, vol. 1 (Cambridge University Press, Cambridge), pp. 279–307.

Breytenbach, C. and Day, P. L. (1995), 'Satan', in Karel van der Toorn, Bob Becking and Pieter van Horst (eds), *Dictionary of Deities and Demons in the Bible* (E. J. Brill, Leiden, New York and Koln), pp. 1369–80.

Bronner, Stephen Eric (2003), *A Rumor about the Jews: Antisemitism, Conspiracy, and the Protocols of Zion* (Oxford University Press, Oxford).

Browning, Christopher R. (2001), *Ordinary Men: Reserve Police Battalion 101 and the Final Solution in Poland*, 2nd edn (Penguin Books, London).

Büssing, Sabine (1987), *Aliens in the Home: The Child in Horror Fiction* (Greenwood, New York and London).

Calmet, Dom Augustine (1850), *The Phantom World*, edited with an introduction by Henry Christmas (Richard Bentley, London).

Canovan, Margaret (1996), *Nationhood and Political Theory* (Edward Elgar, Cheltenham).

Card, Claudia (1996), *The Unnatural Lottery: Character and Moral Luck* (Temple University Press, Philadelphia).

Card, Claudia (2002), *The Atrocity Paradigm: A Theory of Evil* (Oxford University Press, Oxford and New York).

Carroll, Noel (1990), *The Philosophy of Horror or Paradoxes of the Heart* (Routledge, London).

Carroll, Robert and Prickett, Stephen (eds) (1998), *The Bible: Authorized King James Version* (Oxford University Press, Oxford).

Cavallaro, Dani (2002), *The Gothic Vision: Three Centuries of Horror, Terror and Fear* (Continuum, London).

Charlesworth, James H. (ed.) (1983), *The Old Testament Pseudepigrapha*, vols 1 and 2 (Darton, Longman and Todd, London).

Chomsky, Noam (2004), *Hegemony or Survival: America's Quest for Global Dominance* (Penguin Books, London).

Clark, Maudemarie (1998), 'Nietzsche', in Edward Craig (ed.), *The Routledge Encyclopedia of Philosophy*, vol. 6 (Routledge, London and New York), pp. 844–61.

Clark, Stuart (1996), *Thinking with Demons* (Clarendon Press, Oxford).

Clarke, Paul A. B. (1988), *The Autonomy of Politics* (Avebury, Aldershot).

Clarke, Paul Barry (1980), 'Beyond "The Banality of Evil"', *British Journal of Political Science* vol. 10, Part 4, pp. 417–39.

Clarke, Paul Barry (1996), 'Evil', in Paul Barry Clarke and Andrew Linzey (eds), *Dictionary of Ethics, Theology and Society* (Routledge, London and New York), pp. 345–56.

Cole, Phillip (1998), *The Free, the Unfree and the Excluded* (Ashgate, Aldershot).

Cole, Phillip (2000), *Philosophies of Exclusion: Liberal Political Theory and Immigration* (Edinburgh University Press, Edinburgh).

Copjec, Joan (1996a), 'Evil in the Time of the Finite World', in Joan Copjec (ed.), *Radical Evil* (Verso, London and New York), pp. vii–xxviii.

Copjec, Joan (ed.) (1996b), *Radical Evil* (Verso, London and New York).

Cornwell, John (2003), *Hitler's Scientists: Science, War, and the Devil's Pact* (Viking Press, London).

Creed, Barbara (1993), *The Monstrous Feminine: Film, Feminism, Psychoanalysis* (Routledge, London and New York).

D'Entreves, Maurizio Passerin (1994), *The Political Philosophy of Hannah Arendt* (Routledge, London and New York).

Davis, Very Rev. Monsignor H. Francis, Williams, Right Rev. Abbot Aidan, Thomas, Very Rev. Ivo, and Crehan, Rev. Joseph (eds) (1962) *A Catholic Dictionary of Theology* (Thomas Nelson and Sons Ltd, London).

Dostoyevsky, Fyodor (2003), *The Brothers Karamazov* (Penguin, London).

Eley, Geoff (ed.) (2000), *The 'Goldhagen Effect': History, Memory, Nazism – Facing the German Past* (University of Michigan Press, Ann Arbor).

Flint, Valerie (1999), 'The Demonisation of Magic and Sorcery in Late Antiquity: Christian Redefinitions of Pagan Religions', in Valerie Flint, Richard Gordon, Georg Luck and Daniel Ogden (eds), *Witchcraft and Magic in Europe: Ancient Greece and Rome* (Athlone Press, London), vol. 2 of *The Athlone History of Witchcraft and Magic in Europe*, ed. Bengt Ankarloo and Stuart Clark, pp. 277–348.

Forsyth, Neil (1987), *The Old Enemy: Satan and the Combat Myth* (Princeton University Press, Princeton).

Forsyth, Neil (2003), *The Satanic Epic* (Princeton University Press, Princeton, NJ and Oxford).

Frayling, Christopher (1991), *Vampyres: Lord Byron to Count Dracula* (Faber and Faber, London and Boston).

Freud, Sigmund (2003), *The Uncanny*, translated by David McLintock, introduction by Hugh Haughton (Penguin Books, London).

Friedländer, Saul (1997), *Nazi Germany and the Jews: The Years of Persecution, 1933–39*, vol. 1 (Weidenfeld and Nicolson, London).

Gabory, Emile (1930), *Alias Bluebeard: The Life and Death of Gilles de Raiz*, translated by Alban C. Bessie (Brewer and Warren Inc., New York).

Gaita, Raimond (2000), *A Common Humanity: Thinking about Love and Truth and Justice* (Routledge, London and New York).

Galligan, Michael (1976), *God and Evil* (Paulist Press, New York, Paramus and Toronto).

Gardner, Muriel (1985), *The Deadly Innocents: Portraits of Children Who Kill* (Yale, New Haven and London).

Garrard, Eve (1998), 'The Nature of Evil', *Philosophical Explorations*, vol. 1 no. 1, pp. 43–60.

Garrard, Eve and Scarre, Geoffrey (2003), *Moral Philosophy and the Holocaust* (Ashgate, Aldershot).

Gaster, T. H. (1962), 'Satan', in George Arthur Buttrick (ed.), *The Interpreter's Dictionary of the Bible* (Abingdon Press, New York and Nashville), pp. 224–8.

Gelder, Ken (1994), *Reading the Vampire* (Routledge, London and New York).

Gilbert, Martin (1987), *The Holocaust: The Jewish Tragedy* (Fontana Press, London).

Glover, Jonathan (1999), *Humanity: A Moral History of the 20th Century* (Jonathan Cape, London).

Gnoli, Gherardo (1987a), 'Zoroastrianism', in Mircea Eliade (ed.), *The Encyclopedia of Religion*, vol. 5 (Macmillan Publishing Company, New York, and Collier Macmillan Publishers, London), pp. 579–91.

Gnoli, Gherardo (1987b), 'Zurvanism', in Mircea Eliade (ed.), *The Encyclopedia of Religion*, vol. 5 (Macmillan Publishing Company, New York, and Collier Macmillan Publishers, London), pp. 595–6.

Goldhagen, Daniel Jonah (1997), *Hitler's Willing Executioners: Ordinary Germans and the Holocaust* (Abacus, London).

Gould, Stephen Jay (1997), *The Mismeasure of Man* (Penguin revised and expanded edition, London).

Graham, Elaine L. (2002), *The Presentation of the Post/Human: Monsters, Aliens and Others in Popular Culture* (Manchester University Press, Manchester).

Graham, Gordon (2000), *Evil and Christian Ethics* (Cambridge University Press, Cambridge).

Halberstam, Judith (1995), *Skin Shows: Gothic Horror and the Technology of Monsters* (Duke University Press, Durham and London).

Hallie, Philip (1969), *The Paradox of Cruelty* (Wesleyan University Press, Middletown, CT).

Hallie, Philip (1988), 'Response to Jeffrey Burton Russell', in Paul Woodruff and Harry A. Wilmer (eds), *Facing Evil: Light at the Core of Darkness* (Open Court, LaSalle, IL), pp. 62–6.

Haughton, Hugh (2003), 'Introduction' to Sigmund Freud, *The Uncanny* (Penguin Books, London).

Heckel, Robert V. and Shumaker, David M. (2001), *Children Who Murder: A Psychological Perspective* (Praeger, Westport, CT and London).

Heller, Terry (1987), *The Delights of Terror: An Aesthetics of the Tale of Terror* (University of Illinois Press, Urbana and Chicago).

Hobbes, Thomas (1985), *Leviathan*, edited with an introduction by C. B. Macpherson (Penguin, Harmondsworth).

Hobsbawm, E. J. (1999), *Industry and Empire: From 1750 to the Present Day* (Penguin, London).

Hoelzel, Alfred (1988), *The Paradoxical Quest: A Study of Faustian Vicissitudes* (Peter Lang, New York, Frankfurt am Main and Paris).

Human Rights Watch (2004), *The Road to Abu Ghraib* (www.hrw.org/reports/2004/usa0604/).

Hume, David (1975), *Enquiries Concerning Human Understanding and the Principles of Morals*, 3rd edn, edited by P. N. Nidditch (Clarendon Press, Oxford).

Iaccino, James F. (1994), *Psychological Reflections on Cinematic Terror: Jungian Archetypes in Horror Films* (Praeger, Westport, CT and London).

Jackson, David (1995), *Destroying the Baby in Themselves: Why Did the Two Boys Kill James Bulger?* (Mushroom Books, Nottingham).

Jacoby, Mario, Kast, Verena and Riedel, Ingrid (1992), *Witches, Ogres, and the Devil's Daughter: Encounters with Evil in Fairy Tales* (Shambhala, Boston and London).

Jentsch, Otto (1996), 'On the Psychology of the Uncanny', translated by Roy Sellars, in *Angelaki: A Journal of the Theoretical Humanities* 2 (1) pp. 7–16.

Jonte-Pace, Diane (2001), *Speaking the Unspeakable: Religion, Misogyny, and the Uncanny Mother in Freud's Cultural Texts* (University of California Press, Berkeley, Los Angeles, and London).

Jung, C. G. (1970), *Civilization in Transition*, 2nd edn (Routledge and Kegan Paul, London).

Kant, Immanuel (1960), *Religion within the Limits of Reason Alone*, translated by T. M. Greene and H. H. Hudson (Harper and Brothers, New York).

Kast, Verena (1992), 'How Fairy Tales Deal with Evil: Thematic Approaches to the Fairy Tale as a Dynamic Process', in Mario Jacoby, Verena Kast and Ingrid Riedel (eds) (1992), *Witches, Ogres, and the Devil's Daughter: Encounters with Evil in Fairy Tales* (Shambhala, Boston and London), pp. 16–39.

Kastor, Frank S. (1974), *Milton and the Literary Satan* (Rodopi NV, Amsterdam).

Kavolis, Vitautas (1984), 'Civilizational Models of Evil', in Marie Coleman Nelson and Michael Eigen (eds), *Evil: Self and Culture*, vol. 4 of *Self-in-Process* series (Human Sciences Press Inc, New York), pp. 17–35.

Keen, Sam (1986), *Faces of the Enemy: Reflections of the Hostile Imagination* (Harper and Row, New York).

Kekes, John (1990), *Facing Evil* (Princeton University Press, Princeton).

Kelly, Katharine D. and Totten, Mark (2002), *When Children Kill: A Social-Psychological Study of Youth Homicide* (Broadview Press, Peterborough, Ontario).

Koch, Klaus (2000), 'Zoroastrianism', in Lawrence H. Schiggman and James C. VanderKam (eds), *The Encyclopedia of the Dead Sea Scrolls* (Oxford University Press, Oxford), pp. 1010–12.

Krafft-Ebing, Richard von (1965), *Psychopathia Sexualis: With Special Reference to the Antipathetic Sexual Instinct*, translated from the 12th edition by Franklin S. Klaf (Staples Press, London).

Kristeva, Julia (1982), *Powers of Horror: An Essay on Abjection*, translated by Leon S. Roudiez (Columbia University Press, New York).

Lacan, Jacques (1977), *Écrits: A Selection* (Norton, New York).

Langmuir, Gavin (1990a), *History, Religion, and Antisemitism* (University of California Press, Berkeley).

Langmuir, Gavin (1990b), *Toward a Definition of Antisemitism* (University of California Press, Berkeley).

Larner, Christina (1984), *Witchcraft and Religion: The Politics of Popular Belief*, edited by Alan Macfarlane (Basil Blackwell, Oxford).

Lechte, John (1990), *Julia Kristeva* (Routledge, London and New York).

Leiter, Brian (2002), *Nietzsche on Morality* (Routledge, London and New York).

Levack, Brian P. (1999), 'The Decline and End of Witchcraft Prosecutions', in Marijke Gijswijt-Hofstra, Brian P. Levack and Roy Porter (eds), *Witchcraft and Magic in Europe: The 18th and 19th Centuries* (Athlone Press, London), vol. 3 of *The Athlone History of Witchcraft and Magic in Europe*, ed. Bengt Ankarloo and Stuart Clark.

Levi, Primo (1989), *The Drowned and the Saved* (Sphere Books, London).

Lewis, C. S. (2002), *The Screwtape Letters* (HarperCollins, London).

Lifton, Robert Jay (1986), *The Nazi Doctors: Medical Killing and the Psychology of Genocide* (Macmillan, London).

Littler, Jo and Naidoo, Roshi (eds) (2005), *The Politics of Heritage: The Legacies of 'Race'* (Routledge, London and New York).

Marmoy, C. F. A. (1958), 'The "Auto-Icon" of Jeremy Bentham at University College London', in *Medical History*, vol. 2, no. 2, April, pp. 77–86.

Maser, Werner (1979), *Nuremberg: A Nation on Trial*, translated by Richard Barry (Allen Lane, London).

Masters, Anthony (1972), *The Natural History of the Vampire* (Rupert Hart-Davis, London).

Matthews, Roger and Pitts, John (eds) (2001), *Crime, Disorder and Community Safety: A New Agenda?* (Routledge, London and New York).

McDuff, David (2003), 'Introduction' to Fyodor Dostoyevsky, *The Brothers Karamazov* (Penguin, London).

McGinn, Colin (1997), *Ethics, Evil, and Fiction* (Clarendon Press, Oxford).

Megill, Allan (1985), *Prophets of Extremity: Nietzsche, Heidegger, Foucault, Derrida* (University of California Press, Berkeley and Los Angeles).

Midgley, Mary (1984), *Wickedness: A Philosophical Essay* (Routledge and Kegan Paul, London).

Miller, David (1995), *On Nationality* (Clarendon Press, Oxford).

Monter, William (2002), 'Witch Trials in Continental Europe 1560–1660', in Bengt Ankarloo, Stuart Clark and William Monter (eds), *Witchcraft and Magic in Europe: The Period of the Witch Trials* (Athlone Press, London), vol. 4 of *The Athlone History of Witchcraft and Magic in Europe*, ed. Bengt Ankarloo and Stuart Clark, pp. 3–52.

Morrison, Blake (1997), *As If* (Granta, London).

Morton, Adam (2004), *Evil* (Routledge, New York and London).

Nagel, Thomas (1993), 'Moral Luck', in Daniel Statman (ed.), *Moral Luck* (State University of New York Press, Albany), pp. 57–91.

Nash, Walter (1990), *The Language of Popular Fiction* (Routledge, London).

Navarette, Susan J. (1999), 'Unsealing Sense in *The Turn of the Screw*', in Gary Westfahl and George Slusser (eds), *Nursery Realms: Children in the Worlds of Science Fiction, Fantasy, and Horror* (University of Georgia Press, Athens, Georgia, and London), pp. 185–99.

Neiman, Susan (2000), *Evil in Modern Thought* (Princeton University Press, Princeton).

Nelson, Marie Coleman and Eigen, Michael (eds) (1984), *Evil: Self and Culture*, vol. 4 of *Self-in-Process* series (Human Sciences Press Inc, New York).

Newman, Paul (2000), *A History of Terror: Fear and Dread through the Ages* (Sutton Publishing, Stroud).

Nietzsche, Friedrich (1968), *Twilight of the Idols and The Anti-Christ* (Penguin Books, Harmondsworth).

Nietzsche, Friedrich (1996), *The Genealogy of Morals*, translated by Douglas Smith (Oxford, Oxford University Press).

Nissan, E. and Stirrat, R. L. (1987), *State, Nation and the Representation of Evil: The Case of Sri Lanka* (Graduate Division of Social Anthropology, University of Sussex).

Oldridge, Darren (ed.) (2001), *The Witchcraft Reader* (Routledge, London).

Oliver, Kelly (ed.) (2002), *The Portable Kristeva* (Columbia University Press, New York).

Olson, Alan M. (ed.) (1975), *The Disguises of the Demonic: Contemporary Perspectives on the Power of Evil* (Association Press, New York).

Padfield, Peter (1984), *Dönitz: The Last Führer – Portrait of a Nazi War Leader* (Victor Gollancz Ltd, London).

Pagels, Elaine (1996), *The Origin of Satan* (The Penguin Press, London).

Parkin, David (ed.) (1985), *The Anthropology of Evil* (Basil Blackwell, Oxford).

Perkowsky, Jan (1989), *The Darkling* (Slavica, Columbus).

Peters, Edward (2002), 'The Medieval Church and State on Superstition, Magic and Witchcraft: from Augustine to the 16th Century', in Karen Jolly,

Catharina Raudvere and Edward Peters (eds), *Witchcraft and Magic in Europe: The Middle Ages* (Athlone Press, London), vol. 3 of *The Athlone History of Witchcraft and Magic in Europe*, ed. Bengt Ankarloo and Stuart Clark, pp. 174–245.

Philip, Howard (1958), *Jung and the Problem of Evil* (Rockeiff, London).

Pitts, John (2001), 'The New Correctionalism: Young People, Youth Justice and New Labour', in Roger Matthews and John Pitts (eds), *Crime, Disorder and Community Safety: A New Agenda?* (Routledge, London and New York), pp. 167–92.

Pitts, John (2003), *The New Politics of Youth Crime: Discipline or Solidarity?* (Russell House Publishing, Lyme Regis).

Plantinga, Alvin (1975), *God, Freedom and Evil* (Allen and Unwin, London).

Plato (1935), *The Republic* (William Heinemann Ltd, London, Harvard University Press, Cambridge, MA.).

Pocock, David (1985), 'Unruly Evil', in David Parkin (ed.), *The Anthropology of Evil* (Basil Blackwell, Oxford), pp. 42–56.

Radest, Howard B. (1990), *The Devil and Secular Humanism: The Children of the Enlightenment* (Praeger, New York and London).

Rée, Jonathan (2000), *I See a Voice: A Philosophical History of Deafness and the Senses* (Flamingo, London).

Rescher, Nicholas (1993), 'Moral Luck', in Daniel Statman (ed.), *Moral Luck* (State University of New York Press, Albany).

Richards, Norvin (1993), 'Luck and Desert', in Daniel Statman (ed.), *Moral Luck* (State University of New York Press, Albany).

Ricoeur, Paul (1967), *The Symbolism of Evil* (Harper and Row, Boston).

Riley, G. J. (1995a), 'Demon', in Karel van der Toorn, Bob Becking and Pieter van Horst (eds), *Dictionary of Deities and Demons in the Bible* (E. J. Brill, Leiden, New York and Koln), pp. 445–55.

Riley, G. J. (1995b), 'The Devil', in Karel van der Toorn, Bob Becking and Pieter van Horst (eds), *Dictionary of Deities and Demons in the Bible* (E. J. Brill, Leiden, New York and Koln), pp. 463–73.

Robbins, Russell Hope (1972), *The Encyclopaedia of Witchcraft and Demonology* (Crown Publishers Inc., New York).

Rorty, Amelie Oksenberg (2001), *The Many Faces of Evil: Historical Perspectives* (Routledge, London and New York).

Russell, Jeffrey Burton (1977), *The Devil: Perceptions of Evil from Antiquity to Primitive Christianity* (Cornell University Press, Ithaca).

Russell, Jeffrey Burton (1981), *Satan: The Early Christian Tradition* (Cornell University Press, Ithaca).

Russell, Jeffrey Burton (1984), *Lucifer: The Devil in the Middle Ages* (Cornell University Press, Ithaca).

Russell, Jeffrey Burton (1986), *Mephistopheles: The Devil in the Modern World* (Cornell University Press, Ithaca).

Russell, Jeffrey Burton (1988), 'The Evil One', in Paul Woodruff and Harry A. Wilmer (eds), *Facing Evil: Light at the Core of Darkness* (Open Court, LaSalle, IL), pp. 47–62.

Russell, Jeffrey Burton (1989), *The Prince of Darkness: Radical Evil and the Power of Good in History* (Thames and Hudson, London).

Sarna, Nahum M. (1987), 'Biblical Literature', in Mircea Eliade (ed.), *The Encyclopedia of Religion*, vol. 2 (Macmillan Publishing Company, New York, and Collier Macmillan Publishers, London), pp. 152–73.

Semonin, Paul (2000), *American Monster* (New York University Press, New York and London).

Sereny, Gitta (1995), *Cries Unheard: Why Children Kill – The Story of Mary Bell* (Metropolitan Books, Henry Holt and Company, New York).

Shaked, Saul (1984), 'Iranian Influence on Judaism: 1st Century BCE to 2nd Century CE', in W. D. Davies and Louis Finkelstein (eds), *The Cambridge History of Judaism*, vol. 1 (Cambridge University Press, Cambridge), pp. 308–25.

Shandley, Robert R. (ed.) (1998), *Unwilling Germans? The Goldhagen Debate* (University of Minnesota Press, Minneapolis and London).

Sharma, Arvind (1987), 'Satan', in Mircea Eliade (ed.), *The Encyclopedia of Religion*, vol. 13 (Macmillan Publishing Company, New York, and Collier Macmillan Publishers, London), pp. 81–4.

Scharpé, Michiel (2003), 'A Trail of Disorientation: Blurred Boundaries in Der Sandmann', in *Image and Narrative: Online Magazine of the Visual Narrative*, Issue 5. *The Uncanny*, guest editor: Anneleen Masschelein, January 2003 (www.imageandnarrative.be/).

Silber, John (1960), 'The Ethical Significance of Kant's *Religion*', in Immanuel Kant *Religion within the Limits of Reason Alone*, translated by T. M. Greene and H. H. Hudson (Harper and Brothers, New York), pp. lxxix–cxxxi.

Smith, David James (1994), *The Sleep of Reason* (Century, London).

Sprenger, Jakob and Kramer, Heinrich (1971), *Malleus Maleficarum* (Dover edition, New York).

Statman, Daniel (ed.) (1993), *Moral Luck* (State University of New York Press, Albany).

Staub, Ervin (1989), *The Roots of Evil: The Origins of Genocide and Other Group Violence* (Cambridge University Press, Cambridge).

Stein, Murray (1995), *Jung on Evil* (Routledge, London).

Stoker, Bram (1993), *Dracula*, edited by Maurice Hindle (Penguin, Harmondsworth).

Summers, Montague (1996), *The Vampire in Europe* (Bracken Brooks, London).

Tamir, Yael (1993), *Liberal Nationalism* (Princeton University Press, Princeton).

Thomas, Mark (1993), *Every Mother's Nightmare: The Killing of James Bulger* (Pan Books Ltd, London).

Trevor-Roper, Hugh (1978), *The European Witch-Craze of the 16th and 17th Centuries* (Penguin Books, Harmondsworth).

Utting, David, Bright, Jon and Henricson, Clem (1993), *Crime and the Family: Improving Child-Rearing and Preventing Delinquency* (Family Policy Studies Centre, London).

Vardy, Peter (1992), *The Puzzle of Evil* (Fount, London).

Vermes, Geza (1987), *The Dead Sea Scrolls in English*, 3rd edn (JSOT Press, Sheffield).

Vermes, Geza (1994), *The Dead Sea Scrolls: Qumran in Perspective*, rev. 3rd edn (SCM Press, London).

Von Franz, Marie Louise (1983), *Shadow and Evil in Fairy Tales* (Spring Publications, Dallas, TX).

Warner, Marina (1998), *No Go the Bogeyman: Scaring, Lulling, and Making Mock* (Vintage, London).

Wesley, Frank (1999), *The Holocaust and Anti-Semitism – The Goldhagen Argument and its Effects* (International Scholars Publications, San Francisco, London, Bethseda).

Westfahl, Gary and Slusser, George (eds) (1999), *Nursery Realms: Children in the Worlds of Science Fiction, Fantasy and Horror* (University of Georgia Press, Athens, GA, and London).

Wiesel, Elie (1990), 'The Holocaust as Literary Inspiration', in Elie Wiesel, Lucy Dawidowics, Dorothy Rabinowitz and Robert McAfee Brown, *Dimensions of the Holocaust*, 2nd edn, annotated by Elliot Lefkovitz (Northwestern University Press, Evanston, IL), pp. 5–19.

Williams, Bernard (1993), 'Moral Luck', in Daniel Statman (ed.), *Moral Luck* (State University of New York Press, Albany), pp. 35–55.

Wistrich, Robert S. (2002), *Hitler and the Holocaust: How and Why the Holocaust Happened* (Phoenix Press, London).

Woodruff, Paul and Wilmer, Harry A. (eds) (1988), *Facing Evil: Light at the Core of Darkness* (Open Court, LaSalle, IL).

Wright, Dudley (1924), *Vampires and Vampirism* (William Rider and Son Ltd, London).

Young, Alison (1996), *Imagining Crime: Textual Outlaws and Criminal Conversations* (Sage, London).

Zangwill, Nick (2003), 'Perpetrator Motivation: Some Reflections on the Browning/Goldhagen Debate', in Eve Garrard and Geoffrey Scarre (eds), *Moral Philosophy and the Holocaust* (Ashgate, Aldershot), pp. 89–102.

Zola, Emile (1962), *Thérèse Raquin* (Penguin Classics, Harmondsworth).

Index